KV-354-655

Sams
Understanding
Series

Understanding FAX and Electronic Mail

Michael A. Banks

HOWARD W. SAMS & COMPANY

A Division of Macmillan, Inc.
11711 North College, Carmel, Indiana 46032 USA

To Susan and Michael Banks II, for help and consideration above and beyond the call of duty.

First Edition
First Printing—1989

International Standard Book Number: 0-672-27297-0
Library of Congress Catalog Card Number: 89-63713

Acquisitions Editor: *James S. Hill*
Development Editor: *C. Herbert Feltner*
Manuscript Editor: *Sara Black*
Illustrator: *Donald B. Clemons*
Cover Artist: *DGS&D Advertising Inc.*
Cover Photo: *Cassel Productions, Inc.*
Indexer: *Don Herrington*
Technical Reviewer: *Kevin Cole*
Compositor: *Shepard Poorman Communications Corp.*

Contents

Chapter 4 | **Using FAX and PC FAX, *81***

Chapter 5 | **What Is E-Mail?, *101***

Chapter 6 | How E-Mail Works, *119*

Chapter 7 | The Modem/FAX Connection, *145*

Chapter 8 | Using E-Mail and Modem/FAX Service, *161*

Preface

As you read this, several hundred million people throughout the world are communicating with one another. Some are talking face to face or via telephone. Others are writing or reading letters or participating in one-way communication by writing or reading books or magazine articles.

A significant percentage of the communication is by electronic means—what I like to call "electronic communications," or electronic analogs of "conventional" communications activities. Business and hobby computer users are conversing by typing and reading lines sent by telephone lines; individuals are sending memos, letters, and other documents via FAX and electronic mail; researchers are accessing newspapers, magazines, and databases of specialized knowledge via online computer services.

No matter what the medium or the application, communication is the most important single activity in which we participate. Communication is a part of every human activity and has been a keystone in the foundation of every human civilization.

If you doubt this, consider the amount of time we spend learning how to communicate—and the many battles that have been fought to gain the right to learn to communicate. Consider the technological developments related to communication—typesetting, the typewriter, the telegraph, the telephone, the modem—and how rapidly these new technologies were accepted, compared with other technologies.

Consider what would happen to our civilization without rapid, efficient communication—electronic communication in particular. The majority of day-to-day business communication is already conducted via computers and FAX, including ordering and invoicing, routing shipments, and making financial transfers. Without the network of electronic communications that has evolved over the past three decades, business and commerce of all types would probably grind to a halt.

Thus, electronic communications play a more important role in our daily lives than most realize. It doesn't stop there. Electronic communications are *shaping* our society, by affecting the way we work and how we communicate with one another. Thanks to the modem, many people are able to work full- or part-time at home—either for employers or as proprietors of cottage businesses that could not exist otherwise. With electronic communications, we can transfer messages and documents nearly instantaneously. Using the electronic media also means that we control when and how we communicate—which, for many individuals and groups, means communicating and conducting business on their own terms.

Obviously, FAX and electronic mail are important tools for business and personal communication in our society—at least as important as the telephone. While the use of FAX and electronic mail were once restricted to those who could afford and/or understand them, this is no longer the case. Today, with the demand for fast, efficient communication rising in direct proportion to the population, access to FAX and electronic mail is fast becoming an absolute. Electronic mail, once relegated to the province of computer hackers, is now used on a daily basis by millions in their homes as well as in the workplace. FAX, a novelty item in the mid-1980s, promises to proliferate to the point where it will be as common as voice telephones by the mid-1990s. Both FAX and electronic mail have proven their utility in the office and their viability in the marketplace and—like the telephone—have become permanent features on our technological landscape.

In short, electronic communications is not the wave of the future; it *is* the future, and the future is now.

FAX and electronic mail are tools to be mastered. This book is about just that. *Understanding FAX and Electronic Mail* is your guide to putting electronic communications to work for you, so that you, too, can enjoy the advantages of instant, convenient communication in both business and personal applications.

This book shows you what you need to know to use FAX and electronic mail—how they work, the equipment you will need, and the various channels of electronic communications available to you. It does more than merely describe what's out there—it shows you what it's like to use a FAX machine and to send FAX or electronic mail via online services. It also demonstrates how to make the most of the communications resources at your disposal, how to handle problems without panic, and much more.

Welcome to the future!

Michael A. Banks
Cincinnati, Ohio

Trademark Acknowledgments

All terms mentioned in this book that are known to be trademarks or service marks are listed below. In addition, terms suspected of being trademarks or service marks have been appropriately capitalized. Neither the author nor Howard W. Sams & Company can attest to the accuracy of this information, nor can the author nor Howard W. Sams & Company assume responsibility for the recognition of trademarks or service marks unknown as such, or inadvertently not recognized. In sum, the use of a term in this book should not be regarded as affecting the validity of any trademark or service mark.

Academic American Encyclopedia is a service mark of Grolier Electronic Publishing, Inc.

Amerifax and GoFax are trademarks of USSI-Amerifax, Inc.

Amiga, Commodore, Commodore-64, and Commodore-128 are trademarks of Commodore Business Machines, Inc.

AP is a trademark of The Associated Press

Apple, Apple II & III, AppleTalk, and ProDos are trademarks or registered trademarks of Apple Computer, Inc.

AppleLink Personal Edition, PC-Link, and Q-Link are service marks of Quantum Computer Services, Inc.

ASCII Express is a trademark of Southwestern Data Systems Inc.

AT&T, UNIX, and Touch-Tone are registered trademarks of American Telephone & Telegraph

Atari and ST are registered trademarks of Atari Corp.

BIX and Byte Information Exchange are trademarks of McGraw-Hill Information Services

BellSouth is a trademark of BellSouth Corporation

Brother is a trademark of Brother International, Inc.

Canon and Canon Faxphone are trademarks of Canon USA, Inc.

Citifax is a trademark of Citifax Corporation

Citizen is a trademark of CBM America Corporation

Cobra and Cobra Printphone are trademarks of Dynascan Corporation

Compaq is a trademark of Compaq Computer Corporation

CompuServe, EasyPlex, Electronic Mall, FAX-EasyPlex, The Professional Connection, PC3, and VIDTEX, are trademarks or registered trademarks of CompuServe, Inc./H&R Block Company

Comp-U-Store Online is a trademark of Compu-Card of America, Inc.

CoSy is a trademark of the University of Guelph

Courier 2400e is a trademark of USRobotics, Inc.

CP/M is a trademark of Digital Research, Inc.

Crosstalk, CrossTalk XVI, CrossTalk Mark 4, and Mk.4 are trademarks of Microstuf, Inc.

DASnet is a trademark of DA Systems, Inc.

DataPac is a trademark of Bell of Canada

DELPHI is a trademark of General Videotex Corporation

DesqView is a registered trademark of Quarterdeck Office Systems

Dialog and Knowledge-Index are registered service marks of Dialog Information Services, Inc., and a product of United Technologies Corporation

Dow Jones, Dow Jones News/Retrieval, and Text Search Services are registered service marks of and Dow Jones News/Retrieval, Dow Jones News Service, and The Wall Street Journal are registered trademarks of Dow Jones & Company, Inc.

EasyLink is a service mark of and Mailgram a registered trademark of The Western Union Telegraph Company

Epson is a trademark of Epson America, Inc.

EverFAX and Everex are trademarks of Everex

Fujitsu and Fujitsu dex are trademarks of Fujitsu Imaging Systems of America

Galaxy is a trademark of Galaxy Communications

GE Mail, GEMall, GEnie Quik-Gram, LiveWire, and UIK-GRAM are trademarks of the General Electric Company, U.S.A.

Gestetner and Gestetner/Teli Vaxafax are trademarks of Gestetner Corporation

Harris/3M is a trademark of Harris/3M Document Products, Inc.

Hayes and Micromodem are registered trademarks of and Hayes Smartmodem, Smartmodem 300, Smartmodem 1200, Smartmodem 1200B, SmartCom, and SmartCom II are trademarks of Hayes Microcomputer Products Inc.

IBM, IBM PC, AT, OS/2, Portable PC, PS/2, and System/2 are registered trademarks of and PC/XT and IBM Personal Computer AT are trademarks of International Business Machines Corporation

IQUEST is a trademark of Telebase Systems, Inc.

KERMIT is a trademark of Henson Associates

Konica is a trademark of Konica Business Machines USA, Inc.

Macintosh is a trademark licensed to Apple Computer, Inc.

MCI and MCI Mail are registered trademarks of and the MCI logo, MCI Mail, MCI Mail Link, MCI Bulletin Board, and MCI Shared Lists are service marks of MCI Communications Corporation

Microcom Network Protocol and MNP are trademarks of Microcom, Inc.

Minolta is a trademark of Minolta Camera Co., Ltd.

Mirror, Mirror II, and Mirror III are registered trademarks of
SoftKlone Distributing Corporation

Mitsubishi is a trademark of Mitsubishi Electric Sales America

MS, Microsoft Word, MS-DOS, Windows, and XENIX are registered
trademarks of Microsoft Corporation

MultiMate is a trademark of MultiMate International Corp.

Murata is a trademark of Murata Business Systems, Inc.

NEC is a trademark of NEC America, Inc.

Northwestern Bell Phones and Faxline are trademarks of U.S. West
Enterprises, Inc.

OAG and Official Airline Guide are registered trademarks of Official
Airline Guides, Inc.

Olivetti is a trademark of Olivetti USA, Inc.

Olympia is a trademark of AEG Olympia USA, Inc.

Omnifax and Telautograph are trademarks of Omnifax Telegraph
Corporation

Pactel is a trademark of Pacific Telesis Corporation

Panafax, Fax Partner, and Panasonic are trademarks of Matsushita
Electric Corporation of America

PC Paintbrush is a trademark of Z-Soft, Inc.

Pitney Bowes is a trademark of Pitney Bowes, Inc.

ProComm is a trademark of Datastorm Technologies, Inc.

Ricoh is a trademark of Ricoh Corporation

Savin, Savinfax, and Savin Courier are trademarks of Savin
Corporation

Sharp is a trademark of Sharp Electronics Corporation

Tandy, Tandy 1000, TANDYFAX, TANDYFAX 1000, TRS-80, and Color
Computer are trademarks or registered trademarks of Tandy
Corporation

Telenet and TELEMAIL are trademarks of and PC Telemail is a
registered service mark of GTE/Telenet Services, Inc.

Teletypewriter is a trademark of Teletypewriter Corp.

TIE is a trademark of TIE/Communications, Inc.

Toshiba is a trademark of Toshiba America, Inc.

Tymnet is a registered trademark and a registered service mark of
Tymnet, Inc.

UNIVERSAL MAIL SERVICE is a trademark of and Speakeasy is a
service mark of Patelcomp, Inc.

UPI is a trademark of United Press International

Ven-Tel and Half Card are trademarks of Ven-Tel, Inc.

Visa is a trademark of Visa

WordPerfect is a trademark of WordPerfect Corporation

WordStar and WordStar 2000 are trademarks of MicroPro
International Corp.

Xerox and Xerox Telecopier are trademarks of Xerox Corporation

All photographs, and the online menus, screens, and data reproduced in tables and figures in this book are copyrighted in content and/or format by their respective providers and are reproduced by permission. Original data on some screens and all uncredited artwork is copyright © 1990 by Michael A. Banks.

Introduction

Getting Started: What You Will Need

Before you can use FAX or electronic mail, you will need certain pieces of FAX hardware and/or computer hardware and software, as well as ancillary (support) equipment. These are described in the following pages.

Note, however, that you do not need to rush out and buy new equipment to understand FAX or electronic mail. In fact, you should read this book before you buy new equipment or upgrade your existing equipment.

Hardware and Equipment

To use the services described in this book, you will need one or more of the following:

- A FAX machine

- A personal computer equipped with a PC FAX board

- A personal computer equipped with a modem (internal or external)

You may have to add a *serial port* to your computer to accommodate a modem.

You will also need a telephone line and, of course, the standard electrical outlets required by this equipment. No special kind of telephone line or power supply is required; your telephone lines must, however, be equipped with the standard RJ-type modular phone plugs. If your telephone lines are not equipped with this kind of plug, see Chapters 2 and 3 for information on changing them.

Software

If you are using a computer to send and receive FAX with a PC FAX board, you will need special communications software designed for use with a PC FAX board. If you are using a computer to send and receive FAX and/or electronic mail via online services, you will need a standard computer communications software package that is designed for your computer and modem.

Other Items

If you wish to use an online service for FAX and/or electronic mail communication, you will have to establish an account with the service. See Appendix A for more information on contacting online services. You will also need to know the local dial-up number(s) for the service(s) you intend to use.

About This Book

Understanding FAX and Electronic Mail is designed to get you up and running right away and to serve as a continuing reference to FAX and computer communications. In these pages, you will find everything you need to know to become a power user of electronic communications media—including some suggestions on creative applications for FAX and electronic mail and some interesting case histories of successful applications.

Although FAX is fairly straightforward and most electronic mail and electronic mail/FAX systems offer online help, you'll want to keep this manual handy during your electronic communications sessions and refer to it frequently when you're offline. Electronic communications options and features are numerous enough that you'll want a guide to plan your sessions, as well as a record of just what is available.

In addition to serving as a reference for electronic communications, one of this book's major goals is to help you learn as much as possible before you try out FAX or electronic mail. Wherever possible, I have included sample screens from various services, so you'll know what to expect. I have also provided step-by-step instructions for many procedures to show you exactly what you'll see online and how to respond during a procedure.

Special Terms of Reference Used in this Book

A number of special terms are used to describe how to use online services and FAX equipment. These are described below.

A *command* is anything you type on a keyboard to instruct an online service or a computer to take a specific action. Examples of commands are **SEND** and **DELETE**. Certain computer control characters are also commands. Commands may include a modifying word called a *qualifier*, which directs the command to operate in a certain manner. Commands may also be issued by pressing a designated command key or button on a FAX machine or a computer keyboard.

A *menu* is a listing of available commands and other choices.

A *selection* is a choice that is available on a menu. If you choose an item from a menu by typing the item's name, you have *selected* it. A selection may also be an item upon which a command acts. For example, a list of messages in an electronic mailbox are selections and can be manipulated with any of several commands.

Option may be used interchangeably with selection, depending on which online service you're using, but usually it refers to choices that are *not* commands.

A *prompt* is a signal (an audio signal, a flashing light, or a message or character displayed on a computer screen) from a FAX machine or an online service indicating that the machine or service is waiting for you to make a selection, enter information, or type a command. Every online menu has a prompt, and special prompts request special kinds of responses from you.

A *response* is your response to a prompt.

Input is normally text that you type to compose a message or description. Input may also be information or directions that you type in response to a prompt.

Entry may refer to text that you type to compose a message or description or to a message in a group of messages.

When *current* is used with a noun such as "menu" or "message," it refers to an item or entry you *are now or have just completed* reading, transferring, or otherwise manipulating or accessing. For example, "the current message" means a message you are currently reading or have just completed reading.

Commands and Input: Format and Usage

When referring to commands and other information that you provide, this book uses the following conventions:

Commands

Commands—whether they are commands that you type or buttons that you press—are printed in boldface, so you can easily distinguish them from surrounding text. For example, to send the message, type **Send** and press ENTER.

The Enter Key

The key used to send commands or text to your computer or to another computer via a modem is referred to as the Enter key and represented by this symbol: ENTER. This key may be marked ENTER, RETURN, NEW LINE, XMIT, CR, or ↵ on some computer, terminal, or FAX keyboards.

Pressing Buttons

Whenever an operation requires you to press a button to issue a command, the button's label will be printed in bold.

< text >

Text enclosed in greater than/lesser than symbols as in the preceding header means that you should enter the *kind* of information enclosed by the symbols. For example, **Type <addressee>** means that you should type the name, number, or other electronic mail address of the person to whom you are sending a message (*not* the word "addressee").

Entering Numbers

A number sign (**#**) or a lowercase **x** indicates that a number or numbers should be used or will be displayed with the command or option under discussion. *nnnn* is also used to represent numbers.

Organization

This book is organized into three convenient sections:

- The Basics—A guide to how FAX and electronic mail work for beginning and intermediate users.

- Online FAX and Electronic Mail—How to create, send, receive, forward, and store messages and documents, along with previews of electronic mail, general online, and FAX services.

- Reference—Contact information for electronic mail and FAX services, additional information resources on telecommunications, a comprehensive glossary, and answers to the end-of-chapter quizzes.

And now . . . on to the basics of electronic communications!

Chapter 1 | Electronic Communications

About This Chapter

This chapter provides an overview of electronic communications: FAX and electronic mail (E-mail) services. You'll learn a little about how FAX and E-mail work and something of the capabilities of these media.

What Is FAX?

FAX is verbal shorthand for *facsimile*, which alludes to the process of electronically copying and transmitting textual and/or graphic images via telephone lines. FAX is also used to describe messages and other information transmitted via facsimile machines.

Facsimile transmission is accomplished in four stages:

- An electronic image of the document is created, in the form of *binary signals*, by an element of the FAX machine called the *scanner*. This process is called *scanning* the document.

- A special kind of modem built into the FAX machine converts the binary signals to *analog signals* that can be transmitted via telephone lines.

- The modem transmits the analog signals over a preestablished telephone connection to a receiving FAX machine, whose modem converts the signals back to binary form.

- The receiving FAX machine's *printer* reproduces the original document and/or graphics, in effect reversing the scanning process of the sending FAX machine.

The technical details of facsimile scanning, conversion, transmission, and reproduction are discussed in later chapters.

Figure 1.1 shows a state-of-the-art FAX system, including a laser printer.

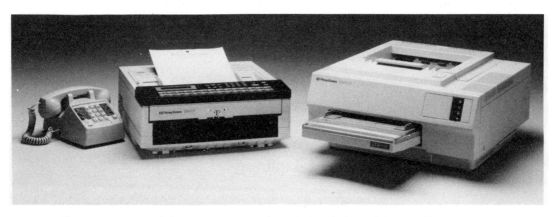

Figure 1.1 State-of-the-art FAX system, integrating dedicated FAX and laser printing.
Photo courtesy of Pitney Bowes Facsimile Systems

FAX Options

FAX machines offer a number of options in delivering documents. Most FAX machines can receive messages unattended. Many have document memory storage and store-and-forward capability and can be set up to send messages unattended—either through repeated calls until the document is delivered or, on more expensive models, through a programming capability that allows the user to store scanned pages in the machine for transmission to one or more FAX machines at a specified time. Similarly, FAX machines with a document memory storage feature can store an incoming document rather than print it immediately.

Some FAX machines also double as copiers and/or voice telephones. A few FAX machines, when connected with like machines, can be switched between voice and FAX communication during a call.

Among FAX's many other options are a variety of message-management and support functions—all detailed in Chapter 3.

Using a FAX Machine

FAX machines are relatively easy to operate. The following steps describe making connections and sending and receiving documents via FAX using very basic machines. The processes can be further simplified by optional features described in later chapters.

Making Connections

Standard FAX protocol always has the calling machine send the document.

If you need to send a document, just dial another FAX's phone number or instruct your FAX machine to do so. The two machines will take care of establishing and maintaining data communications. If you are receiving a document, the sender's FAX will telephone your machine, which will answer and establish the connection.

Sending a Document

After the connection is made, sending a document involves nothing more than inserting the pages to be transmitted into the scanner, one at a time, and waiting for the signal to insert the next page. This instruction assumes that you aren't using a more advanced machine that can be programmed to store and send the document later. With properly equipped FAX machines, you don't even have to feed pages into the scanner; special hardware does this for you.

Receiving a Document

Receiving a document via FAX is even easier than sending one. All you have to do is have your FAX machine connected to a telephone line, turned on, and stocked with paper for printing the incoming document. When the sending FAX machine calls, your machine answers the phone, establishes the connection, and receives and prints the document. That's all there is to it.

PC FAX Boards

PC FAX boards enable computers to send and receive FAX messages. A PC FAX board converts a computer's binary data into the kind of analog signals that a FAX machine uses to send data over a phone line, and vice versa. Sending a document to a FAX machine from a computer using a PC FAX board typically requires that you start a special program, specify a prepared file to send, and tell the program the number of the FAX machine to which the FAX is to be sent.

PC FAX boards can handle both text and graphics.

What Is Electronic Mail?

Electronic mail, more commonly known as E-mail, is private electronic messaging via computer. E-mail is typically handled by an intermediary computer (e.g., a computer bulletin board or—more often—an online service such as MCI Mail or CompuServe). Such intermediary computer systems are also called *host systems*.

A computer must have a modem to communicate with E-mail host systems. The modem communicates with the host system via voice telephone lines. Figure 1.2 shows a modem. The technical details of computer communication are detailed in later chapters.

Figure 1.2 A dial-up computer modem. *Photo courtesy Radio Shack, a division of Tandy Corporation*

Standard E-mail consists of textual messages addressed to a specific online *address* on the host system. This address is also known as an account, a user ID, and a username. If a message is to be delivered to the recipient via computer, both the sender and the receiver must have accounts on the host system. If the message is to be delivered by other means—FAX, hardcopy, U.S. Mail, or courier service—the recipient doesn't have to have an account on the host system.

In practice, the person sending the E-mail message enters a command to create a message, after which the sender receives a prompt to enter the online address of the recipient, along with a subject header. After entering this information, the sender composes the message online or transfers (uploads) a prepared message to the host system, then sends it using the command appropriate to the host system. Instructions involving handling options (e.g., sending the message to multiple recipients or sending it to a FAX machine) may be entered before or after the message is entered, depending on the host system.

E-mail delivery is not restricted to computers.

Depending on the handling options specified and the capabilities of the host system, the message may be handled in any of several ways:

- The message may be copied into a storage area referred to as the recipient's *electronic mailbox.* (This is analogous to a mailbox to which only the recipient has the key.) Optionally, it can be sent to one or more additional recipients.

- The message may be sent to one or more FAX numbers. If the FAX number is busy, the host system tries again at specified intervals until it can deliver the message. This is known as the "store-and-forward capability," an option with some FAX machines.

- The message may be sent to one or more Telex machines. The store-and-forward procedure is used here, too.

- The message may be printed out in the city nearest its destination and delivered via U.S. Mail or a courier service.

The sender may retain a copy of the message and receive a delivery receipt, again depending on options specified by the sender and the capabilities of the host system.

If the message is sent to an electronic mailbox, the recipient has a number of possible options, including replying to the message, storing it in a file area on the host system, copying it to the computer's disk drive, and deleting the message.

Some host systems can transmit graphics and computer data files.

As you can see, E-mail is a very versatile service, offering all the benefits of conventional text communication and some special advantages of its own.

What You Have Learned

- FAX, or facsimile transmission, is the process of transmitting text and/or graphics ("documents") via telephone lines.

- Before transmitting a document via FAX, an electronic image of the document is created by scanning the pages. This electronic image is converted to a different format for transmission via telephone lines.

- A properly equipped FAX machine can scan and store a document for transmission at a later time, double as a copier, and perform many other tasks related and unrelated to FAX transmission.

- When a FAX machine receives a document, it prints out the document using a built-in printer.

- A PC FAX board enables a personal computer to send and receive FAX messages.

- E-mail is private electronic messaging via computer.

- E-mail messages consist of files created with a computer.

- Most E-mail is carried by intermediary, or host, computer systems.

- The majority of E-mail consists of text messages, but graphics and data files can also be transferred via E-mail.

- E-mail delivery is not restricted to computers. E-mail messages can be delivered in hardcopy form via U.S. Mail or courier services to FAX machines or to Telex machines.

That's electronic communications in a nutshell. Now, take the quiz on the following page, then move on to Chapter 2 and the basics of FAX!

Quiz

1. Before a document can be transmitted by FAX, an electronic image of the document is created by a process called:

   a. Transmitting
   b. Printing
   c. Scanning
   d. Connecting

2. Which element of a FAX machine handles the actual transmission of a document?

   a. The printer
   b. The modem
   c. The scanner
   d. The memory

3. When a FAX machine receives a document, what does it do with the document?

   a. Scans it
   b. Converts it to binary signals
   c. Prints it out on a printer or stores it in memory
   d. Sends it to a modem

4. PC FAX boards enable a computer to:

   a. Print graphics
   b. Send and receive FAX messages
   c. Access E-mail services
   d. Convert text to graphics

5. PC FAX boards can send and receive documents containing:

   a. Text
   b. Graphics
   c. Text and graphics
   d. All of the above

6. E-mail is private electronic messaging via computer. What handles E-mail?

   a. An intermediary, or host, computer system
   b. FAX or Telex machines
   c. Specialized software
   d. Binary data

7. Which of the following is required to communicate with E-mail host computer systems?

   a. A parallel port
   b. A modem

    c. A printer

    d. A scanner

8. How does a computer communicate with an E-mail system?

    a. Via telephone lines

    b. Via radio waves

    c. Via disk transfer

    d. Via FAX

9. E-mail messages are generated by computer but can be delivered to:

    a. FAX and Telex machines

    b. Other computers

    c. Street addresses

    d. All of the above

HOWARD W. SAMS & COMPANY

♫♫♫

Bookmark

DEAR VALUED CUSTOMER:

Howard W. Sams & Company is dedicated to bringing you timely and authoritative books for your personal and professional library. Our goal is to provide you with excellent technical books written by the most qualified authors. You can assist us in this endeavor by checking the box next to your particular areas of interest.

We appreciate your comments and will use the information to provide you with a more comprehensive selection of titles.

Thank you,

Vice President, Book Publishing
Howard W. Sams & Company

COMPUTER TITLES:

Hardware
- ☐ Apple 140
- ☐ Macintosh I01
- ☐ Commodore I10
- ☐ IBM & Compatibles I14

Business Applications
- ☐ Word Processing J01
- ☐ Data Base J04
- ☐ Spreadsheets J02

Operating Systems
- ☐ MS-DOS K05
- ☐ OS/2 K10
- ☐ CP/M K01
- ☐ UNIX K03

Programming Languages
- ☐ C L03
- ☐ Pascal L05
- ☐ Prolog L12
- ☐ Assembly L01
- ☐ BASIC L02
- ☐ HyperTalk L14

Troubleshooting & Repair
- ☐ Computers S05
- ☐ Peripherals S10

Other
- ☐ Communications/Networking M03
- ☐ AI/Expert Systems T18

ELECTRONICS TITLES:
- ☐ Amateur Radio T01
- ☐ Audio T03
- ☐ Basic Electronics T20
- ☐ Basic Electricity T21
- ☐ Electronics Design T12
- ☐ Electronics Projects T04
- ☐ Satellites T09

- ☐ Instrumentation T05
- ☐ Digital Electronics T11

Troubleshooting & Repair
- ☐ Audio S11
- ☐ Television S04
- ☐ VCR S01
- ☐ Compact Disc S02
- ☐ Automotive S06
- ☐ Microwave Oven S03

Other interests or comments: _____

_____

Name_____

Title _____

Company _____

Address _____

City _____

State/Zip _____

Daytime Telephone No. _____

A Division of Macmillan, Inc.

4300 West 62nd Street Indianapolis, Indiana 46268

27297

Bookmark

BUSINESS REPLY CARD
FIRST CLASS   PERMIT NO. 1076   INDIANAPOLIS, IN

POSTAGE WILL BE PAID BY ADDRESSEE

HOWARD W. SAMS & COMPANY
ATTN: Public Relations Department
P.O. Box 7092
Indianapolis, IN 46209-9921

HOWARD W. SAMS
& COMPANY

Part **1** | The Basics

This section builds on the groundwork laid by the Introduction and Chapter 1 to provide you with the basic and advanced knowledge you need to understand and use FAX and electronic mail effectively. Several chapters include hands-on guides.

You may wish to read chapters selectively. If you're more interested in FAX than electronic mail, you'll find the coverage of FAX in Chapters 2, 3, and 4 most useful. If you want to learn more about E-mail, read Chapters 5, 6, and 7. Chapters 7 and 8 cover topics of interest to both FAX and E-mail users.

Here's a chapter-by-chapter preview of the section.

Chapter 2, entitled "What Is FAX?," explains basic FAX concepts and terminology, FAX applications, and equipment used in facsimile transmission. It also explains how FAX messages are transmitted, the capabilities and limitations of FAX, and what to expect from FAX.

Chapter 3, entitled "How FAX Works," explains the inner workings of FAX machines. You'll learn about scanners; data conversion and storage; modems, data transmission, and reception; and FAX printers. Also detailed are FAX hardware types and FAX features and options. PC FAX boards are introduced in Chapter 3 as well, and you'll learn how PC FAX boards work and what they have to offer. Finally, it helps you decide whether you need a dedicated FAX machine or a PC FAX board.

Chapter 4, entitled "Using FAX and PC FAX," gives you all the information you need to install, set up, use, and maintain a FAX machine. You'll also learn how to install and use a PC FAX board—as well as support software and hardware such as graphics conversion programs and optical scanners.

Chapter 5, entitled "What Is E-Mail?," introduces electronic mail (computer communication via modem), beginning with its origins and evolution and basic E-mail concepts. The chapter then discusses the capabilities and limitations of E-mail.

Chapter 6, entitled "How E-Mail Works," continues E-mail coverage with detailed explanations of how computer communication works, presenting the technical elements of modem operation in a nontechnical manner. You'll also learn about the features and options available in computer communications hardware and software, and basic E-mail features and options, as well as command structure.

Chapter 7, entitled "The Modern/FAX Connection," discusses how to send FAX messages without a FAX machine. You'll learn everything you need to know about the hardware, software, and intermediary online services involved. You'll also learn about networks for dedicated FAX machines and the comparative advantages and disadvantages of FAX versus modem/FAX messaging.

Chapter 8, entitled "Using E-Mail and Modern/FAX Services," delves deeper into computer communication by showing you how to get started using E-mail services, general online services, and modem/FAX services. Of special interest are sample E-mail and modem/FAX sessions.

Chapter

2 | What Is FAX?

About This Chapter

This chapter describes the following:

- Basic facsimile terminology
- Applications for facsimile transmission
- How FAX machines "see" graphic images
- Equipment associated with facsimile transmission
- FAX communications channels
- Capabilities and limitations of facsimile transmission

Getting the Words Right

Before proceeding, I'll introduce some terms you'll see frequently in this book and in other literature about FAX.

Text and Graphics

The terms "text" and "graphics" describe two entirely different types of visual material but are sometimes confused. Even though a dedicated FAX machine does not distinguish between the two, it is often important to speak of each as discrete elements.

Text

When discussing facsimile transmission, text means letters, words, numbers, and spaces (also referred to as characters) that are combined to form words or numeric data. Examples of text characters are those characters found on a standard typewriter keyboard.

In general, text consists of machine-produced or -generated characters (i.e., typewriter or computer printer output or characters generated by a computer and stored in the computer's memory or on disk). Handwritten text is generally regarded as graphics. As you will learn later, these two distinctions are important, particularly where sending FAX via PC FAX boards or online services are concerned.

Graphics

Graphic material is any visual image that does not consist exclusively of machine-produced text characters. Graphics can include lines, curves, angles, lettering, dots, varying tones or color intensity, halftones, cursive, designs, and logos. Graphics to be scanned and transmitted by FAX can be produced or generated by any of several methods (individually or combined):

- Human drawing or writing (freehand, or with the use of drafting equipment or other aids)
- Computer printers (dot-matrix, ink-jet, and laser)
- Photography
- Photocopying existing graphics
- Computer programs (for storage and later transfer via a PC FAX board or an online service)

Pages, Documents, Messages, and Images

The terms "page," "document," "message," and "image" often appear to be used interchangeably—and often are. The following explanations demonstrate how the terms are distinguished from one another, and how they are used in this book and in other venues.

Note: FAX refers to both machines and documents.

Page

Page generally refers to a sheet of physical paper scanned or printed by a FAX machine. Page also describes a unit of information transmitted via FAX (i.e., the information content of a sheet of paper, which can be text, graphics, or both).

Document

A *document* is a page or group of pages transmitted by FAX, which can also be described as the sum total of information transmitted during a single FAX transmission. Here again, the information can consist of text and/or graphics.

Message

Message is also used frequently to refer to a page or group of pages transmitted by FAX but is usually used with reference to a document of one or two pages. As is the case with document, message does not refer exclusively to a text-only message.

Image

Image alludes to the contents of a page or, more often, the electronic form of a scanned page (i.e., the binary or analog data in which a page is stored and transmitted).

Group x FAX Machines

You will see many references to "Group 3 FAX" in product literature and advertisements and some references to Groups 1, 2, and 4 FAX machines. Simply explained, the number in the phrase "Group x FAX" refers to the generation or sequence in the evolution of FAX technology in which the machine in question belongs. The numbers match the age of the technology—Group 1 being the oldest and Group 4 being the newest.

The technology itself is defined by the graphic resolution (the detail of the image), the speed at which data is transmitted, how data is scanned and stored in preparation for transmission, and other elements.

With rare exception, the technology used in FAX machines (the means whereby images are scanned, encoded, transmitted, and decoded for printing) follows a set of recommendations formulated by the Consultive Committee on Telegraphy and Telephony (CCITT), an international organization that also sets standards for modem and other kinds of electronic communications. This means that modern FAX machines the world over are *compatible* (able to communicate) with one another.

Group 3 is the most common type of FAX machine currently in use. (Industry estimates indicate that 90% of the FAX machines in use in the world are Group 3.) Group 3 FAX machines scan and store images as *digital* data; earlier FAX machines used strictly *analog* scanning techniques. Group 3 FAXes boast a finer resolution than that of Group 1 or Group 2 FAX machines, as well as higher speeds in scanning and transmitting images.

> **Note:** While Group 3 machines use digital scanning and storage techniques, they must still transmit image data as *analog* signals, due to the nature of the voice telephone network. This, as you will learn, is why FAX machines have built-in modems.

If you expect to communicate with Group 2 FAX machines, make sure your FAX machine can recognize Group 2 FAX machines. Group 2 capability is not available on all Group 3 machines.

Group 3 FAX machines are 100% compatible only with other Group 3 FAX machines. This means they may not be able to communicate with Group 1 or 2 machines. Some Group 3 machines can recognize transmissions from Group 2 machines and can thus receive documents from the older machines. Some Group 3 machines can also send documents in a format recognized by Group 2 machines. Very few Group 3 FAX machines can communicate with Group 1 machines.

In general, incompatibility between older FAX machines and Group 3 machines is not an issue. As previously indicated, the majority of FAX machines in use today are Group 3 machines, so you have little need to be concerned about the compatibility of a recently purchased dedicated FAX machine. In fact, PC FAX boards and modem FAX services are set up to communicate with Group 3 FAX machines, and some may communicate with Group 2 machines, as well.

Group 4 FAX machines are extremely expensive and specialized communications tools. When they transmit data many times faster and with less chance of error than Group 3 machines, they communicate in a digital rather than analog fashion. Group 4 FAX machines are not generally compatible with Group 3 machines and require a special digital telephone network, referred to as ISDN (Integrated Service Digital Network). Due to the fact that Group 4 FAX machines require such digital links and cannot use the existing voice-telephone network, it will be several years before they become a significant force in the marketplace. Specifically, when the large-scale ISDNs now planned and under construction are in place (near the end of the 1990s), Group 4 FAX will be widely available and affordable and the general FAX user will be interested in it. Because it is so specialized, Group 4 FAX is beyond the scope of this book.

FAX Applications

Specific applications for FAX transmission are virtually endless. Due to the fact that the initial cost of FAX machines was relatively high until recently, most FAX transmissions are business oriented. However, as with computers, consumer demand and manufacturer competition are resulting in price reductions, making FAX more accessible to the public. More and more FAX machines are being used for personal and hobby applications.

Business Applications

Typical business applications for FAX include transmitting drawings, photographs, signed contracts, memos, letters, and lengthy documents (with or without graphics). There are several advantages to being able to send graphic images and documents by FAX:

- FAX delivery is nearly instantaneous; even next-day delivery services cannot compete with FAX in delivery time.

- You can send and receive FAX messages at your convenience; you do not depend on the schedules of next-day delivery services.

- FAX delivery is, in general, less costly than other forms of rapid delivery. Four-hour delivery of a ten-page printed document (when available) would cost approximately $150.00; overnight delivery of the same document currently costs between $9.00 and $15.00. FAXing a ten-page printed document might cost between $2.00 and $5.00 during business hours, less during evening, nighttime, and weekend hours.

- Even though electronic mail offers instant delivery of documents, most E-mail systems cannot transmit graphics—the few that do are restricted to very specialized types of computer-generated graphics.

  Note: With reference to signatures on FAXed contracts, while they are accepted as binding by the parties to such a contract, the question of their legality is still a gray area as far as the courts and most attorneys are concerned. In general, FAXed signatures have been regarded by the law as being in the same category as photocopied signatures.

While there is some precedent for signatures on FAXed contracts being accepted as valid by individuals, attorneys, and courts, there is no legislation determining their legitimacy. The absence of such legislation will undoubtedly be noticed by the legal community at large and rectified in the next couple of years, but for now most attorneys are of the opinion that there is a chance that FAXed copies of contracts and other signed documents may well be disregarded in any legal proceedings involving them.

When possible, it is best to "back up" a FAXed contract with the original, which can be delivered by conventional means.

FAX Abuse

As with the telephone, many enterprising (and some desperate) individuals and organizations have devised ways to use FAX communications for commercial enterprise—much to the annoyance of tens of thousands of FAX users. Specifically, advertisements and other useless information are being broadcast to known FAX telephone numbers. Fortunately, there are ways to avoid being victimized by such FAX junk mail. These are discussed in Chapter 4.

Personal Applications

Personal applications for FAX are somewhat limited. Because FAX machines are not as prevalent as telephones, and because it is easier to use a telephone for local and long-distance personal communications (most personal communications are strictly words—i.e., voice), individuals have been largely without real incentives to buy FAX machines, aside from as a novelty item or out of curiosity.

Some individuals use FAX machines in the workplace and at home to send advance lunch orders to local restaurants, requests to radio stations, and the like. FAX is also becoming a popular substitute for ordering and paying for goods and services by telephone or mail, where credit cards are involved, because with FAX one can include an authenticating signature.

Hobby Applications

The major hobby applications for FAX seem to be the novelty of using FAX, finding new applications for FAX, and modifying FAX machines and/or interfacing them with other electronic devices.

It's All How You Look at It: Text Versus Graphics and FAX

As you are aware, both text and graphics can be transmitted via FAX. However, you may not be aware of an important fact: Both text and graphics are the same where FAX is involved, because a FAX sees both text and graphics as graphics. That is, when a FAX machine scans and records a character (a letter or number), it is not treating it as a letter; instead, it is treating the character as an element in a picture, just as it would treat a small sketch or hand-written character. Further, the graphics are perceived and printed as patterns of dots.

The software behind PC FAX boards and modem FAX services perceives characters as characters. When the characters are translated to FAX format, they are seen as graphics.

FAX Equipment

Three categories of equipment are used to originate and receive FAX messages: *dedicated* FAX machines, computers equipped with *PC FAX boards*, and computers equipped with modems that use *online services* to transmit FAX messages.

Dedicated FAX Machines

A dedicated FAX machine is exactly what the name implies: a piece of equipment designed and used primarily or solely for facsimile transmission.

Dedicated FAX machines are similar in appearance to business telephone sets or photocopiers. A typical FAX machine is shown in Figure 2.1. The primary elements of a FAX machine are a scanner, a modem, a printer, and the telephone interface. The scanner reads words and images from a sheet of paper and converts them to electronic signals. A modem, as described in Chapter 1, converts the electronic signals to a format that can be transmitted by telephone line. In the case of received FAX messages, a modem converts the signals back to the electronic format used by the scanner. A printer converts the electronic signals supplied by the modem into words and images on paper, and the telephone interface handles dialing.

Optional dedicated FAX machine elements may include a memory for storing telephone numbers and/or FAX messages, a programming element (actually, a small dedicated computer) to set up delayed message transfers, automatic paper feeders, a display to provide call-status information, and other hardware to support standard or optional fea-

Figure 2.1 A dedicated FAX machine. *Photo courtesy of Panasonic*

tures. Dedicated FAX machine options are described in detail in Chapters 1 and 3.

The vast majority of FAX messages are transmitted using dedicated FAX machines. This is primarily because it requires less knowledge to operate a dedicated FAX machine than to operate a computer and because FAX-by-computer was not possible until relatively recently.

PC FAX Boards

A PC FAX board translates computer text and graphics contained in a computer's memory or stored on a computer disk into the kind of binary signals used by FAX machines. Special software that works with the PC FAX board reads the text or graphics. A built-in FAX-type modem translates these signals into the analog form used by FAX machines for telephone-line transmission, then transmits the text and/or graphics that comprise the pages of the FAX message. When the receiving FAX machine receives these signals, it sees them as the all-graphics format used by FAX, whether text or graphics are involved. In other words, it doesn't make distinctions as to the source of a message.

PC FAX boards receive FAX messages in a manner similar to that of dedicated FAX machines. The big difference, of course, is that received text and/or graphics are stored in the computer's memory or on disk. Once a message is stored, it can be accessed with any of a variety of computer programs, printed, or retransmitted.

A useful feature of PC FAX boards is their ability to translate and transmit (or receive) graphic image files created by popular personal computer graphics programs.

PC FAX board-equipped computers are not limited to transmitting only computer-generated text and graphics. If you have a scanner, you can scan paper documents and drawings, which are stored on computer disk and can then be accessed by the PC FAX board's software just like any other disk file.

As shown in Figure 2.2, PC FAX boards are similar in appearance to other add-on boards. The electronic components are mounted on a printed-circuit board, and an edge connector on one side of the board connects it with the computer.

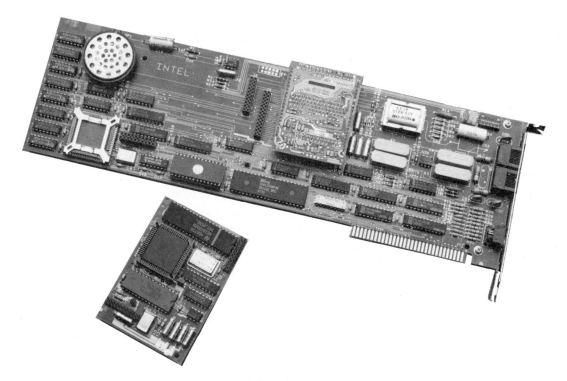

Figure 2.2 A PC FAX board. *Photo courtesy of Intel PECO*

PC FAX boards are popular among computer users for several reasons:

- A PC FAX board provides FAX access at a cost equivalent to or less than that of a dedicated FAX machine, without cluttering the computer user's desk top with another piece of equipment.

- Using a PC FAX board saves time and trouble by eliminating the need to print text or graphics, then scan the printed pages with a dedicated FAX machine.

- Most PC FAX board/software combinations can be directed to send or receive FAX transmissions automatically, without supervision.

- Graphics that might otherwise be inaccessible due to a lack of the appropriate printer type can be delivered via FAX.

- Veteran computer users find PC FAX boards easier to learn to use than standalone FAX machines. Doing FAX-related work from their computers is more efficient than switching gears to another machine.

FAX via Online Services

Online services are telecommunication networks capable of communicating with computers or dedicated FAX machines and PC FAX board-equipped computers via telephone lines.

Two kinds of online services handle FAX traffic: online services for modem-equipped computers and online services that can communicate with FAX machines. Both kinds of online services are based on and controlled by computers.

Computer FAX via Online Services

If you have a computer, a word processing program, a communications program, and a modem, you can send text FAX messages via almost any online service (e.g., AT&T Mail, CompuServe, DELPHI, MCI Mail) to any FAX machine in the world. This kind of FAX communication, also referred to as *modem/FAX* service, is extremely useful to computer users—many of whom, unfortunately, are unaware of it.

The logistics of sending a message to a FAX machine via an online service are fairly simple. You transmit a message from your computer to the online service and enter the telephone number of the FAX machine that is to receive the message. The online service's computer calls the designated number and transmits the message. The order of message- and telephone number-entry may be reversed on some services.

> **Note:** Depending on the word processor you use, you may need to make certain changes to documents produced with it before you can send the documents as a FAX message via an online service. This is discussed in more detail in later chapters.

The major differences between transmitting a FAX message via an online service and via a FAX machine or PC FAX board are these:

- You can send only text on most services.

- You cannot receive FAX messages on most services.

- The text you send must be in a file on your computer's disk.

- Messages are not transmitted directly from your equipment (your computer) to the receiving FAX machine; instead, they are stored for a short period, then forwarded to the designated recipient.

> **Note:** Several online services can transfer graphic images created with popular PC graphics software, and a few allow you to receive text messages sent from dedicated FAX machines or PC FAX boards. There is currently a trend toward offering FAX reception and graphics transfer, which should culminate in virtually all online services offering such services.
>
> You can also transfer files to several services from popular word processors without preparation, which translate the files and send them to a specified FAX number.

When you transmit a message to an online service and specify FAX delivery, the message is stored until the service's computer calls and connects with the FAX machine designated as the receiver. How often and for how long the online service's computer will attempt to deliver your FAX message can vary, depending on which service you use. Some services allow you to specify the duration and interval of retries.

You can, by the way, specify more than one FAX telephone number on almost all the services when you send a message by FAX. Being able to do this means you can send the same message to multiple recipients without having to transmit the same message more than once. This is a distinct savings of time and effort.

When a connection is made with the receiving FAX machine—which may be minutes or hours after you transmit it to the online service, depending on whether the receiving FAX machine is online and not busy—the host computer sends your stored message to the receiving FAX in the special format required by FAX machines. You don't have to worry about the conversion; it's handled automatically.

When a receiving FAX machine receives a message from the online service's computer, it sees it in the all-graphics format used by FAX, whether text or graphics are involved, and reproduces the message just as it would a message from a dedicated FAX machine. In other words, the receiving FAX machine doesn't make distinctions as to the origins of a message. Thus, when printed by the receiving FAX machine, a message sent in this manner looks like any other text-only FAX message.

Figure 2.3 shows a FAX message as it might be entered on a screen while on an online service.

Sending a FAX message via an online service has several advantages:

- You do not have to worry about whether the receiving FAX machine is connected, and you do not have to wait until the FAX machine isn't busy. As previously indicated, the online service will

```
create, delete, get, help, profile, quit, read, show
Command: .create
To: FAX!3175551212
Attention To: Alan Rodgers
To:
Cc:
Subject: Relays
** Enter message followed by a .COMMAND or .
Alan,
        I checked on the overpour relay for the new EDI system; you
were right.  It is sticking, which means that whenever it's used to
override the system limit, the limit is effectively set 1.5 times
higher.
        I wonder if there is something that can be done to
prevent this?  While the problem was due to a faulty relay, it
seems that proper design could have prevented it from causing as
much trouble as it did.  Specifically, can we add a circuit that
senses whether the relay doesn't release (perhaps with a second
latching relay) and warns the operator?
```

Figure 2.3 A FAX message being input on an online service.

continue trying to deliver your message for a set period of time and at specific intervals.

- For those who create documents via computer, using an online service to deliver a message or document to a FAX machine can save time and trouble. You don't have to print the document, and you don't have to run it through a FAX machine's scanner.

- You can easily send the same message to multiple FAX machines, in a fraction of the time it takes to send the same message manually.

FAX via an online service is ideal for those modem-equipped computer users who primarily need to *send* FAX messages and/or whose FAX traffic is perhaps too small to justify investing in a dedicated FAX machine.

Radio-FAX Transmission

Some products can transmit FAX via radio; however, these are intended mainly for licensed amateur radio hobbyists. Various manufacturers have indicated an interest in marketing consumer versions of radio-FAX devices, which would operate in much the same manner as cellular telephones (and may double as cellular telephones). Watch for such products to appear on the scene by 1995.

Note: FAX transmission via telephone line sometimes involves transmission via radio during some stages of the transmission, especially over very long distances. Some elements of the telephone-line link may involve sending the signals via microwave radio transmission rather than telephone wires (telephone company microwave relays). Also, if one end of a FAX link involves a cellular telephone, radio transmission is used. However, these elements are transparent to you, the FAX user. As far as you're concerned, there is one wire connection between your machine and the FAX machine with which it is communicating.

Telephone Lines: The FAX Communication Channel

As implied in the preceding section, there is really only one FAX communications channel: the worldwide voice telephone network. Group 4 FAX uses a telephone network, even though the ISDN required to support Group 4 technology is not yet widespread enough to make Group 4 FAX competitive with Group 3 technology. Even international FAX is now available on a low-cost basis, thanks to special international packet-switching network FAX gateways.

Accessibility: The Secret of FAX's Success

No matter what you use to send or receive FAX messages, the messages are carried over ordinary telephone lines (radio-FAX transmission excepted, of course). This is the main reason FAX has become so popular; anyone who has access to telephone service has access to FAX service. For the purposes of this book, microwave and other nonwire links in the telephone network are considered to be one with telephone lines.

> **Note:** FAX transmissions are vulnerable to line noise, which can cause data loss, and even disconnection. If you are concerned with poor connections, use voice telephone to call the receiving FAX's area before calling via FAX. Listen for line noise or cross talk. If the line quality is poor, wait half an hour and try again.

FAX Dimensions and Limitations

While FAX is a marvelous tool, its capabilities are not unlimited. We'll take a look at just how far FAX goes in the final section of this chapter.

How Much Can You Send?

There is no limit to the quantity of information that can be sent via FAX. Transmission speeds may vary, based on the equipment being used and the quality of the telephone connection, but you can transfer as many pages of text and/or graphics as you wish during a FAX session.

Can You Send and Receive During the Same Call?

With a few exceptions, most FAX machines only transmit *or* receive during a call. Some machines can be *polled*, which means that another FAX machine can call them and request that a document be sent. Even so, once a FAX link is established, the sending and receiving machines remain in their respective modes.

Certain advanced FAX machines can change transmission direction during a call, thus saving the time, trouble, and potential long-distance expense involved in making a second call. This feature will most likely become standard over the next 2 years.

How Fast Is FAX?

To be considered Group 3 FAX, a FAX machine must be able to transmit data at a minimum rate of 2400 bps.

The speed at which FAX messages are sent is determined by the FAX's modem speed. For Group 3 FAX machines, this is a maximum of 9600 bps (data bits per second). Data bits are explained in detail in Chapter 3. Group 3 FAX machines can send a page in 15 to 20 seconds, depending on the contents of the page. If the connection between the sending and receiving FAX machines is poor, the time can double or quadruple, because the FAX modem will fall back to slower transmission speeds— 7200, 4800, or 2400 bps.

> **Note:** FAX transmissions can be slowed by a bad telephone connection or poor line quality. When static or line noise is encountered, FAX modems automatically fall back to a slower transmission speed, which may be one half or even a quarter of the normal transmission speed.

PC FAX board modems and online services transmit translated FAX messages at the same speed as dedicated FAX modems.

> **Caution:** Do not transmit FAX messages during a thunderstorm in your area or in the area of the FAX machine to which you're connected. Lightning and high winds create line noise.

What Kinds of Information Can Be Sent?

Anything that you write, print, paint, or photocopy on a sheet of paper of standard thickness (16- or 20-pound bond paper or standard typing paper) can be FAXed.

If you have to FAX material from paper that is too thick or too thin, use a photocopier to copy it onto standard-size paper.

The images created by FAX machines are not unlike those of standard photocopiers. In fact, many FAX machines use photocopier technology and double as photocopiers. Thus, you cannot transmit color images via standard FAX; only black-and-white images or images with varying shades of gray can be transmitted and printed by FAX printers. If you scan a color image, the colors will be transmitted and printed out in black and white or in shades of gray.

How Much Per Page?

The physical dimensions of the paper that a FAX machine can scan and print vary from one machine to another and depend in part on the physical makeup of the FAX's scanner. I'm referring to dedicated FAX machines here. The page size of PC FAX board and modem/FAX messages are determined in part by the software involved and in part by the printer on the receiving FAX.

Paper Size Limitations

Use standard typewriter margins to leave roughly ½ inch of empty space on the top, bottom, and sides of the page. These margins eliminate lost letters or portions of a drawing.

If you don't know whether a scanner will capture the entire page, use a reducing photocopier for a slightly smaller page.

Scanners that require you to insert the paper between a platen (roller) and a scanner or between two platens will typically take paper that is 8 ½ inches wide (the width of a standard sheet of typewriter or copier paper). Not all such machines will accommodate the full 11-inch length of a standard sheet of typewriter paper, however. Refer to your FAX machine's operation manual for information on the size paper you can scan. The maximum size of a page may vary (one popular machine will accept sheets 8.7″ wide by 39.5″ long), but machines that use sheet feeders typically accept standard 8 ½″ × 11″ paper.

Scanners that are configured like photocopiers (i.e., you place the page to be scanned on a flat, clear glass or plastic surface, under a cover) can usually scan any size paper up to the size of the surface on which you must place the paper to be scanned. However, there may be limitations on the *area* of a page scanned, so you should leave wide margins on the paper.

Machines with either type of scanner may have *minimum* limits, as well. One popular FAX machine requires that a document page be no smaller than 5.8″ × 2.9″.

Note: FAX machines in England and other European countries and in most Asian countries use a metric paper size referred to as A4, the dimensions of which are 8.3″ × 11.7″. This may affect the format (page margins) and the amount of data you can transmit to FAX users in other countries.

Printed Page Size

Very large documents or drawings may have to be sent in several pieces. They can be reassembled after the pages are printed by the receiving FAX machine.

The size of a printed page varies from one FAX machine to another. Some dedicated FAX machines can print on standard-size bond paper, but the majority use thermal paper on rolls or—less frequently—in sheets. The printing process is the same as with thermal calculators. No matter what the physical size of the page from which a FAX message was scanned, a receiving machine will reduce it as necessary to fit its printer's paper.

How Good Will It Look?

The quality of graphic images (be they letters or drawings) sent by FAX—referred to as the *resolution*—is another element that varies from one machine to another. The resolution depends on three elements:

- The resolution mode in use (standard or fine)

- The quality of the sending FAX machine's scanner (discussed in Chapter 3)

- The type and quality of the receiving FAX machine's printer (again, discussed in Chapter 3)

FAX printers of all types create an image by placing dots on paper, the locations of which are based on information generated by the sending machine's scanner. Each dot is called a *pixel* (short for picture element), which is the smallest possible unit of a picture.

Resolution

In FAX, resolution machine refers to the detail of scanned and printed images. That is, it refers both to how closely a FAX machine scans a page and to the relative density of dots in its printouts.

Most modern FAX machines have a Standard resolution of 98 × 203 lpi (lines per inch) and a Fine resolution of 196 × 203 lpi. You will find a few more advanced FAX machines capable of what is called Super-Fine mode, which produces a resolution of 391 × 203 lpi.

In each instance, the first number is horizontal and the second number is vertical. The horizontal measurement is actually the maximum number of dots in a horizontal line an inch wide (left to right). The vertical measurement can be interpreted as the number of lines *or* dots per vertical inch (top to bottom). Standard resolution is of a higher quality than either standard dot-matrix printers or computer monitors. Even Fine resolution does not produce as good a quality an image as a laser printer, which can produce an image of 300 × 400 dpi (dots per square inch) or higher. Interestingly enough, some high-end FAXes use laser printers. They can not only reproduce Super-Fine resolution scans but also enhance the appearance of Standard and Fine resolution scans. In contrast, the density of a standard typeset page is approximately 1000 × 1200 dpi.

When communicating with Group 2 FAX machines, resolution will drop to 98 × 98 lpi. Documents and graphics sent via PC FAX boards or modem/FAX services are normally Fine resolution.

It's worth noting here that a low-quality or Standard-resolution printer will not reproduce the resolution of an image scanned by a Fine-resolution scanner. Similarly, a Fine-resolution printer cannot make a page scanned with a poor-quality or Standard-resolution scanner look as good as the original. In other words, the quality of a printed FAX message can be no better than the FAX machine's printer is capable of producing and no better than the scanned image that is sent to it.

What You've Learned

This chapter has taught you the following:

- While text and graphics are distinct entities, both are perceived and handled by FAX scanners and printers as graphics composed of dots.

- Information transmitted by FAX can be referred to as pages, documents, messages, or images, depending on the specific usage.

- The four types of FAX machines are referred to as Group 1, Group 2, Group 3, and Group 4. Each group is newer in time and technology than its predecessor, and each is distinguished by the speed of data transfer, graphic resolution, and other elements.

- The most common type of FAX machine currently in use is Group 3.

- Individual Group 3 FAX machines may not be able to communicate with Group 1 or Group 2 machines.

- Most applications for FAX machines are business related.

- The three categories of FAX equipment are dedicated FAX machines, PC FAX board-equipped computers, and modem-equipped computers.

- The vast majority of FAX transmissions use the worldwide voice-telephone network.

- There is no limit to the amount of information (number of pages or length of a document) that can be sent during a FAX transmission. The physical size of a scannable page is, however, limited.

- Most dedicated FAX machines can either send or receive during a call; they cannot reverse roles until a new call is made. If you wish to receive a document from another FAX machine after sending a document to it, you must hang up and allow the other machine to call your FAX.

- The time required to transmit the contents of a typical page via FAX is 15 to 20 seconds.

- Anything that can be printed on paper can be sent via FAX, including text, artwork, handwriting, and photographs.

- Although you can scan color images, only black-and-white images and images in varying shades of gray can be output by a FAX printer.

- Most FAX machines' scanners accept standard-size paper 8½″ ×

11 ″ in the U.S. and a metric size called A4 in European and Asian countries.

- Because of variances in scanners, printers, and the alignment of pages when scanned, you should leave reasonable margins on all sides of a page to be scanned and transmitted.

- A receiving FAX resizes the images it receives to fit the paper used by its printer.

- The quality of a FAX's output is referred to as its resolution. Among Group 3 FAX machines, there are two common levels of resolution: Standard, which is printed with a matrix, or array, of 98 × 203 dpi, and Fine, which is printed with a matrix of 196 × 203 dpi. Some upper-end machines feature a Super-Fine resolution of 196 × 391 dpi.

Now that you have a basic understanding of the methods and equipment used in facsimile communication and the capabilities and limitations of FAX, test your knowledge with the following quiz. Then, move on to Chapter 3, where we'll examine in detail just how FAX works and what's available in terms of FAX features and options.

Quiz

1. Which is currently the most popular type of dedicated FAX machine?

   a. Group 1
   b. Group 2
   c. Group 3
   d. Group 4

2. What kinds of documents can you send via FAX?

   a. Typed letters and memos
   b. Mechanical drawings
   c. Photographs
   d. All of the above

3. How do FAX scanners and printers see text and graphics?

   a. Both text and graphics are scanned and printed as graphics.
   b. Text and graphics are handled differently.
   c. It varies, depending on the machine in use.
   d. Special FAX machines are required to handle graphics.

4. A machine that is designed primarily or solely to send and receive FAX messages is called:

   a. A PC FAX board
   b. A dedicated FAX machine
   c. A Group 2 FAX machine
   d. A modem/FAX machine

5. The element of a FAX machine that converts the material on a page into electronic signals for transmission is called the:

   a. Printer
   b. Scanner
   c. Modem
   d. Image

6. The element of a FAX machine that sends and receives (transmits) electronic signals is called the:

   a. Printer
   b. Scanner
   c. Modem
   d. Image

7. The element of a FAX machine that outputs received images to paper is called the:

   a. Printer
   b. Scanner

   c. Modem

   d. Image

8. FAX that originates on a computer and is transmitted via an online service is called:

   a. Modem/FAX

   b. PC FAX board

   c. PC/modem

   d. Standalone FAX

9. What is the communications channel (or physical carrier) for FAX transmissions?

   a. Serial cables

   b. Standard telephone lines

   c. Radio waves

   d. Modem

10. The resolution of a FAX printout is measured by a density of dots referred to as lpi. What does "lpi" stand for?

   a. lines per inch

   b. lines per iota

   c. lines pel inch

   d. labels per inch

11. Which of these densities is referred to as Fine resolution?

   a. 196 × 203 lpi

   b. 200 × 200 lpi

   c. 300 × 200 lpi

   d. 200 × 400 lpi

12. The speed at which a FAX machine's modem transmits data is measured in bits per second (bps). What is the highest transmission rate for Group 3 FAX (assuming the modem doesn't fall back to a slower speed to compensate for a poor connection)?

   a. 1200 bps

   b. 2400 bps

   c. 4800 bps

   d. 9600 bps

Chapter **3** | **How FAX Works**

About This Chapter

If you're interested in the technical end of facsimile transmission, the first part of this chapter will satisfy your curiosity. The rest of the chapter covers the various features and options available for dedicated (conventional) FAX machines, PC FAX boards and how they work, and modem/FAX services. The discussions of available features include relative advantages and disadvantages.

> **Note:** If you're intimidated by things technical, don't worry. I'll provide the technical information necessary to understand FAX transmission in an easy-to-understand manner. You don't have to read all of this chapter, although I recommend it. While it isn't necessary to understand how FAX works, the additional knowledge it will make you a more effective FAX buyer and user.

Conventional FAX: How It Works

As you know, conventional facsimile transmission is accomplished in four stages:

- A document (text, graphics, photograph, etc.) is translated into binary signals by a FAX machine's scanner.

- The FAX machine's modem converts the binary signals to analog signals that can be transmitted via telephone line.

- The modem transmits the analog signals over a preestablished telephone connection to another FAX machine, where another modem converts the signals back to binary form.

- The receiving FAX machine's printer reproduces the original document and/or graphics, in effect reversing the scanning process of the sending FAX machine.

Let's take a look at each of these steps in detail.

Scanning

A scanner is a device that converts the characters, lines, etc., on a sheet of paper or photograph into electronic signals, which are sent to (or temporarily stored in) the FAX's modem for transmission. When a dedicated FAX machine is used, a sheet of paper containing the material to be transmitted (text and/or graphics) is moved past a scanning device, or vice versa.

The scanning device uses *photoelectric elements* (typically, *photodiodes*) that allow current to flow or not flow depending on whether a high or low intensity of light reaches their surface. A simple scanner sees a page as thousands of tiny points, each of which is perceived and recorded as either white or black, based on the amount of light reflected from or passed through the page at the point being scanned.

This simple *two-state* scanning system is used in the transmission and reproduction of FAXed material, as well. As you'll soon see, more sophisticated scanning techniques are used by FAX machines that can distinguish various shades of gray in addition to black and white.

Pixels, the points on a page that are scanned by the photoelectric elements, are the smallest elements of a picture. You may be familiar with the term and concept as applied to television or computer monitors.

The size of pixels—and the distance between them—is determined by the resolution capability and setting of the scanner. As you learned in Chapter 2, a Group 3 FAX scanner can perceive 98 or 203 pixels in a horizontal inch, and 98, 196, or 391 pixels in a vertical inch. The number of pixels per inch is dictated by the increments in which the paper is moved past the scanner (or vice versa) and the sensitivity of the photoelectric elements in use.

The status of a pixel—black or white—is mirrored by a representational electrical state in the FAX machine's circuitry, which is called a *binary digit* or *bit*. At the same time, the location of the pixel is recorded, which uses additional bits and creates strings or groups of binary digits called *bytes*. The process of *encoding* such information about a picture element is called *digitizing*.

How Scanning Works

The scanner senses whether points on a page are light or dark.

When a page is scanned, the scanner moves over a dark point on the page, and no current flows through the photoelectric element. This registers as a black pixel and is recorded as such in the binary data format used by the FAX machine. When the scanner moves over a light point on a page, current flows through the photoelectric element, and the pixel is recorded as white. Figure 3.1 is a simplified representation of the scanning process.

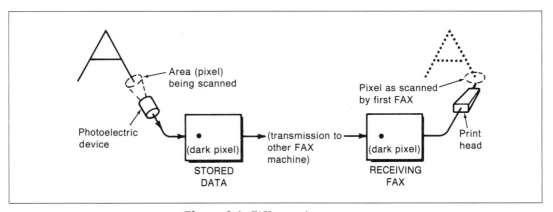

Figure 3.1 FAX scanning process.

Conventional Two-State (Black-and-White) Scanning In the scanning process, only two states are perceived: white and black. Because of this, most light gray pixels register as white when scanned, and most dark gray pixels register as black. In binary terms, a pixel is either on or off.

Just how dark a pixel must be before it registers as black can vary greatly, depending on the sensitivity of the scanner. The sensitivity of some scanners is adjustable. If you increase a scanner's sensitivity, it will perceive almost all gray areas as black. The higher the sensitivity, the lighter the pixels perceived as black can be. It's like selecting a "Light Original" or "Darker" setting on a photocopier; make the scanner more sensitive, and you get more black pixels in the scanned and transmitted image. This is also known as "contrast control."

Halftone and Gray Scale

More sophisticated scanning techniques are used to perceive more than two states in scanning and recording pixels, by distinguishing the *relative* lightness or darkness of a pixel. FAX machines that can perceive varying levels of gray are said to have *halftone* or *gray scale* capability, and their scanners can distinguish 8, 16, 32 or even 64 different shades (scales) of gray. Such scanners are most useful in transmitting black-and-white or color photographs or any graphic image whose details depend on varying shades and contrast. Without halftone capability, most of the detail in such an image is lost, relegated to plain black and white.

When time is more important than document quality, set machine to the lowest resolution.

The varying shades are perceived through the use of analog sensing by photoelectric elements. The analog-sensing process uses photodiodes which are able to sense the relative shades and record them using the same binary data format used to record pixels as straight black or white.

FAX machines that offer halftone capability can usually be switched between standard black-and-white scanning and halftone scanning, to accommodate transmissions to machines of lesser capability.

The quality of a halftone scan when printed depends entirely upon the capability of the printer on the other end—which may not be able to reflect varying shades of gray by using different sizes of dots when printing or by increasing or decreasing the density of the dots.

Binary Data and Signals

As previously mentioned, a scanned image is recorded electronically in binary data format. Binary data has two states—which means it can be used to represent a high or a low value, the absence or presence of something, or an off or on state.

The process of scanning a page creates electrical current at low- and high-voltage levels or, in some cases, the absence or presence of voltage. This provides the basis for a two-state or *binary* data structure. When a FAX scanner senses a dark pixel, it stores the pixel as a low voltage, which is referred to as a binary 1; a light area is stored as high voltage, or a binary 0. Where halftone scanning is involved, multiple bits are used to record the gray scale value of a pixel.

These binary representations of pixels are encoded and transmitted in bytes, which a receiving FAX machine decodes and uses to direct its printer to print dots (pixels) in the proper locations on its printout of the FAXed document. The order and placement of bits within a byte carry the information necessary for a receiving FAX machine to reconstruct the location and shade of a pixel.

Note: For a more complete discussion of binary data, see *Understanding Data Communications* (Howard W. Sams & Company, 1987).

Binary Signals When a scanner sends data to a modem (or a modem to a printer), the bits are transmitted as *binary signals*. The signals are literally a series of negative and positive voltages, as illustrated in Figure 3.2. The negative state represents a binary 1, while the positive state represents a binary 0.

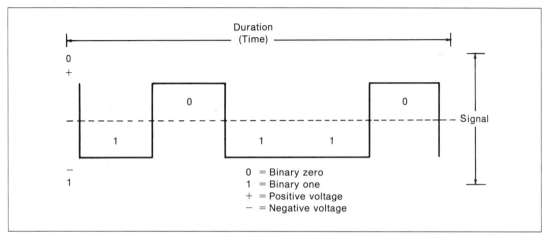

Figure 3.2 A binary signal.

Data Conversion with a Modem

A modem (the word is a contraction of the phrase "*mod*ulate/*dem*odulate device") is a device that converts binary signals to analog signals, and vice versa. The conversion is necessary because the worldwide voice-telephone network was designed to carry analog signals: it cannot carry binary data reliably.

Strictly defined, an analog signal is a signal that varies in a continuous manner, as opposed to a digital signal, which varies in a discontinuous manner. Figure 3.3 provides a visual comparison of analog and digital signals.

As Figure 3.3 illustrates, analog signals vary continuously between their minimum and maximum values, while digital signals do not vary between values. A digital signal is always at either a minimum or a maximum level or value (or in one state or the other); there is no in-between state. Analog signals, on the other hand, cover the entire range between maximum and minimum values.

The analog signal in Figure 3.3 is in the form of a sine wave, while the binary signal is a square wave. It may help to think of binary signals as *digital* or electronic signals, and analog signals as electric signals.

Modems convert the binary data produced by FAX scanners into a form that can be transmitted via telephone lines and convert incoming analog data back into binary data.

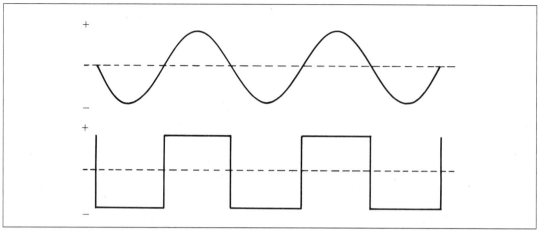

Figure 3.3 Analog and binary signals.

A modem converts the bits that compose binary data signals into analog signals by changing elements or characteristics (e.g., strength and frequency) of a *carrier wave*. A carrier wave is a constant signal that is already present on an analog circuit (in this case, a telephone line).

The carrier wave is altered in a pattern that mimics the distinction between the binary 1s and 0s in the binary data being transmitted. Figure 3.4 illustrates how an analog carrier wave can be made to vary in a manner that approximates the variations of a digital signal.

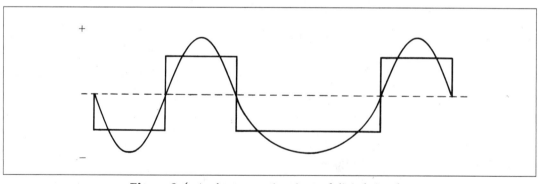

Figure 3.4 Analog approximations of digital signals.

Placing information on a carrier wave in this manner is called *modulation*.

Data Transmission and Reception

Once the data from a scanned page has been converted from digital to analog signals, it is transmitted over a telephone line—either the public voice-telephone network or, in the case of many Group 4 FAX machines and some Group 3 machines, what are known as *dedicated telephone lines*. Dedicated telephone lines are phone links that are used only by the communications devices to which they are connected—FAX machines in this instance—and that are always connected.

> **Note:** *Digital networks* accommodate direct transfer of binary information for Group 4 FAX, but these are presently extremely expensive and are used only in applications where high speed and accuracy are necessary.

A telephone link does not, by the way, consist solely of telephone wires. Electromechanical, electronic, and computer-switching equipment are involved, as are microwave radio relays, transmitters, and satellite links. For the purposes of this book, however, such elements will remain transparent.

If you frequently transmit FAX over long distances and are using a long-distance carrier whose lines are of poor quality, consider changing to a carrier whose connections are of better quality.

A modulated analog signal is carried by voice-grade telephone lines as a series of tones. The tones vary as the modulation varies. The frequency of the tones is limited to the range used by the voice-telephone data network, which in turn limits the speed at which FAX modems can transmit data to 9600 bps. Special fiber-optic networks or dedicated telephone lines can transfer FAX two to four times faster, but they are very expensive.

At the receiving end of a FAX transmission, incoming tones are converted to binary data in a process that is basically the reverse of the process used to modulate the carrier wave. This process is called *demodulation*, and it recreates the binary data that the sending FAX's modem converted to analog data.

> **Note:** Most dedicated FAX machines can either transmit or receive during a call; they cannot do both. If you dial up another FAX machine and send a document, you have to disconnect and call again to receive a document. However, *turnaround polling*, an increasingly popular feature on more advanced FAX machines, enables you to both send and receive documents during the same call.

At this point, the receiving FAX has in its circuitry a copy of the binary data the sending FAX's scanner generated and can either store the data or output the data to its printer.

Physical Connections

As previously indicated, a FAX machine is directly connected to a telephone line. Modern FAX machines have a jack (receptacle) designed to accommodate the standard telephone-line connector, the RJ-11 plug. An RJ-11 jack is the plastic connector found at either end of a telephone line. One end is plugged into the telephone wall outlet, and the other end is plugged into the telephone or, in this case, the FAX machine.

Because virtually all FAX machines are equipped with an RJ-11 jack, your telephone line should terminate in an RJ-11 or similar plug. If the line does not have an RJ-11 plug, ask your telephone company to upgrade the telephone line. You can do this yourself, if you wish; the conversion is quite simple. Most telephone companies, electronics stores such as Radio Shack, and telephone specialty stores sell kits with which you can convert any telephone line or outlet to use RJ-11 plugs and jacks. Either way, you will have to have a telephone line that terminates in an RJ-11 plug to connect a FAX machine to your telephone line.

Other Modem Functions

In addition to data conversion and transmission, FAX modems handle these tasks:

- Establishing and maintaining the telephone link between FAX machines
- Checking data for errors

Establishing and Maintaining a Telephone Link

Just as a FAX's modem communicates data via tonal signals, it also uses tones to establish and maintain communication with another FAX machine's modem. In fact, if you are using a speaker-equipped FAX machine (or dial up a FAX machine with a telephone and listen), the first thing you will hear is a high-pitched squeal. This is an identifying tone to which a calling FAX's modem must respond with a similar tone before a communications link is established. Carrier tones are a bit quieter.

FAX modems perform the housekeeping chores of transmitting a tone that turns off the *transponders* (special kinds of signal boosters used on telephone circuits to eliminate data alteration) and keeping the communications link open by generating an "empty" carrier wave when data is not being sent. If no carrier wave is present, a modem will either quickly drop a connection or disconnect.

More intelligent FAX machines not only handle initiating and maintaining the communications link but also dial phone numbers. This feature, called *auto-dialing*, is becoming more and more common, even on low-end FAX machines. Some will even dial numbers and send documents at preset times, unattended. This feature works best if the FAX machine has a memory in which a document can be stored.

Error Checking

A relatively recent innovation in FAX is *error checking*. Dubbed *Error Correction Mode*, or ECM, this is an optional feature whose operation has been standardized by the CCITT so that FAX machines made by different manufacturers can use it. With ECM, each page is checked automatically for errors. The receiving FAX machine communicates information about the data it has received to the sending machine, which checks the information against its own information. If an error is corrected, the page is sent again.

Printing FAXed Documents

After a signal is received and converted from analog back to digital format, it is sent to the FAX's printer (or, with some machines, stored in memory to be printed later). The printer reproduces the pattern of dots recorded by the sending FAX's scanner as closely as possible by printing arrays of dots on paper. In other words, the pattern and density of dots printed reflects the pattern and density of the dots as seen by the sending machine's scanner.

The resolution and detail of the printout depends entirely upon the capability of the receiving FAX's printer. If, as mentioned earlier, a halftone scan is transmitted to a FAX whose printer cannot reproduce the varying shades of gray in a halftone, the quality will be about the same as a Standard scan. If a 196 × 203-lpi scan is transmitted to a FAX whose printer is capable of 98 × 203-lpi output, then the image will be printed in 98 × 203-lpi resolution.

How the dots are placed on the paper varies, depending on the type of printer used. There are four types of printers used by FAX machines.

Conventional FAX: Hardware Features and Options

The range and variety of features available on dedicated FAX machines are almost endless (and some are useless). However, you should be familiar with a number of basic and advanced features.

Whether the features discussed in the following pages are standard or optional (or even available) with a specific FAX machine is entirely up to the machine's manufacturer.

Telephone-Related Features

How a dedicated FAX uses and interacts with the telephone system is important. Certain telephone-related features can make using FAX easier and less time consuming, and some are vital for frequent FAX users.

Auto-Answer

The ability to answer an incoming call is vital and almost omnipresent with modern FAX machines. An auto-answer FAX machine typically answers the phone on the first or second ring. It then emits the characteristic high-pitched identifying tone, after which a communication link is established if another FAX machine is calling.

You should be able to disable a FAX machine's auto-answer feature, in case the FAX shares a phone line with a voice telephone, or if you want to take the machine off line to avoid incoming FAX junk mail.

Auto-Dial

As explained earlier, auto-dial is the ability of a FAX machine to dial telephone numbers on its own, without the aid of a telephone set. This feature is invaluable; without it, you have to connect a telephone set to the FAX machine. FAX machines with auto-dial capability have a numeric keyboard, similar in appearance to the layout of buttons on a push-button telephone, which is used to dial numbers.

Dialing Features

In addition to the auto-dial capability, more sophisticated FAX machines offer many of the same features as advanced office telephones, such as tone/pulse dialing, memory dialing, and other features described below.

Tone/Pulse Dialing Depending on the area in which you live—or if you use a FAX machine in more than one location (especially a portable FAX machine)—you may need both tone and pulse dialing capability. Pulse dialing is required where only old-fashioned rotary dial phone service is available.

Memory Dialing FAX machines with auto-dial capability often offer the ability to store frequently called telephone numbers and dial them when a single button or a two-button combination is pressed. Known as memory dialing, single-key dialing, or speed dialing, this is probably the most useful dialing feature you can have. Be sure the memory can hold enough digits to handle all of your long-distance calls. Long-distance calls within the United States require eight to 11 digits, and calls to other countries can require 15 or more digits. If you're using an alternative long-distance service, you'll have to add the local phone number and access code digits to the dial string.

Automatic Callback Single-key automatic callback is usually included with FAXes that offer memory dialing. This feature redials the most recently dialed number (whether it is dialed directly or from memory).

Repeat Dialing Repeat dialing is another feature that may accompany memory dialing and is a subfeature of automatic callback. If a number is dialed and is busy, a FAX machine with this feature will wait a specified amount of time, then try the number again. It will repeat this process a specified number of times or until a connection is made.

Backup Number Dialing This feature is one for high-volume FAX usage. If a number is dialed and is busy, a FAX machine with backup number dialing will dial a designated backup number. This feature is useful when you need to send a document to someone who has two or more FAX machines that are frequently in use.

Other Dialing Features Some nice extras that may not be included on a FAX machine equipped with memory dialing include an LED or liquid-crystal display that shows the number being dialed and/or a name associated with it. Another extra is the ability to search for and dial numbers based on the entry of a letter or two (or a number that represents a letter).

If you intend to use a FAX machine in an office with a PBX system, you'll want to be sure it has pause capability (e.g., the ability to pause between digits when dialing a number). Most PBX systems require that you dial a number such as 9 before you can call out, and you usually have to wait a second or two before you get a dial tone. Thus, you must be able to direct an auto-dial machine to pause as necessary.

Telephone Jack

A *telephone jack* (a receptacle into which you can plug an outgoing telephone line to connect to a telephone set) enables you to use a single telephone line for either FAX or voice-telephone communications without having to disconnect the FAX machine. Even if you have a dedicated FAX line, you should still have this option; sooner or later you'll want to use it. You should, of course, be able to disable the FAX machine's auto-answer feature or to toggle a switch from "FAX" to "Telephone" to accommodate the use of a voice telephone.

This feature can also be used to share a phone line with a modem. When you already have either a modem or a FAX machine on a dedicated line, and want to add the other communications device, this situation is very common.

> **Note:** Some basic FAX machines require that you plug a telephone set into a jack provided by the manufacturer to make a call.

Voice/Data Switching

If your auto-answer FAX machine shares a line with a voice telephone (whether the phone is plugged into a phone jack on the FAX or on an extension), voice callers will be rudely greeted by the FAX's answering squeal—and probably hang up before you can disable the FAX and answer the phone—unless you disable the FAX machine. This can be done by turning the FAX off or by manual or automatic voice/data switching.

Manual voice/data switching is accomplished via a toggle switch or setting on the FAX machine. Set it to "FAX," and the FAX's modem will answer when someone calls; set it to "Voice," and the phone will ring until you answer it or the calling party hangs up.

Many upper-end FAX machines handle voice/data switching automatically. Machines with automatic voice/data switching can determine whether an incoming call is FAX or voice. If a carrier wave is detected when the FAX answers the call, the FAX's modem answers the machine; if not, the phone is allowed to ring.

> **Note:** Some FAX machines that have automatic voice/data switches still answer a call with the squeal that is characteristic of a FAX machine, and some don't. You'll most likely prefer to use a FAX that doesn't insult your voice callers by squealing at them.

Telephone Function

Many FAX machines like the one shown in Figure 3.5 combine a telephone set with a FAX machine. Having this configuration is advantageous when you must share a telephone line between a FAX and a voice telephone, because it combines both into one compact unit, and you don't have to worry with extra connections.

Some machines limit this feature to using the FAX machine as a telephone *or* a FAX. On more advanced machines, you can interrupt a FAX transmission to talk with the party on the other end of the connection, then resume FAX communication. The other FAX machine must, of course, have the same capability.

FAX/voice phone combinations typically offer all the dialing features previously discussed and can, in fact, serve in lieu of an advanced office telephone. If you need office telephone features, consider buying a FAX/voice phone. While more expensive than a FAX-only machine, the combination is less costly than buying a FAX and telephone separately.

Scanner Features

The ability to switch resolution levels is important.

The most important feature on a scanner is its maximum level of resolution—transmitting graphics-rich or even text-only documents will sometimes require as much detailing as possible.

In addition to resolution, important features to consider in a scan-

Figure 3.5 A telephone/FAX combination. *Photo courtesy of Brother International Corporation*

ner are halftone capability, contrast control, how the scanner physically handles pages, and page reduction and enlargement.

Halftone Capability

As explained earlier, a scanner with halftone (or gray scale) capability can distinguish more than two image states. That is, instead of just perceiving black-and-white pixels, a scanner with halftone capability perceives and records up to 64 shades of gray.

If you intend to FAX copies of black-and-white photos, color artwork or photos, and/or shaded line art of any type, you should buy a FAX machine with halftone capability. Remember, however, that halftone transmissions to FAX machines that do not have halftone capability will not be of the best quality.

> **Note:** FAX machines that have scanners with halftone capability also have printers with halftone capability.

Contrast Control

The contrast control lets you decrease or increase the sensitivity of the scanner's photoelectric sensing elements. This means you can remove some darkened areas from a dark image to increase its clarity (select greater contrast) or darken the lines in a light image (select lesser contrast).

> **Note:** FAXed images are often reproduced darker than the original, destroying some of the detail. If detail is lost when you FAX an image, set the sending FAX machine's contrast control to increase the contrast. If the FAX has no contrast control, create a lighter version using a photocopier with a contrast control.

Page Handling

How a FAX machine handles pages to be scanned is very important, because the physical configuration of a scanner can both limit and enhance the usefulness of your FAX machine, depending on your applications. There are two common physical configurations for scanners: sheet and flatbed.

Sheet Scanners The sheet scanner configuration is the most common among low- and medium-priced FAX machines. This configuration uses a roller or rollers (platens) to move pages to be scanned past the scanner. Sheet scanners usually require you to insert the pages of a document manually, although some have automatic *document feeders* that will accept several standard (8½" × 11") pages stacked in a tray and move them through the scanner themselves.

The maximum-size page accepted by a sheet scanner is usually standard or legal size. However, some will accept standard width pages that are up to 39" long (sheets of this size require manual insertion).

If you intend to FAX only standard- or near-standard-size pages and want to save money, a FAX machine with a sheet scanner is your best bet.

Flatbed Scanners Flatbed scanners are used almost exclusively with higher-priced FAX machines. The flatbed consists of a flat sheet of glass on which pages to be scanned are placed. This configuration is the same as that of most photocopiers and may include an automatic sheet feeder of the type used in many photocopiers.

If your FAX machine has a flatbed scanner, keep the glass surface clean. Streaks or smears can obliterate sections of a document page totally.

The maximum-size page that a flatbed scanner can scan is limited by the size of the glass. In addition, most flatbed scanners will not scan the entire width and length of the glass area. So, in addition to making the usual allowances for the possibility of unscanned margins (i.e., allow for ½" of unscanned space all the way around), you will have to follow the manufacturer's instructions as to the maximum-size page that can be scanned.

Document feeders are an option with most flatbed scanners, but they are standard for some. If your FAX traffic volume is high, it's best to have a document feeder in any case.

Flatbed scanners are best if you will be scanning oversize pages frequently; the extra cost is more than offset by the convenience of not having to cut down or otherwise resize documents that won't fit a sheet feed scanner. You also have the advantage of being able to scan thicker pages or even books.

Page Reduction

As noted earlier, all FAX machines reduce the size of a received image, if necessary, to fit the size of paper they use. However, there are some situations in which it may be useful to reduce the size of a page *before* it is transmitted (e.g., when you want to FAX a large spreadsheet). Some flatbed scanners have an option that enables them to scan a larger area than they normally would and proportionally reduce the size of the material on the page. The reduced image is transmitted and printed in a proportionally smaller format by the receiving FAX machine. This eliminates your having to prepare the drawing with an interim step such as copying it on a reducing photocopier.

Page Enlargement

Some documents can benefit from being enlarged—in particular, extremely detailed line art. Some scanners (both flatbed and sheet feed) can enlarge a drawing by a set or a specified percentage, in much the same manner as an enlarging photocopier enlarges copies.

Enlargement is limited by the maximum size of a scannable page. If, for instance, you scan a drawing that fills a page, you are going to get very little in the way of enlargement.

Modem Features

Group 3 FAX modems offer four options: speed, the absence or presence of error checking, automatic fallback, and compatibility with Group 1 or Group 2 FAX machines.

Speed

As noted earlier, the maximum speed of a Group 3 FAX is 9600 bps. This does not, however, mean that all Group 3 FAX machines are capable of transmitting at this speed. The *minimum* transmission speed for a Group 3 FAX machine is 2400 bps; for some low-end Group 3 machines, this is also the maximum speed. Such machines can still communicate with 9600-bps FAX machines; the faster machines merely fall back to the lower speed.

If you are going to be doing a lot of long-distance FAX communication, be sure to get a machine with 9600-bps capability; you'll cut your long-distance FAX phone bills by 50 to 75%. If most or all of your FAX communications will be local, you might consider saving on the initial investment with a 2400-bps machine.

Error Checking

As noted earlier, Error Correction Mode, or ECM, is an option that helps eliminate errors in FAX transmissions—even when there's a bad connection or lots of line noise. ECM is enabled only when both the sending and receiving FAX machine has ECM capability. If one or the other of the FAX machines doesn't have ECM capability, transmission proceeds normally.

While it may seem an "iffy" option, since not all FAX machines have ECM capability, you should seriously consider buying a FAX machine with ECM capability. It appears that ECM is on the way to becoming a standard feature on all Group 3 FAXes. Since ECM is based on an international standard (which means that any ECM-equipped FAX machine can transmit in error-checking mode with any other ECM-equipped FAX), and more and more FAXes are being equipped with ECM, it's a good idea to jump on the bandwagon in preparation for the time when all FAX machines will use error checking.

Automatic Fallback

Although FAX modems initiate transmission at the highest possible speed (i.e., the highest speed of the slower of the modems), transmission may be garbled or terminated by poor connections or line noise. In dial-up telecommunications operations such as FAX communications, the faster the rate of data transfer, the more opportunity there is for error.

To compensate for this, most FAX modems automatically reduce the transfer speed, or fallback, to a slower speed when delays in transmission are detected. These fallbacks are typically in increments of 2400 bps. Automatic fallback can serve as a replacement for or adjunct to ECM.

Group 1 and Group 2 Compatibility

While the vast majority of FAX machines currently in use are Group 3, you may find it necessary to communicate with a Group 1 or Group 2 FAX machine. Many older FAX machines (mainly Group 2) remain in service because of their original high initial cost, the reluctance of those who use them to upgrade, or other reasons.

Group 1 and Group 2 compatibility involves both transmission speed and transmission techniques and can be an expensive option because a special modem is required. If there are certain companies or individuals with whom you know you will be exchanging documents by FAX, it is a good idea to find out whether they use Group 3 FAX, to determine if you'll need Group 1 and/or Group 2 compatibility.

Printers

Until the 1980s, most FAX machines used thermal printers, because this was the only truly cost-effective means of printing graphics. Other kinds of output—including video—might have been used, but the cost of FAX machines was already priced as high as the market would bear. Thanks to the development of relatively low-cost, high-quality printing technologies for personal computers, however, several options are now available to the FAX buyer in terms of printed output.

Other printer-related options are also available, some likewise thanks to computer technology.

Printer Types

Four basic types of printers are available with FAX machines: thermal, electrostatic, dot-matrix, and laser. Figure 3.6 contains a sample of each.

Thermal Printers You are probably familiar with thermal printers from using "inkless" printing calculators or early computer printers. Thermal printers print characters and images on heat-sensitive paper. The paper is called, appropriately enough, thermal paper.

An array of electrically charged wires (or, sometimes, one wire) is used to place miniscule dots on the thermal paper in locations corresponding to pixel locations in a transmitted image. When a dark pixel occurs, the print head is charged at the appropriate location on the paper. This generates heat and darkens the area of the paper adjacent to the wire.

Thermal printers offer several advantages. Thermal printing is a fast and virtually soundless process. You don't have to worry about running out of ink, toner fluid, or ribbon, because thermal printers use none of these. Some thermal printers use single sheets, but many use paper that comes on a roll and feeds through the machine on its own. Using this type of paper means you don't have to keep a constant watch on an incoming document. There are few moving parts to break down or wear out. Finally, a thermal printer is the least-expensive kind of printer to have.

```
                                       FAX COVER PAGE


         Date:                   Fri Aug 18, 1989,  5:55 pm EDT

         To:                     Ralph W. Roberts

         Destination Fax:        915-581-2360


         From:                   Michael Banks

         Subject:                Septor press release


         Number of pages excluding cover page:  0.5

         Number of delivery attempts:  1
```

*This facsimile message was electronically transmitted by **MCI Mail**®*

*Call 800-444-6245 for information about **MCI Mail**®*

Figure 3.6 Sample FAX printer output (first part).

Because images on thermal paper can deteriorate rapidly, photocopy any FAXed documents that you wish to keep for more than a few weeks.

On the negative side, thermal paper is somewhat more expensive than normal paper, and it tends to deteriorate after a time. If exposed to direct or indirect heat—even sunlight on a hot day—thermal paper darkens, which means you can lose a valuable document (or lose your stock of blank thermal paper) if you don't handle it with care. Many thermal printers use a narrow roll paper that, combined with relatively low resolution, makes for a nonprofessional appearance. You have to cut continuous roll thermal paper (or add a *paper cutter* to your FAX machine) if you prefer to have the pages of your documents in individual sheets. Single-sheet thermal paper doesn't have to be cut, but it must be fed into the machine manually, unless you add a *sheet feeder*.

```
ATTN: Mr. Ralph W. Roberts
Septor Electronics
4605 Ripley Drive
El Paso, TX  79922

Dear Mr. Roberts:

     I recently received your press release regarding Septor
Electronics Corporation's joint venture with the Soviet Union.  I
found the concept of Septor's self-aware controls most
interesting, and would like to include information on Septor's
products, as well as the joint venture, in an article we are
developing for the March issue of Intelligent Control Systems
Journal.
     Please send product photos and any additional brochures or
other product information you have available; after receiving
this material, I'll be in touch with you by phone with additional
questions.
     Thank you for your cooperation.

M.A. Banks, Associate Editor
Intelligent Control Systems Journal
P.O. Box 312
Milford, OH  45150
(513) 555-1212
```

Figure 3.6 Sample FAX printer output (second part).

With superior FAX printer technologies emerging, thermal printers can be recommended only if cost is an issue.

Electrostatic Printers The electrostatic printing process is the same one used by photocopiers to place images on specially coated or regular bond paper. A black pigment ("toner" fluid or powder) is attracted and bonded to the paper whenever an electrical charge is generated by the printer's print head. The print head is so activated wherever a pixel occurs, attracting the fluid or powder to the paper at that point, printing a dot on the paper (the image is later fixed by fusing the pigment to the paper with a small amount of heat).

The paper used by electrostatic printers is typically less expensive than thermal paper. Because electrostatic printers use individual sheets of paper, you don't have to worry about cutting documents into manageable sheets. Images are less likely to be destroyed, because the paper is not sensitive to heat and deteriorates very slowly.

Unfortunately, electrostatic printers are more complex than thermal printers and, thus, more expensive and somewhat more prone to breakdowns. Too, you must replenish the supply of toner fluid or ink periodically (and a few do require special paper). The sheets of blank paper used by electrostatic printers must be fed by hand, which means that someone has to attend the FAX machine's paper needs, unless you add a sheet feeder to the machine.

Dot-Matrix Printers Dot-matrix printers used with FAX machines operate in the same manner as the ubiquitous dot-matrix computer printers. Very fine wires in the print head are driven against a ribbon, on the other side of which is a sheet of paper. Each time a wire impacts the ribbon, a dot is placed on the paper. Each wire is, in effect, an electromagnet's core and is activated when electrical current is passed through the wire surrounding it. A wire is activated whenever it is in the location where a pixel occurs. Because the wire actually strikes the ribbon, this kind of printer is more properly known as an *impact* printer.

Dot-matrix printers are fairly reliable mechanically and use just about any kind of paper (even colored paper). They are, however, slower and noisier than thermal or electrostatic printers, and ribbons must be replaced periodically. Unless a sheet feeder or (more typically) a *tractor feed* mechanism is used, you must feed blank paper by hand.

A variation on impact dot-matrix printers is the ink-jet printer. Ink-jet printers place dots on paper using jets of ink activated by current flow, a process that is quieter and faster than impact printing. Like impact dot-matrix printers, ink-jet printers can use almost any kind of paper, but the ink supply must be replenished periodically.

Laser Printers The laser printing process, originally developed for use with computers, has been adapted for use with photocopiers and FAX machines. Laser printing uses a process similar to that used by electrostatic printers, but augmented by the use of a tiny laser beam to create the necessary electrostatic charge. The laser beam speeds up the printing process and, more importantly, creates more sharply focused images for higher resolution.

Laser printers provide the best of all worlds where printing is concerned. They use standard paper, are fast, use inexpensive pigments, and are silent. And, best of all, they produce the highest resolution of any FAX printing process.

Though expensive (adding $2000.00 or more to the price of a FAX machine), laser printers are rapidly gaining acceptance among FAX manufacturers and users. Advances in technology and increasing demand among computer, FAX, and other office machine users will eventually lower the price of laser printers, but it is unlikely that laser printers will be as common as thermal printers on FAX machines until next century.

Printer-Related Features

The major printer enhancements and options available for FAX machines are paper cutters, sheet feeders, and document feeders. FAX machines that can store documents in memory typically store them automatically if paper runs out.

Paper Cutter A paper cutter is a manual or automatic device used to cut a continuous roll of thermal paper into individual sheets after FAX images have been printed on it. Depending on the machine, a paper cutter may not cut a printed document into sheets automatically and may not allow you to specify the size of those sheets.

Sheet Feeder A sheet feeder inserts individual sheets of blank paper from a stack (in a *tray* or *bin*) into a FAX machine's printer as called for by the printer. Sheet feeders typically handle one standard paper size, though some are equipped to handle several different sizes of paper. Sheet feeders can be used with single-sheet thermal paper or with standard paper.

Sheet feeders are especially useful in high-volume, unattended FAX operations, although some are limited to as few as five sheets of paper.

Document Feeder A document feeder operates like a sheet feeder, except that it supplies paper to the scanner rather than to the printer. A document feeder's job is to pick up pages to be scanned from a stack and run them through the scanner sequentially. Ideally, a FAX machine that is equipped with a document feeder is also supplied with a catch bin, into which documents are dropped after being scanned.

As with sheet feeders, document feeders are useful in high-volume, unattended FAX operations.

Automatic Storage on "Paper Out" When a FAX machine runs out of paper, it usually stops operation and may alert the operator. However, if an unattended FAX machine runs out of paper, no one will be available to resupply the paper. Important document transfers may be missed.

Fortunately, a FAX machine that can store documents in memory is usually equipped with an option that diverts an incoming FAX to memory storage when its supply of paper runs out.

This is an especially important option where unattended FAX operation is necessary (as with FAXes that must be left on 24 hours a day). And, human nature being what it is, automatic memory storage is a good idea for any high-volume FAX operation; after all, people do forget.

Copier Function

Many FAX machines can be used as photocopiers. It's a simple option to implement—a matter of sending a scanned document directly to the FAX's printer, rather than to the modem. Depending on the kind of printer used by the FAX, the quality of the copy may not be the best, but if you don't have a photocopier, FAX-copying beats having to run down to the quick-print shop whenever you need a copy.

> **Note:** Some FAX machines have a self-test feature that, while it isn't referred to as a copier function *per se*, scans and prints a document, which is the same thing as a copier feature.

Document Storage (Memory)

One of the most pragmatically *useful* FAX options is the ability to store incoming or outgoing documents in memory. This feature, used alone or in conjunction with other features, enhances a FAX machine's ability to operate unattended.

Being able to store scanned documents in memory (rather than transmitting them as the pages are scanned) means you can scan a document now and send it later. This is useful for those times when you won't have the time to scan the document when it's time to transmit it. Many memory-equipped FAX machines also have a programming feature that allows you to specify when a document is transmitted, which means that you can scan a document when it's convenient for you, then have the FAX machine transmit it at an appointed time—either for the convenience of the recipient or to take advantage of reduced late-night long-distance telephone rates.

Finally, being able to store a document in memory makes it very easy to *broadcast* the document to more than one other FAX machine. Broadcasting is nothing more than programming a FAX machine to dial up more than one number and deliver the same document. You only have to scan the document's pages once, after which it can be sent at will to as many FAX machines as you desire—either by manually dialing or by using a built-in broadcast capability that is available with most programmable, memory-equipped FAX machines.

With a FAX machine that can store incoming documents in memory (rather than printing them out immediately), you don't have to worry about running out of paper or being on hand when a document is received. Nor do you have to be concerned with incoming documents being read by anyone who happens to be near the FAX machine; you can print documents at your convenience.

With many memory-equipped FAX machines, you can not only print incoming documents from memory, but also direct the FAX to forward stored documents to other FAX machines, on an individual or broadcast basis. You simply dial up another FAX machine and transmit the document as you would a scanned document stored in memory. This application eliminates the tedium of scanning and rescanning a document that your FAX has received and printed out.

Scheduled Transmission and Other Programmable Features

FAX machines that feature document storage in memory may also offer other options that make use of memory—specifically, memory that you can program to send documents unattended when and where you wish.

Scheduled/Delayed Transmissions

The most useful (and used) programmable FAX feature is scheduling document transmissions. If you scan a document into a memory-equipped machine and program it to dial up and transmit the document at a specific time (or after a certain period of time has passed), you can enjoy the ultimate in unattended FAX operation.

This feature can be used with broadcast FAX and may be backed up by automatic redialing and/or backup number dialing. It may also be available on machines with document feeders.

Broadcast FAX

A silly, pretentious, and confusing misnomer, *broadcast* FAX is nothing more than calling and delivering the same message to one FAX machine after another. In the true sense of the word, "broadcast" implies simultaneous delivery.

Broadcast FAX is typically used to send a document that is stored in a FAX machine's memory. To broadcast, a FAX must have enough memory to store all the numbers to be dialed and the ability to be programmed to dial them in sequence and automatically transmit the document in memory. Broadcast FAX may be used in conjunction with scheduled transmissions, automatic redialing, backup number dialing, and store-and-forward.

Note: In addition to being a misnomer, broadcast FAX is also a frequent tool for delivering FAX junk mail.

Polling

Polling is the ability of one FAX machine to dial up another and request that a document stored in the called FAX's memory be sent to it. This is the reverse of conventional FAX communication, in which the calling machine always sends. In most cases, the machine to be called must be set up to send a document when called; this involves scanning a document into memory (or placing a document's pages in a document feeder) and selecting the FAX's "Poll" function. The calling machine may have to be set to Poll mode, as well.

Turnaround Polling

As has already been established, each machine in a conventional FAX communication is assigned a role: the calling machine sends a document, while the machine being called receives the document. However, a FAX machine with turnaround polling capability can reverse roles during a call and receive a document after sending one. This is a convenient feature that can also save money on long-distance calls, since a certain amount of time is wasted during the initial connection and recognition process.

Store-and-Forward

Store-and-forward is a sophisticated feature that turns around a received document and transmits it to another FAX machine. Store-and-forward requires document memory storage capability, of course, and may be used in conjunction with scheduled transmissions, automatic redialing, backup number dialing, and broadcast.

Support and Miscellaneous Functions

More sophisticated FAX machines—typically, those with memory and programming functions—offer a variety of functions that support FAX management and recordkeeping and/or provide other convenient information.

Transaction Journal/Activity Report

An important support feature for high-volume FAX operations is the ability to generate records of transactions or FAX calls and other activities. A typical transaction report (shown in Figure 3.7) is generated by pressing a button on the FAX machine and consists of detailed information on recent incoming and outgoing calls. Such information is valuable in controlling FAX access, as well as in analyzing FAX costs and efficiency.

```
** COMMUNICATIONS REPORT **        AS OF  AUG 23 '89 16:42  PAGE.01

                                        PRODUCT MANAGEMENT

    TOTAL PAGES                         TOTAL TIME

        SEND    : 0001                      SEND    : 00'00"22
        RECEIVE : 0002                      RECEIVE : 00'00"42


    DATE  TIME         TO/FROM     MODE   MIN/SEC PGS    CMD#  STATUS
 01  8/23 16:29 PITNEY BOWES NYD   UF--R  00"42   02           OK
 02       16:39 EQUIP CONTROL      UF--S  00"22   01           OK
```

Figure 3.7 FAX transaction report. *Courtesy of Pitney Bowes Facsimile Systems*

Security Features

With FAX handling an ever-increasing percentage of business, government, professional, and personal communications, the security of FAX messages both incoming and outgoing has become a subject of concern. Thus, many medium- and higher-priced FAX machines offer some of the following security features:

- Requiring certain recognition codes before sending a document to a FAX that calls and polls for document transmission

- Encrypting data during transmission

- Requiring password entry via a numeric keyboard before stored documents can be printed (or before the FAX machine can be used at all)

The first two features normally require that the two machines involved use the same code-exchange or encryption protocols, which usually means they must be made by the same manufacturer.

In addition to these built-in, active security features, you can implement passive or indirect security features by tracking FAX activity through transaction reports and by restricting on-site physical access to FAX machines.

Automatic Cover Sheets and Document Headers

Many high-end FAX machines can transmit information about a document along with the document, in the form of a cover sheet (separate from and preceding the document itself) that contains information pertaining to the source and intended recipient of the document.

Some of these machines can also generate document headers that contain such information as the date and time the document was received, a running title, and a page number, as well as internal reference numbers. This may be done automatically or on request.

Self-Testing

The ability to perform a self-test is a handy feature, because it provides a quick way to determine whether a transmission or printing problem is the result of a problem with your machine, the fault of the machine with which you are communicating, or a poor connection. Self-testing can eliminate down time and money wasted on needless service calls.

A typical self-test consists of the FAX machine performing some "invisible" internal tests, then printing out a scanned document.

Most FAX machines with self-testing capability initiate a test in response to a button being pressed (either at startup or after being in use). A few machines perform a self-test automatically at startup.

If self-testing is initiated manually and involves scanning and printing a document, it can be used to make a FAX machine serve as a copier.

Information Display

A frequently seen feature on high-end FAX machines is a digital display, which is used to display information such as the date and time. Such displays may provide several lines of information and, in addition to the date and time, provide information on the operating status of the FAX machine—including but not limited to the telephone number being dialed, whether the machine is sending or receiving, programming and memory data, and other information. (The dedicated FAX machine shown in Figure 3.5 has a 16-digit liquid-crystal display that displays information of this type.)

Serial Port

A relatively rare feature on FAX machines is a *serial port*. This is a standard RS-232C connection that can be used to connect a FAX machine to other devices capable of serial communication—including dial-up modems and computers. (An RS-232C serial port translates data from an electronic device into a form that can be transmitted and shared with other devices.) A FAX machine that is equipped with a serial port can be used to communicate with dial-up modem services or as a printer for a computer.

PC FAX Boards

A PC FAX board is a computer communications device designed to send and receive FAX documents. A PC FAX board works in conjunction with special software to convert computer-generated text and graphics into the format used by dedicated FAX and to convert the FAX transmissions it receives into the format used by its host computer.

PC FAX boards are internal devices, which means they are installed inside a personal computer's housing. In appearance, a PC FAX board is similar to other internal devices (e.g., disk drive controllers and internal modems). As shown in Figure 3.8, a typical PC FAX board consists of a printed-circuit board that is stuffed with microprocessors and other components required to do its task.

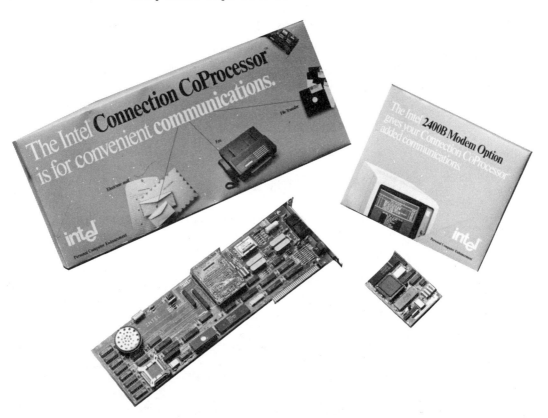

Figure 3.8 PC FAX board. *Photo courtesy of Intel PECO*

A PC FAX board is connected to its host computer via *edge connectors* (a series of conductors along one edge), which fit into a slot that likewise has connectors. The edge connectors provide the physical path whereby the PC FAX board communicates with the computer and receives its power.

To communicate with dedicated FAX machines, a PC FAX board must use a FAX-type modem; this is built into the PC FAX board. The PC FAX board's main external connection (i.e., connection with a device other than the host computer itself) is a telephone line jack—an RJ-11 jack into which you can plug a telephone line. Other external connections may not be present, but the telephone-line jack is present on every PC FAX board, since FAX communication is via telephone line.

How a PC FAX Board Works

A PC FAX board's primary jobs are:

- Converting data stored in its host computer's memory or in a disk file to the format used by FAX machines

- Converting incoming FAX transmissions to the format used by its host computer

- Establishing communications links with FAX machines or with other PC FAX board-equipped computers

- Sending and receiving documents in FAX format

- Printing and/or storing FAXed documents

Data Sources and Conversion

The source of a document to be sent via a PC FAX board can be a disk file, an area of the computer's memory in which text or graphics are being created, or (with PC FAX boards that will transmit the contents of the computer's screen) the computer's screen memory. If an optical scanner is being used to scan a paper document, some PC FAX boards use the scanner's data directly. Scanner data is usually handled by storing it in a file, then reading and sending the file contents.

No matter what the source of the document, PC FAX boards accomplish data conversion in a manner that is different from conventional FAX machines. Data conversion when an optical scanner is used is another matter and is discussed later. Rather than scanning a physical page and converting the pixels perceived into electronic signals that represent the pixels' location and state, a PC FAX board and its software must first read and interpret binary computer data. It must then convert it into a reasonable facsimile of what the same data would look like if it were printed out and scanned by a dedicated FAX scanner.

Computer Data Format Like FAX data, computer data is binary in nature, consisting of groups of 1s and 0s arranged in groups called *bytes*, each of which represents a character. Depending on the type of computer, there may be 128 or more possible characters. Some of these characters are letters and numbers. Some are *graphics characters*—individual lines, curves, and shapes that can be used together or separately as elements of a picture. Still other computer characters are what are called *control-characters*. These are characters that communicate information or signal a computer's operating system or a program when a file ends, where page breaks occur in a document, what the formatting elements in a text or graphic file are, etc.

FAX data is simple in contrast, consisting as it does of nothing more than bytes that contain information about the relative position and degree of darkness of dots.

The bottom line is that computer data represents each character with an assigned byte (group of binary digits), while FAX data represents each character (element of an image) as a group of dots (individual binary digits). FAX data—text or graphics (and most computer graphics data)—is stored and transmitted in what is known as *bit-mapped* format, which means that each bit is set to 0 or 1 to represent a dark or light area on a map of the image.

How PC FAX Converts Data Obviously, the task faced by a PC FAX board when sending a file is converting the bytes that represent computer characters into groups of binary digits (1s and 0s) that represent these characters—*and* their relative locations—in a dot-by-dot or pixel format.

The conversion and encoding is accomplished in the computer's memory and/or in temporary disk files, with the PC FAX board's circuitry and its attendant software working together to perform the conversion. Such a conversion involves a process that is in effect scanning the textual and graphic elements of the file and arbitrarily assigning pixels to create the equivalent of the image as it would appear when printed. The pixel types and locations are stored in a reasonable facsimile of the binary format created by FAX scanners.

Many elements of PC FAX hardware/software combinations are proprietary, but the end result is always the same: a disk file or a file stored in memory that contains the data in a format equivalent to that created by dedicated FAX machine scanners.

When receiving a FAX document, a PC FAX board and software has to interpret the pixel-oriented binary data and convert it into the binary format used by its host computer.

Special Note: Converting FAX Text Images to Computer ASCII Characters. Almost without exception, PC FAX boards use a time-saving shortcut and automatically store an incoming document as a graphic image—even if it contains only text. This is fine if all you need to do is view or print out the document. However, if you want to access the text with a word processor or other text-based program, you'll have to use special software to scan the graphic image of the text and convert it to a true text file, using the proper ASCII equivalents of the characters in the file.

The software you'll need is called optical character recognition (OCR) software. OCR programs scan the graphic image of the characters in a FAX document and convert them into standard ASCII characters. Some PC FAX boards include OCR software, and some don't. Either way, you should have OCR software if you're using a PC FAX board because you'll have a use for it sooner or later.

This software is built into or included with some PC FAX boards, providing optional or automatic conversion of text in FAX documents.

Establishing and Maintaining Communications Links

PC FAX board modems handle communications in the same manner as dedicated FAX machine modems. The only difference is that all PC FAX boards have auto-dial and auto-answer capabilities, in addition to any other dialing/telephone options they may sport.

Data Transmission and Reception

PC FAX board modems basically operate in the same manner as dedicated FAX modems (explained in detail earlier in this chapter). When sending a document, the modem varies a carrier wave on a telephone line in a pattern that imitates the pattern of the binary data composing a stored document. When receiving a document, the modem creates binary data based on the analog patterns it receives via the telephone line.

Printing and Storing Incoming FAX Documents

When a FAX document is received by a PC FAX board, it can be handled in any of several ways:

- The document may be routed directly to the printer, as a graphics image or as text (provided the board has performed the necessary OCR conversion first).

- The document may be displayed onscreen.

- A file may be created and the document stored in it, for later print-ing and/or OCR or graphics conversion.

Note that a dot-matrix or laser printer is required to print an in-coming FAX message in its native graphic format.

PC FAX Boards and Scanners

As implied earlier, documents that you wish to FAX via PC FAX board and computer don't have to be computer generated. With the addition of an optical scanner (Figure 3.9), you can input text and graphics into your computer for storage in memory or on disk. Once data is input in this fashion, it can be handled just like computer-generated text and graphics.

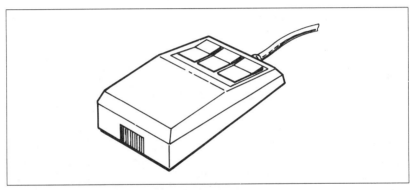

Figure 3.9 Optical scanner for computer. *Courtesy of KYE International Corp.*

With some PC FAX boards, you can route scanner input directly through a modem to a receiving FAX. With others, scanning is a separate operation, and scanned images are stored in a file that can then be trans-mitted like any other file.

Note that most optical scanners offer a maximum resolution (300 to 400 dpi) that is far beyond the capabilities of current Group 3 FAX machines, so some of the detail of scanned documents that may be visible on a computer screen or when a scanned document is printed will be lost.

Note: You can use a dedicated FAX machine that is equipped with an RS-232C port as a scanner for a computer. Connect the FAX machine to the computer's serial port, direct the FAX machine's output to the RS-232C port, and scan a document. Appropriate scanner and/or OCR software is required.

Direct Transmission of Scanner Input

If you have no reason to retain a computer file version of a document scanned with a computer scanner, having to store it on disk before you can transmit it is a somewhat useless step. You can eliminate this step and save time with a PC FAX board that will transmit a document *as you scan it*. Ironically, this makes the computer/PC FAX board/scanner operate in effectively the same manner as a dedicated FAX machine.

> **Note:** There are two kinds of computer optical scanners on the market: handheld and flatbed. Handheld scanners are usually limited to a 4-inch scan width. Flatbed scanners can scan a full page (or more). If you plan to do a lot of scanning, it is best to buy a flatbed scanner.

PC FAX Board Features and Options

PC FAX boards offer many of the same features and options as dedicated FAX machines—and a few that are unique.

Hardware and Software Compatibility

When selecting a PC FAX board, there are several compatibility issues, which we'll examine here, to consider.

The primary compatibility consideration is compatibility with your computer. The PC FAX board should naturally be designed to work with the type of computer you have (IBM or compatible, Macintosh, etc.), but there's more to it than that. If your computer has only half-size slots available, you'll want to buy a half-card-size board. You should also check the board's power requirements to make sure it doesn't exceed your computer's power supply capabilities, since all PC FAX boards draw their power from the host computer.

FAX compatibility is important if you're going to be exchanging documents with Group 1 and Group 2 FAX machines. You'll need the capability built into the PC FAX board and/or its software. Group 3 capability should not be an issue with PC FAX boards, although you should double-check to make sure you're not buying a PC FAX board that is compatible only with certain other PC FAX boards used in a local area network (LAN).

Printer compatibility is, perhaps, an obvious issue. You'll most likely need a printer with graphics capability (dot-matrix, ink-jet, or laser) to print incoming FAX documents. If you already have such a printer or have in mind a specific model to buy, make sure the PC FAX board and/or its software supports the printer in question.

Scanner compatibility should be checked. Whether you're going to buy a scanner with the board or think you'll never need one, you should still ascertain whether the board can be used with the more popular brands of scanners.

Software compatibility may be important, if you wish to use FAXed images with specific graphics or desktop publishing programs, and if you wish to transmit graphics created with those programs. Compatibility with operating environments (e.g., as Windows or DesqView for MS-DOS computers) is a very important issue.

Modem and Dialing/Calling Options

The modem and telephone-related options available with PC FAX boards are pretty much the same as those available for FAX machines. However, most of these options are standard with PC FAX boards.

Speed As noted earlier, not all PC FAX boards can communicate at FAX's top speed of 9600 bps. As with dedicated FAX machines, if your FAX transmissions will consist solely of local calls, or infrequent long-distance calls, you will be happy with a slower (4800-bps) machine. If you do a lot of long-distance FAX communication, however, a 9600-bps machine will more than pay for itself in long-distance savings.

Error Checking Error checking is an option that may not be present in a PC FAX board. If it is included, it may be a proprietary kind of error checking that is active only when the PC FAX board in question is communicating with the same make and model PC FAX board.

Automatic Fallback Automatic fallback to a slower transmission speed is standard with PC FAX board modems.

Polling Almost all PC FAX boards are capable of the same kind of polling operations as dedicated FAX machines—including turnaround polling.

> **Note:** While document memory storage is an option with dedicated FAX machines, it is standard on every PC FAX board-equipped computer, since documents can be (and usually are) stored in a computer's memory or on disk. This means that virtually all FAX options that require document storage in memory are standard with PC FAX boards.

Number Storage, Phone Lists, and Distribution Lists Like many dedicated FAX machines, PC FAX boards can compile lists of FAX numbers to be called. The numbers are typically stored in a searchable directory format, and you can specify one or more numbers to be called from such a list—as well as document(s) to be sent to the specified FAX machines.

A subset of the phone list feature is the ability to create what are called *distribution lists*. Distribution lists are groups of phone numbers that can be specified as the destination or address of a document. Each number is called in sequence, and busy numbers are redialed as necessary until the specified document has been FAXed to all the numbers on the list.

Broadcast FAX Any PC FAX board that has distribution list capability can perform broadcast FAX operations.

Scheduled Transmissions Almost all PC FAX boards provide some means of scheduling document transmission or polling at specific times. This feature is often accompanied by a background operation option.

Store-and-Forward Store-and-forward operations, which typically make use of document storage in memory and scheduled transmission capabilities, are possible with any PC FAX boards that offer those capabilities.

Other Phone-Related Features Automatic callback of busy numbers, alternate number dialing, and other dialing options discussed for dedicated FAX machines are usually available with PC FAX boards.

Tone and pulse dialing are available with all PC FAX boards, as is pause capability.

Scanner and Transmission Features and Options

Many optical scanners offer document resizing. Some allow you to compress extra-wide documents, like spreadsheets, for transmission to any FAX machine. A very few PC FAX boards will resize documents or transmit extra-wide documents at their full size to specific PC FAX boards.

Contrast is an option available with (and necessary for) most optical scanners.

Halftone capability is an option on high-end scanners.

Some PC FAX boards that have *dithering* (halftone or gray scale capability) sometimes offer you the option of specifying the image type of a graphic image to be transmitted (photo or line drawing). This affects how the conversion to FAX data format is handled and, ultimately, the resolution of the printout at the other end of a FAX connection.

Some PC FAX boards allow you to adjust the aspect ratio of documents.

Printers

If you use a computer, you know that you cannot print graphics with a daisy-wheel printer. If your incoming FAX documents consist only of text and you have OCR software or capability to translate the FAX images into ASCII files, you'll be able to print the text messages. This is a rather expensive and time-consuming way to go about it. If you already have a daisy-wheel, you should at least pick up an inexpensive dot-matrix printer to use in printing FAX documents. You're going to want to handle graphics eventually, in any event.

Most standard dot-matrix, ink-jet, and laser printers will print FAX images (text and graphics). It is recommended that you use one of the more familiar brand-name printers (e.g., Apple, Epson, IBM), because these are the printers specifically supported by PC FAX boards and their software.

You can use a thermal printer to print FAX images from a computer—if you can find one for your computer and if your PC FAX board's software supports the printer. Most thermal printers for computers are cantankerous beasts and have been replaced, for the most part, by dot-matrix printers.

Resolution

PC FAX boards offer the same resolution options as dedicated FAX machines. Most transmit or receive at Standard and Fine resolution, as directed. As with dedicated FAX machines, Super-Fine resolution is a relatively new innovation for PC FAX boards.

Interestingly enough, the resolution of computer-generated text and graphics is better than that of data scanned by a FAX or computer scanner. This is because a scanner cannot record every bit of an image, while each and every bit of computer-generated data is included in the conversion process.

However good the conversion process may be, the FAXed image is only as good as the receiving FAX machine's graphics-translation abilities and printer. So, unless you are transmitting to a dedicated FAX machine with laser printer or to a computer with a PC FAX board and a laser printer, the quality of the graphics you transmit will not be any better than from any other source.

Halftone (Gray Scale)

About half of the PC FAX boards on the market will send and receive halftone images. These are naturally the more expensive models.

Note: Halftone or gray scale is sometimes called "dithering" when discussed in the context of PC FAX boards.

Automatic Cover Sheets and Document Headers

Most PC FAX boards are capable of generating cover sheets and page headers on outgoing documents, as well as document and page headers on incoming documents. There is far more flexibility in the layout and content of cover sheets and headers generated by PC FAX boards than of those generated by dedicated FAX machines, because you have the specialized text-input resources of a computer at your disposal. With a dedicated FAX machine, you are limited to a prepared cover sheet (and perhaps a built-in cover sheet format) and to headers whose layout and content are determined by formats built into the FAX machine.

Transaction/Activity Reports

Here again, most PC FAX boards can generate the same kinds of FAX activity reports as dedicated FAX machines.

> **Note:** The following features are unique to PC FAX boards, and in many cases their absence or presence may be dictated by how you use the PC FAX board.

Software

A few PC FAX boards are not accompanied by the software necessary to operate them. In some cases, the software is supplied by the PC FAX board manufacturer but sold as a separate item or (rarely) offered by third party. Because PC FAX boards cannot operate without specialized software, you should not purchase a PC FAX board that does not include software. Selling software separately is tantamount to price gouging, and not providing software at all casts aspersions on the quality of the board in question.

Note that the better PC FAX boards include part of their operating software in ROM (i.e., coded into chips on the board itself). This is a good feature; it means faster software access and operation, and that much more disk space can be allocated for software.

As a bonus, some PC FAX boards are bundled with popular graphics or OCR software, and some include scanner software and scanners.

Graphics Format Conversion

If you use graphics programs to create FAX images to send or wish to incorporate FAX images in graphics created with such programs, you'll find *graphics conversion* an important option. This option translates *graphics files* (files received via FAX or those created with a graphics program) into formats used by specific graphics or desktop publishing programs.

Graphics conversion is necessary, because—in the MS-DOS world in particular—PC FAX boards usually use their own proprietary methods in storing FAX documents on disk. These proprietary methods are not normally readable by software other than that used by the PC FAX board in question.

The programs whose formats are supported will vary depending on the type of computer you're using, but they are typically the most popular (best-selling) graphics programs.

Screen Print Send

If you want to send a number of brief messages by FAX or send specific screen displays, being able to transmit the contents of the computer screen is an extremely useful option. This is faster than creating a document, saving it to disk, then transmitting it from disk. This feature allows you to eliminate the save-to-disk operation, so that scanning and converting onscreen text is much faster than scanning and converting a disk file.

A typical screen print send works on a memory-resident basis. In other words, when you press the keys that cause a screen to be dumped to your printer, the output is intercepted and sent to a FAX machine with which your PC FAX board is currently communicating. Alternatively, this function may store the contents of a screen in a file for later sending.

This feature requires *background operation* and is used in part by some PC FAX board *text editors*.

Printer Output to FAX

This option is similar to a screen print, except that it intercepts text and/ or graphics that a program is sending to the printer. The data is converted and transmitted to a FAX machine with which the host computer's PC FAX board is communicating.

Background Operation

Simply explained, background operation is the ability of a computer program to perform a task on its own while you use another program. Background operation is a popular and sometimes indispensable feature with computer users, because it allows them to use their computers for interactive tasks (e.g., word processing) instead of waiting for a program to complete a noninteractive task (e.g., printing, converting, or transmitting a file). Having background operation is like having two computers.

Some PC FAX boards and their software offer a background operation option. This is extremely useful when you have to FAX a large file or a large number of files to one or more FAXes. Simply set up the *transmission parameters*—the file(s) to be transferred and the number(s) to call—exit the PC FAX program, and you're free to use your computer for other purposes while the PC FAX board works away in the background.

The background operation option can also be used to receive FAX transmissions. Set up the board on "standby," and it will answer the phone, establish contact, and receive and store FAX documents automatically.

If it is at all possible, buy a PC FAX board with this option; otherwise, you'll be locked out of using your computer when you wish to use FAX functions. This is an inefficient situation when you consider the fact that the PC FAX board requires your interaction only at the beginning and end of a FAX transmission. Your computer will effectively become a FAX machine, unable to perform other tasks.

Text Editor

Among the more useful options offered by PC FAX boards is a text editor. A PC FAX board text editor is a simplified word processor that you can use to create text-only documents for immediate FAX transmission. This option is especially useful for those whose FAX applications require a lot of communication via short memos. With this option, you can create a message and send it right away, without having to go through the process of storing and reading it.

Some PC FAX board text editors will also store the documents they create on disk and/or print them.

Onscreen Document Display

Because FAX transmissions are graphic in nature, use a monitor and display card capable of displaying graphics. The display system can be either monochrome or color.

PC FAX boards will display a document onscreen in lieu of printing it—useful for previewing purposes.

Various enhancements to onscreen display include scrolling, color changing, rotating, zooming (focusing on and enlarging one element of a drawing), and extracting a portion of a document to a separate file.

An interesting option that's not always included among a PC FAX board's features is the ability to display incoming FAX documents onscreen in realtime (i.e., as it's received).

Dial-Up Telecom Modem

A few PC FAX boards combine the "best of both worlds" in telecommunications by including a standard dial-up modem. This offers some cost advantage over buying both a PC FAX board and a modem. You won't normally be able to use both at once, unless you have a separate telephone line for each of the telecommunications devices, a PC FAX board that is capable of multitasking and background operation, and the appropriate modem communications software.

Miscellaneous PC FAX Board Features and Options

Custom Fonts Because text in FAX documents is really graphics, a PC FAX board can be set up to display and print text in almost any form. Thus, some PC FAX boards offer a selection of text *fonts*, or type styles. This feature is mainly useful when you are printing documents for distribution to others and wish to lend them an impressive or appropriate appearance.

Onscreen Help Following the lead of the more successful MS-DOS and Macintosh software packages, as well as that of high-end modems, some PC FAX boards offer *online help*—abbreviated explanations of specific operations that are called up when a certain key combination is issued or via menu selection. A few PC FAX boards offer *context-sensitive help*, which means the help information displayed is keyed to the current operation.

Security Features

PC FAX boards offer varying levels and kinds of security. Some PC FAX board software can be set up to require a password before allowing access to its function. Data encryption is also offered by some PC FAX board packages.

PC FAX Board or Dedicated FAX Machine?

In addition to a PC FAX board or a dedicated FAX machine, you have a third option: modem/FAX, which is discussed in Chapters 7 and 8.

If you have a computer, you may be wondering, even after reading the preceding paragraphs, whether a PC FAX board is for you. The answer to that question depends on your applications and on the options included with the PC FAX board you select.

In general, if you have a lot of computer-generated material to transmit, you can benefit from using a PC FAX board. However, some obvious and not-too-obvious limitations and advantages to using a PC FAX board are detailed below and should figure in your decision.

PC FAX Board Limitations

In case you missed the stated and implied (and potential) limitations of PC FAX boards earlier, here's a roundup:

- Like dedicated FAX machines, not all PC FAX boards can communicate at the maximum Group 3 transmission speed of 9600 bps. Many lower-priced PC FAX boards are limited to half that speed.

- Some PC FAX boards have an upper limit on the number of pages that can be transmitted as one document. Very few documents will exceed such limits, which many be anywhere between 300 and 999 pages. This is not much of a limit if your FAX needs are small, but it could be a deciding factor for those who send really large documents.

- Unless you have an optical scanner (a separate item), you cannot scan and send hardcopy documents via a PC FAX board. Alone, PC FAX boards are capable of sending only the contents of a computer's memory (working RAM or screen memory) or disk files. With an optical scanner you can scan and transmit virtually anything scannable, but you will have to spend several hundred to more than one thousand dollars to be able to do so.

- Since PC FAX boards commonly receive, recognize, and store *all* elements of an incoming FAX document as graphic in nature—including text—you may need to add an OCR software package to your system to convert the text in FAX messages into ASCII characters that a word processor or other program can read. This is another extra cost item.

- If you do not have a hard disk on your computer, you will have to add one to use a PC FAX board effectively. The size of the operating and support software for a PC FAX board, as well as the size of stored incoming and outgoing documents, demands far more space than a typical floppy disk.

- Unless you buy a PC FAX board with background operation capability, your computer will be tied up whenever you want to send or receive FAX messages.

- PC FAX boards and their software are not compatible with *all* software—even when operating in background.

- If you want to make full use of a PC FAX board's graphics capability, you will have to buy a graphics software package.

PC FAX Board Advantages

PC FAX boards offer a number of potential advantages over dedicated FAX machines. Here's the overview:

- With a PC FAX board, you can transmit computer-generated text and graphics without having to print them first. The copy will be at the best possible resolution.

- PC FAX board-equipped computers provide automatic document storage in memory.

- You can merge text and/or graphics from FAXed documents into word processing, desktop publishing, or graphics files for later printout or transfer. To do the same thing with FAX documents received via a dedicated FAX machine, you would have to go through the additional step of scanning the printed document into your computer, perhaps losing some data in the process.

- A PC FAX board that can operate in the background gives you the best of both worlds: fully automated two-way FAX communication and the use of your computer for other tasks.

What You've Learned

This chapter has taught you the following:

- There are four steps in transmitting a document via FAX:

    1. Scanning the document and converting it to binary data

    2. Converting the document from binary data to analog data

    3. Transmitting the analog data via telephone lines

    4. Reversing the data conversions and printing the document

- A scanner is a device that uses photoelectric elements to convert images into electronic signals. The scanner does this by sensing whether specific points on a page, referred to as pixels, are light or dark. After a page has been scanned, it is sent to the FAX's modem for transmission or stored in memory for later transmission.

- There are two kinds of scanning: black and white (two-state) and halftone (gray scale). All scanners are capable of black-and-white scanning, but halftone scanning requires a more sophisticated device. In black-and-white scanning, the scanner perceives a page as composed of only black or white pixels; even gray shades are perceived as either black or white. A scanner capable of halftone scanning is able to perceive between 8 and 64 shades of gray, depending on the sophistication of the scanner.

- Scanned images are recorded as electronic signals that represent the pixels on a page; the signals consist of either high or low voltages and are referred to as binary data.

- A modem's primary jobs are converting binary data to analog data, and vice versa, and transmitting that data.

- In addition to data conversion and transmission, modems are responsible for establishing and maintaining communications (telephone) links and—if properly equipped—may check transmitted data for errors.

- FAX images are transmitted by placing analog data on a telephone carrier wave in a process called modulation. This modulated signal is carried via voice-grade phone lines to a receiving FAX's modem.

- When a FAX document is received, the receiving FAX's modem demodulates the analog data it receives, recreating the binary data created by the sending FAX's scanner. This data is sent to the receiving FAX's printer, which prints a facsimile of the original scanned document.

- Most modern FAX modems are able to dial numbers automatically and answer the phone; these capabilities are called auto-dial and auto-answer, respectively.

- A wide variety of telephone-style options are available for FAX machines, including memory dialing (sometimes referred to as dialing list capability), automatic callback, repeat dialing, backup number dialing, and tone/pulse dialing, as well as the ability to pause between digits when dialing a number and to display the number being called.

- Most FAX machines can be used with or as a telephone, via a telephone jack or a built-in telephone set.

- Advanced FAX machines can be switched between FAX and voice telephone operation during a call. Many are able to distinguish whether an incoming call is FAX or voice and respond accordingly.

- FAX scanner features may include multiple resolution levels, half-tone capability, contrast control, page reduction, page enlargement, and a document feeder to feed document pages to the scanner.

- The physical configuration of a scanner is either page or flatbed.

- FAX modem options include high-speed (9600-bps) transmission, error-checking capability, automatic fallback to lower transmissions when poor connections are encountered, and Group 1 and/or Group 2 FAX compatibility.

- There are four types of FAX printers: thermal, electrostatic, dot-matrix, and laser. Of these, thermal printers are the most common. Some printers use continuous paper on a roll, while others use single-sheet paper.

- FAX printer options include paper cutters (for printers that use roll paper), sheet feeders to feed paper to the printer, and automatic storage in memory when the paper supply runs out.

- Many FAX machines can be used as photocopiers. This option is sometimes an element of a machine's self-test function.

- Among the more useful FAX options is the ability to store incoming and outgoing documents in memory. This supports several other options, including scheduled transmissions, broadcast FAX transmission, and store-and-forward transmission.

- While the roles of calling and answering FAX machines are traditionally sending and receiving documents, respectively, some machines can call a FAX machine and receive a document through a process called polling. More sophisticated FAX machines can both send and receive documents during the same call, via what is called turnaround polling.

- Optional support functions provided by some FAX machines include reports on calls, password and data-encryption security, generation of cover sheets and document headers, self-testing, and the display of information such as the date, time, and current status of a call.

- Some FAX machines are equipped with a serial port through which they can be connected to computers or other communications devices.

- A PC FAX board is an add-on device for a computer that converts computer-generated computer text and graphics into a format that can be transmitted to and understood by dedicated FAX machines, and vice versa.

- PC FAX boards offer virtually all the options available on dedicated FAX machines, plus some unique features.

- Some PC FAX boards can operate in the background, which means you can use your computer for other purposes while sending or receiving documents via FAX.

- You can scan hardcopy documents for transmission via a PC FAX board-equipped computer with an optical scanner.

- Some PC FAX boards will convert and transmit data from an optical scanner as it is sent to the computer, eliminating the need to store the scanned data in a disk file before sending it.

- All elements of a FAX document, including text, are treated as elements of a graphic image by a PC FAX board; therefore, you may have to use special software to convert text in a FAXed document into a format that is usable by word processors and other computer programs.

- PC FAX board software is usually included with the board; such software is sometimes partially built into the board.

- All PC FAX boards offer document storage in memory, via their host computers' memory and disks.

- Graphics received via PC FAX boards can be imported into computer desktop publishing and graphics programs, provided the PC FAX board's software is capable of converting FAX documents to the appropriate format.

- Among the many useful options offered by PC FAX boards are text editors for creating instant messages.

- Documents received via PC FAX boards can be displayed on-screen, stored in disk files, or printed.

- Efficient use of a PC FAX board requires a hard disk.

Now you are familiar with the technical aspects of FAX communication and are aware of the features and options available with both dedicated FAX machines and PC FAX boards, as well as various FAX services designed to increase the convenience and efficiency of FAX. Test your knowledge with the following quiz. Then, move on to Chapter 4, where we'll take a hands-on look at setting up, using, and maintaining dedicated FAX machines and PC FAX boards.

Quiz

1. What is a pixel?

   a. The smallest element of a picture or image
   b. An element of binary data
   c. A sensing device
   d. A measure of voltage

2. Conventional FAX scanners perceive a scanned page as:

   a. Numbers
   b. Groups of light and dark dots
   c. Electrical charges
   d. A matrix

3. After a page has been scanned and converted to binary data format by a scanner, it is:

   a. Printed
   b. Transmitted to another FAX machine via a modem or stored in memory for later transmission
   c. Read by electronic circuitry and converted to strings of 1s and 0s
   d. Erased

4. What is the ability of a FAX machine to distinguish shades of gray called?

   a. Dot-matrix
   b. Halftone
   c. Two-state scanning
   d. Binary data

5. In addition to transmitting data, a modem's primary job is to convert data from binary to _____ format, and vice versa.

   a. Analog
   b. Voltage
   c. Textual
   d. Graphic

6. Placing information on a carrier wave is called:

   a. Encryption
   b. Modulation
   c. Scanning
   d. Dithering

7. What is the name of the adjustment on some FAX machines that can be used to make a scanned FAX image lighter or darker?

   a. Gray scale

    b. lpi
    c. Sheet feed
    d. Contrast

8. Dedicated FAX machine scanners come in two configurations: page and _____.

    a. Image
    b. High-density
    c. Flatbed
    d. Graphic

9. How many types of FAX printers are there?

    a. One
    b. Two
    c. Three
    d. Four

10. The ability of a FAX machine to call another FAX machine and request that a document be sent is called:

    a. Memory
    b. Polling
    c. Forwarding
    d. Broadcasting

11. A properly equipped and supported PC FAX board can do which of the following?

    a. Send and receive text and/or graphic documents via FAX
    b. Send scanned hardcopy documents
    c. Merge text or graphics into files created with other programs
    d. All of the above

12. Which of the following can you *not* do with a PC FAX board?

    a. Display FAX messages on a computer screen
    b. Print graphics
    c. Make a voice telephone call
    d. Convert FAX graphics to and from various computer graphics formats

13. Which kinds of printers can be used to print FAX graphics (all that apply)?

    a. Dot-matrix
    b. Daisy wheel
    c. Ink-jet
    d. Laser

14. The ability of a PC FAX board to send and receive FAX documents

while you are using your computer for other purposes is called what?

    a. Foreground operation
    b. Ready mode
    c. Background operation
    d. Environment operation

15. Special software that converts text from the graphic image format used by FAX to a computer's standard ASCII format is called what?

    a. File-conversion software
    b. Optical character recognition software
    c. Graphics translation software
    d. Background software

4 | Using FAX and PC FAX

About This Chapter

This chapter is a general user's guide to dedicated FAX machines and PC FAX boards. It covers the following:

- What hardware, software, equipment, and supplies you'll need to use a dedicated FAX machine or PC FAX board

- How to install and maintain a dedicated FAX machine

- How to scan, send, and receive documents with a dedicated FAX machine

- How to install and set up a PC FAX board and its operating software

- How to send and receive documents with a PC FAX board-equipped computer

- How to use a PC FAX board's advanced features

- How to install and use an optical scanner with a computer

- What kinds of support software are available for a PC FAX board

- How to protect yourself against FAX junk mail

Getting Started

By now, you probably have an idea of whether a dedicated FAX machine or a PC FAX board will best serve your FAX needs. With that in mind, we'll take a look at what it's like to install, set up, and use each.

Dedicated FAX Machines

If you're like the vast majority of FAX users, your first (and perhaps only) choice will be a dedicated FAX machine.

What You Will Need

To use a dedicated FAX machine, you will need the following items:

- The FAX machine itself

- A telephone line with an RJ-11 jack

- A grounded 110-volt power supply (standard AC house outlet)

- A supply of paper for the FAX machine's printer

You'll also need a document to transmit and the number of a FAX machine to send it to (or someone with a FAX machine to call your machine and transmit a document).

Optional items you may wish to obtain include:

- Power-line surge protector (necessary if you live in an area where voltage drops and surges are common)

- Telephone-line surge protector, which guards the FAX modem and other internal components against electrical surges on telephone lines

- Power- and/or telephone-line extension cords (It is recommended that these not be used, if possible.)

- A telephone set and connecting line, if you are using a FAX machine without a built-in telephone and want the FAX to share the phone line with a voice telephone

- An uninterrupted power supply (UPS), which provides uninterrupted electrical power when there is a power outage (This is an extremely expensive item, but it may be worthwhile if it is critical to maintain FAX communications.)

Installing a FAX Machine

If your FAX traffic is heavy, install a separate telephone line for the FAX machine.

Installing a FAX machine involves little more than selecting an appropriate location, plugging in the power supply, plugging in the telephone line, and loading the paper roll or sheets into the printer. Some thermal or electrostatic printer paper requires that a certain side—usually the shiny side—be facing the printer. Consult your FAX's manual for details.

Location

Locate your FAX machine so that you can easily reach both the scanner paper feed and the printer output; there should also be ample room for any document and/or printer paper bins. Leave enough room around the FAX machine so that there is adequate ventilation (excess heat is one of the banes of electronic equipment). Avoid locations that expose the machine to excessive dust or direct sunlight.

Testing

The final step in installing a dedicated FAX machine is testing. As explained in Chapter 3, many FAX machines have a self-test mode that you can use to ensure that the machine is operating properly. If you need a "live" test, you can exchange test messages with a friend or associate who has a FAX machine.

Keeping It Running: FAX Machine Care and Maintenance

Once your FAX machine is set up, it should require very little maintenance. Electrostatic and laser printers do require routine maintenance, but you can handle most other maintenance yourself. (Most of it is common sense.)

Don't Use It for a Shelf

A common problem with FAX machines (and all electronic equipment) is that they tend to be convenient temporary resting places for papers, books, and other items. Try to resist the temptation to place objects on top of your FAX machine just because you're not using it at the moment, no matter how convenient it is. Even if the machine is turned off, too much weight can cause the casing to flex and damage internal components. Buttons and switches can be damaged by constant pressure, as well. If the machine is turned on, there's no telling what you might activate by placing objects on it, and you may block incoming calls.

Electricity and Coffee Don't Mix

Keep liquids (e.g., coffee and soft drinks) away from the machine. Such liquids can not only short out electronic components but also cause corrosion.

Keep It Clean

As with any piece of electrical or electronic equipment, FAX machines run better when clean. A lot of dirt and dust can cause heat build-up. Dirt and dust can also infiltrate moving parts (e.g., scanners and printers) and slow or damage them. Dirt and dust on scanning elements will reduce the quality of scanned images, too.

FAX manufacturers usually provide cleaning recommendations, and special FAX cleaning kits are available. In general, a mild, nonabrasive liquid spray cleaner, used with a soft rag or paper towel, will work fine for cleaning the exterior surface. To clear dust from the exterior and interior, you can use a small vacuum cleaner (with a *plastic* cleaning attachment). Alternatively, you can use low-pressure compressed air. In particular, you should vacuum the printer frequently to remove paper dust that tends to collect.

Other Precautions

Always use the printer paper recommended by the manufacturer, and never try to force too large a document through a page scanner. If you encounter resistance when feeding a document into a scanner or if the printer or any other element jams, kill the power to the FAX machine immediately. This can prevent damage and stop the jam-ups from becoming hopeless.

When loading paper for the printer (or untangling paper jams), make sure the power is off.

Do not use a FAX machine during a thunderstorm—especially when lightning is present. As with any sensitive electronic equipment, electrical surges on the power line or telephone line can damage a FAX machine. It may be a good idea to disconnect your machine during an electrical storm. Even surge protectors may not protect your equipment from a massive surge of the kind that accompanies lightning strikes.

Using a Dedicated FAX Machine

Using a FAX machine's basic send and receive features is a pretty straightforward process. With most machines, you can probably figure out what to do by just looking at the machine, although it's best to read the manual.

The following instructions on sending and receiving documents apply to basic FAX machines only and do not take into account advanced features such as sheet or document feeders and memory.

Sending a Document

Although there is more to it than this (as described in Chapter 3), sending a document involves two steps:

1. Connecting with the receiving FAX machine

2. Scanning the pages of the document to be sent

Connection is made automatically. All you have to do is dial a number—either manually (using an attached phone, built-in phone, or built-in telephone number keypad) or automatically (using a phone list or one-key dialing feature).

Once connection is made, your FAX machine will signal you with light and/or sound when it is ready to transmit. (Basic FAX machines may rely on the squeal of the answering modem carried by the FAX machine's speaker to alert you to the fact that connection has been established.) At this time, insert the first page of the document into the scanner and press the button to start transmission. This will be labeled "START" or something similarly appropriate. The FAX machine will scan the page, then transmit and eject it. It may not signal you when it is ready for the next page. If there is no prompt, just insert the next page. Figure 4.1 shows a page in a scanner.

When all the pages of the document have been sent, press the appropriately labeled button to terminate the FAX communication. This will carry a label like "END," "DISCONNECT," "TERMINATE," or something similar.

> **Note:** A few older, more primitive FAX machines will transmit no more than one page at a time, after which you must redial the receiving FAX machine to send the next page.

Receiving a Document

All FAX machines have auto-answer capability and will automatically print document pages as they are received. Thus, all you need to do to receive a document from a FAX machine is have your machine turned on, connected to the phone line, and loaded with paper. If you aren't using a machine with roll paper or a sheet feeder, you should be ready to feed blank paper into it when prompted or whenever the printer is finished printing a page.

When a FAX machine calls, your machine will answer and begin

Figure 4.1 Document page in a scanner. *Photo courtesy of Sharp Electronics Corporation*

printing the transmitted document immediately. Figure 4.2 shows a FAX machine printing a document.

When all the pages of the document have been sent, the sending machine will disconnect, and your machine will sense the lack of a carrier wave (or dropped carrier) and release the phone line.

> **Note:** Call-waiting can disrupt or terminate a FAX transmission. If you have call-waiting, ask your local phone company how to disable call-waiting temporarily. (This option is not available in all areas.) You could also consider doing away with call-waiting or installing a separate line for your FAX machine.

Using Advanced Features

If you read Chapter 3 and the two sections immediately preceding, you have a good idea of how to use features such as one-key dialing and programmable features such as scheduled transmission and document

Figure 4.2 FAX printer printing an incoming document.

storage in memory. Because FAX machines vary in how they operate, it is beyond the scope of this book to instruct you on how to use each of these features with every FAX machine on the market. Refer to your FAX machine's manual for detailed instructions.

PC FAX Boards

If you already have a computer (and particularly if you are using a modem for some of your communications), you may wish to use a PC FAX board to integrate all your data processing and communications facilities. Doing so can result in time savings, increased efficiency, and—in the long term—cost savings.

What You Will Need

You need the following to be able to use a PC FAX board:

- The card itself

- The card's operational software (Only a very few PC FAX boards come with software completely built-in.)

- The card's support software, which may include graphics-conversion and/or scanner support software

- A computer with at least one empty expansion slot (to accommodate the card)

- Sufficient computer memory (RAM) to run the PC FAX board's software (A minimum of 640K RAM is recommended.)

- At least one floppy disk drive (A hard disk is recommended.)

- A telephone line with an RJ-11 plug

You'll also need a file to transmit, the number of a FAX machine to send it to, and, depending on your application, one or more of these items:

- A dot-matrix, ink-jet, or laser printer, if you intend to print FAX documents

- An optical scanner and its operating software, if you wish to scan hardcopy documents for FAX transmission

- Support software, which may include OCR software and/or graphics-conversion software

- Various connecting cables for the peripherals (e.g., printer and scanner), and power and phone extension cords

- Power- and/or telephone-line surge protectors

- An uninterrupted power supply

Installing a PC FAX Board

There are two separate elements to PC FAX board installation:

- The physical installation of the board itself

- Computer configuration and software setup

Physical Installation

If you buy a PC FAX board from a reputable computer dealer, installation, software setup, and testing should be included in the cost of the board.

Although installing a PC FAX board is not particularly difficult, you may be uneasy about getting into your computer's innards, or you may not have the time to install the board. However, if you install the board yourself, you will gain an additional level of understanding about its operation.

Installing a PC FAX board in a computer is basically the same as installing any other board or card in a computer. First, *turn off the computer and unplug it and any peripherals connected to it* (e.g., printer and modem). Then open the computer's *case* (the box to which your keyboard, monitor, printer, etc., are connected). This usually involves removing four to eight screws. Refer to your computer's hardware manual for the locations of the screws.

You'll probably have to push out a knock-out plug or unscrew a cover plate on the back of the computer to make room for the external connecting jacks or plugs on the card.

After removing the screws, slide or pull the case from the computer, as necessary. You'll see a metal chassis with a number of printed circuit boards and one or more empty expansion slots. Figure 4.3 shows a typical computer expansion slot.

Your PC FAX board's instruction manual will tell you in which slot to install the board. You may have to configure the software so that it knows where to find the board. Line up the board's card-edge connectors with the slot, oriented as instructed in the board's manual. There's usually only one way the board will fit, anyway. Then press the edge connectors into the slot, using a gentle, even pressure, until they bottom out. Fasten the board to the computer chassis if so instructed and connect cables as necessary. The board is physically ready to use.

After installing a PC FAX board, test it before you replace the computer's cover in case you've made a mistake or neglected something.

After the board is physically installed and connected, you may have to set *dip switches* to customize it for your system—telling it how to communicate with your computer, listing which features it can use, etc. Dip switches are small rocker-type switches set in a block on the PC FAX board. The board's documentation will tell you in which position (ON or OFF) to set each switch to activate specific settings, operating modes, and features.

System Configuration and Software Installation

Virtually all PC FAX boards require that you configure your system to accommodate their operation and enable the computer to recognize and work properly with them. Such a configuration may include but is not limited to:

- Setting the number of files and buffers and/or assigning a device driver in your system's CONFIG.SYS (or similar) file (Files of the CONFIG.SYS type set certain system operating parameters when the computer starts.)

- Setting your system's AUTOEXEC.BAT (or similar) file to run a special program and/or set a directory path name (Files of the AUTOEXEC.BAT type issue operating system commands when the computer starts.)

These files may go under different names (the examples above represent MS-DOS computer files), but in most cases they are text files, easily created with an ASCII text editor. The better PC FAX board operational software packages will handle creating these files for you during an automated installation process. If not, the PC FAX board's documentation will tell you how to create them.

After you've configured your system, you'll have to install the PC FAX board's operational software. This is typically an automated or semiautomated process that involves running a specified program or selecting a menu item after you start the PC FAX board operating program.

Elements that you will have to specify during the installation process vary, but may include:

- The type of printer in use

- The disk drive and/or directory in which FAX documents are stored

- The disk drive and/or directory in which the operational software is stored

- Background or foreground operation mode

- Screen color combinations

- The physical location (slot) of the PC FAX board

- Other elements, determined by the features and options offered by the PC FAX board and its operating software

Using a Dedicated PC FAX Board

Almost all PC FAX board operations are initiated via operating software's menu selections or by typing commands. This means that, to use a PC FAX board, you must start the software, make your selections, and provide information such as numbers to call and names of files to be transmitted when prompted. Then you must wait while the PC FAX board carries out your instructions—unless your board is capable of background operation. Figure 4.3 shows a PC FAX board software menu.

Document File Preparation

Text documents to be sent must be prepared using a PC FAX board's built-in text editor or a word processor that produces 7-bit ASCII text. If the text is not in the format used by the PC FAX board's text editor (if any) or in 7-bit ASCII text, it will not be interpreted properly when scanned.

A few PC FAX boards are capable of reading text produced by popular word processing programs (e.g., Microsoft Word, MultiMate, and

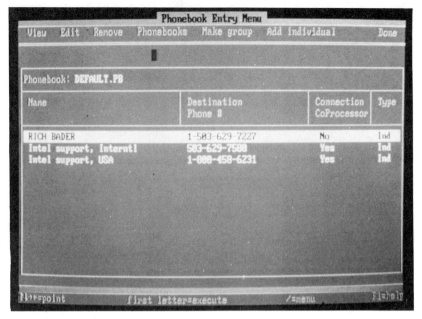

Figure 4.3 PC FAX software menu. *Photo courtesy of Intel PECO*

WordStar) in their native format, translating them to FAX format, and formatting the documents for transmission.

Graphics should be prepared using one of the formats recognized by the PC FAX board's software. This may require that you convert the graphics, using the PC FAX board's support software or other support software. The graphic formats are those used by programs designed for use with the kind of machine you use.

Optical scanner input may have to be converted, as well. Scanner input is typically stored in one of the popular graphics program formats.

Sending a Document

The steps involved in sending a document with a PC FAX board vary, depending on the document's source. All normally begin with a call to the receiving FAX machine, which may be a dedicated FAX machine, another computer equipped with a PC FAX board, or a PC FAX service. The call is made by selecting or typing a Call command and entering the number to be called, using the PC FAX board's operating software. Depending on the operating characteristics of the PC FAX board in use, the software may have to be loaded first. If the software is memory resident or running in background, a certain key-combination may have to be entered to activate the software.

Sending a Prepared File Sending a prepared file normally involves selecting or typing `Send` or a similar command, and specifying a file to be sent. The file name may be typed with a command (`SEND FILE.EXT`), typed after the command is selected or typed, or selected from a list.

Alternatively, some PC FAX boards send a file by intercepting it as it is being sent to the printer by another program. They then issue the program's Print command, and the PC FAX board's software takes the output, converts it to FAX format, and transmits it.

Sending an Instant Message An *instant message* is a brief document, typically consisting of text only. Depending on the capabilities of your PC FAX board, you can send a message after it is created with the PC FAX board's text editor (without having to save it) or by displaying what you want to send on your screen and issuing the command that does a screen dump. In each case, your PC FAX board may not be connected to another FAX machine.

Sending Scanner Input If you have an optical scanner, your PC FAX board may be able to transmit data as it is scanned. To do so requires that you connect with the receiving FAX machine, set your software to transmit the scanner input, then scan the document.

Receiving a Document

Receiving a document via a PC FAX board involves nothing more than having your computer on and running, the telephone line connected, and the PC FAX board online. If the PC FAX board cannot run in the background, you will have to start the software and wait for the other FAX machine to call and the document to be transferred. If the PC FAX board can run in the background, you may have to start the PC FAX board's operating program and set it up to receive a call—after which you can use your computer for other applications.

Once a document is received, it may be displayed onscreen (Figure 4.4), stored in a file, or sent to a printer, depending on the options offered by the PC FAX board's operating software.

Using Advanced Features

If you read the two sections immediately preceding and Chapter 3, you have a good idea of how to use advanced PC FAX board features such as store-and-forward and scheduled transmission. PC FAX boards vary in operation, so it is beyond the scope of this book to instruct you on how to use each advanced feature with every PC FAX board on the market. Refer to your FAX machine's manual for detailed instructions. However,

Figure 4.4 Displaying an incoming FAX document. *Photo courtesy of KYE International Corp.*

using these features is largely a matter of selecting menu items and entering information at prompts.

Optical Scanners

Computer optical scanning is a topic worthy of a book in itself, but I will provide basic information about computer optical scanners here.

Most optical scanners scan only in black and white or in shades of gray (e.g., halftone, gray scale, or dithering). Color images are scanned as black and white or halftone. If you have to scan color images frequently, it is best to get a scanner that is capable of halftone scanning. A color scanner cannot add to the quality of an image scanned for FAX transmission.

Optical scanners come in two physical configurations: handheld and flatbed.

Handheld Scanners

A handheld scanner, as illustrated in Figure 4.5, consists of a handheld scanning device, which is connected to its host computer or board with a cable. Handheld scanners can usually scan an area approximately four inches wide by 12 or 14 inches long at one time, so you will have to make several passes over a page to scan it completely.

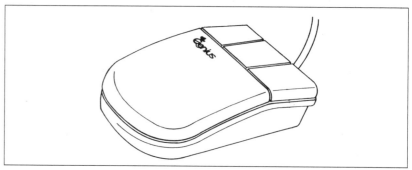

Figure 4.5 A handheld scanner. *Courtesy of KYE International Corp.*

Handheld scanners can scan anything you can pass them over, including books.

Flatbed Scanners

Flatbed scanners are somewhat similar to photocopiers; the page to be scanned is placed on a glass sheet, and the scanner is moved past the page, or vice versa. Figure 4.6 shows a typical flatbed scanner.

Figure 4.6 A flatbed scanner. *Photo courtesy of Radio Shack, a division of Tandy Corporation*

While more expensive than handheld scanners, flatbed scanners are worth the extra cost if you do a lot of scanning.

Flatbed scanners can scan anything you can place on the scanning glass.

Installing an Optical Scanner

A few optical scanners plug directly into a computer's serial port. Installing this kind of scanner consists of nothing more than plugging it into the serial port.

Most optical scanners, however, connect with a board installed in the host computer. The board is installed in the same manner as a PC FAX board; see the scanner's instruction manual for additional installation information.

Optical scanners usually require special software to operate. (A very few PC FAX boards provide software that accommodates scanners.) This software will have to be installed, and special computer system configurations may have to be set up, as described for PC FAX board operating software.

Using an Optical Scanner

Using an optical scanner normally involves loading and running the software that comes with the scanner, specifying the name of a file in which a scanned document should be stored, then passing the scanner over the page(s) of the document (handheld scanner) or placing the document on the scanner's surface (flatbed scanner).

Special software setup may be required for scanner software and/or PC FAX board software to enable a PC FAX board to transmit data from a scanner as it is scanned.

PC FAX Support Software

Depending on the capabilities of a PC FAX board and its operating software and on your applications, you may need to have one or more of the following kinds of software:

- Text conversion (to convert some word processing programs' 8-bit or binary files to 7-bit ASCII text), also known as OCR

- Graphics conversion (to convert graphics created by a graphics or desktop publishing program—or graphics scanned by an optical scanner—to a format that the PC FAX board's software can read)

- Multitasking environment (to enable you to use your computer for other tasks while using a PC FAX board that will not operate in the background mode)

Protecting Yourself from Junk Mail

As noted earlier in this book, FAX broadcast capability is sometimes used to send advertisements, solicitations, and other commercial messages to FAX machines on a wholesale basis. This can be as annoying as automated voice-telephone sales. While the person or organization sending such FAX junk mail is paying to send it, you pay, too—in tied-up telephone lines and wasted paper. If your FAX machine is frequently left on and unattended, you could miss important messages because your line is busy and/or your machine is out of paper. PC FAX boards tied up with receiving a FAX message can tie up your computer, or slow it down and waste disk space.

To protect yourself against FAX junk mail, maintain control of your FAX telephone number. Do not give it out indiscriminately. It may not be a good idea to put it on your business card. Do not give it to FAX directory solicitors who offer "free" FAX listings, and specify that the number be unlisted in your local telephone company's directory. If your FAX traffic is light, disconnect your FAX machine or disable your PC FAX board when you're not using it. Send and receive FAX messages at prearranged times.

If your FAX machine or PC FAX board has security features, you may use these to lock out calls from unauthorized FAX machines. A calling FAX can be required to transmit its phone number, and/or a security password, before your machine will accept a transmission from it.

When you do receive FAX junk mail, contact the sender immediately and request to be removed from the sender's phone list. If FAX junk mail continues to come in from the same source, notify your telephone company. Most telephone companies have strict guidelines regulating commercial solicitation via telephone.

What You've Learned

This chapter has taught you the following:

- To use a dedicated FAX machine, you need the machine itself, a power supply, a telephone line, a supply of blank paper, and any of several optional pieces of equipment, depending on your application.

- Installing a FAX machine consists of selecting an appropriate location, loading the machine with a supply of paper, and plugging in the power and phone lines.

- A FAX machine should not be located in areas where there is likely to be excessive dust, heat, clutter, or sunlight, and where all of its operating elements are easily accessible.

- FAX machines operate best when clean.

- You should not use a FAX machine during an electrical storm.

- FAX machines handle the logistics of establishing and maintaining a connection automatically (with the exception of those machines that require you to dial a number manually). To send a document via FAX, all that's required is to connect with the receiving FAX machine, then scan the pages of the document to be sent.

- To receive a FAX document, you need only make sure your machine is supplied with paper, turned on, and ready to answer the phone.

- In addition to a telephone line, to use a PC FAX board, you need the board, its operating software, and a computer with an empty slot and enough memory and disk space to accommodate the board and its operating requirements.

- Installing a PC FAX board is not unlike installing any other board or card in a computer's expansion slot.

- Some PC FAX boards may require you to prepare text and/or graphics by converting them to alternate formats before they can be transmitted.

- Prepared files, instant messages, and scanner input may be transmitted with PC FAX boards.

- Receiving a FAXed document with a PC FAX board is an automatic process; received documents can be stored on disk, displayed on-screen, or sent to a printer.

- Computer optical scanners come in two configurations: handheld and flatbed.

- Most optical scanners require a board and/or software to operate.

- Among the support software you may need to use a PC FAX board are text- and graphics-conversion programs, and multitasking software.

- The best way to protect yourself against FAX junk mail is to not give your FAX telephone number out indiscriminately.

This chapter concludes our examination of dedicated FAX machines and PC FAX boards. Test your knowledge with the following quiz, after which you'll learn the basics of electronic mail (E-mail) in Chapter 5.

Quiz

1. The basic items required to use a dedicated FAX machine are a power supply, a supply of paper, and:

   a. A surge protector
   b. A telephone line
   c. A modem
   d. A FAX directory

2. The greatest enemy of electronic devices is:

   a. Static
   b. Light
   c. Heat
   d. Dirt

3. Where is a PC FAX installed?

   a. Next to the host computer's monitor
   b. Inside a telephone
   c. Inside the host computer's cabinet
   d. Inside a dedicated FAX machine

4. PC FAX board installation involves:

   a. Installing the board itself
   b. Plugging in a scanner
   c. Installing operating software and making necessary system configuration changes
   d. a and c

5. Most PC FAX boards come with operational software of varying capability. Which of these tasks can PC FAX software perform?

   a. Graphics format conversion
   b. Word processing
   c. Number dialing
   d. All of the above

6. Software that is not directly associated with FAX transmission, but which performs related tasks such as file conversion, is called:

   a. Support software
   b. Graphics software
   c. Communications software
   d. Installation software

7. Computer optical scanners come in two configurations: handheld and flatbed. What is the major limitation of handheld scanners, compared to flatbed scanners?

   a. Limited width of scan

b. The inability to do halftone scanning
c. The extra software required
d. The extra hardware required

8. Computer optical scanners may require which of the following items?

   a. Supporting software
   b. A power supply
   c. A telephone line
   d. A color monitor

9. Which of the following *cannot* be considered support software for a PC FAX board?

   a. Graphics-conversion software
   b. Multitasking software
   c. Database software
   d. Text format conversion software

10. FAX junk mail is best avoided by:

    a. Not giving out your FAX telephone number indiscriminately
    b. Keeping your FAX telephone number unlisted
    c. Not giving your FAX telephone number to individuals or organizations offering free FAX directory listings
    d. All of the above

Chapter **5** | # What Is E-Mail?

About This Chapter

This chapter provides an overview of electronic mail (E-mail). In it, you will learn what E-mail is, its capabilities, and its applications. The purpose of this chapter is to give you a basic, nontechnical understanding of E-mail. For details on how E-mail works and specific information on the computer hardware you'll need to access it, see Chapter 6—but read this chapter first.

Electronic Mail—Origins and Development

E-mail's origins can be found in mainframe computer file transfer. Almost as soon as there was more than one computer, a need to share programs and information between computers developed. But, while program listings and documents were easily stored and accessed within a computer as *files*, transferring them to another computer was another matter. In the early days of computing, duplicating a file's contents in another computer was a time-consuming process that could be accomplished in one of two ways:

- By manually entering the contents of the file into the receiving computer based on memory and/or a hardcopy listing of the file's contents

- By copying the file to storage media (e.g., punched tape and magnetic tape), then physically transferring the media to the receiving mainframe computer.

Figure 5.1 illustrates a mainframe computer.

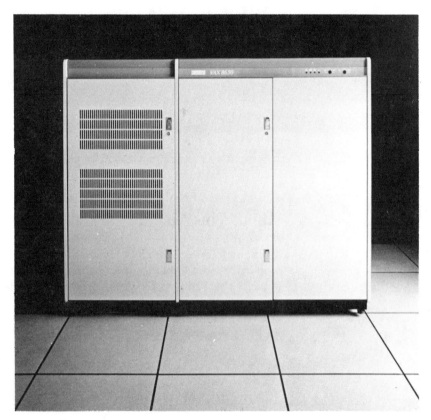

Figure 5.1 Mainframe computer. *Copyright of Digital Equipment Corporation 1989*

File Transfer

There had to be a better way to transfer files between computers, so a better way was developed. Early computer engineers devised methods of transferring files directly between two computers by connecting them with a special kind of cable. Such connections transferred data from one computer's memory to another's in the binary format used by the two computers.

These direct connections were limited; data became lost or garbled if the connection was too long. It would be impractical to run hundreds (or thousands) of miles of cable to connect computers even if the data signals weren't degraded by the distance involved.

A perhaps obvious solution to the problem of connecting computers many miles apart was to use the existing network of telephone wires that girdled the country. That still left the problem of signal degradation, to which modems provided the solution. Figure 5.2 shows a modem.

Figure 5.2 Modem. *Photo courtesy of Hayes Microcomputer Systems*

Computer Messaging

As the problems of long-distance computer communication were being solved, computer users and programmers were busy inventing interesting ways to enhance the ability of mainframe and minicomputer terminal users to communicate with one another. These users typically shared working program and data files, some of which were text. Why not, it was reasoned, take file sharing one step farther and set up special areas to share *messages* among the group of users? Databases were developed to contain the messages, which one could read and respond to (a.k.a. posting messages). A few lines of program code made it possible for the message-handling program to keep track of the messages read by a specific user, thus enabling the user to read only new messages without having to wade through previous messages.

Computer messaging systems—at first a novelty, their creation perhaps inspired by boredom—quickly gained popularity as practical replacements for paper memos and sharing longer documents in the computer workplace. This, in turn, inspired more development.

Computer Bulletin Boards

A little more programming resulted in headers for computer messages, which allowed the inclusion of a sender's name, a subject, and the name of the person to whom a message was directed (although anyone could read it). Since the group of messages was stored as one large database, it was possible to extend the program's capability to allow users to search for specific messages, to read only those messages addressed to them, to read messages on specific topics, and more. Thus, *computer bulletin boards* (electronic analogs of the corkboards in laundromats, community centers, and the like) were born.

With messages present on computer systems and message-handling capability at such a level of sophistication, it naturally occurred to users and programmers to create more private bulletin boards. Privacy was handled in two ways:

1. Access to certain message databases (or to messages within a database on certain subjects, from certain users, etc.) was restricted to users with certain access levels.

2. A security feature, which enabled a person posting a message to instruct the computer system optionally to display it only to the person to whom it was addressed; was implemented.

Electronic Mail

With messages and message-handling software present on computer systems and message privacy a recognized and desirable option, special user-to-user messaging systems were the logical next step. Software capable of delivering messages to a specified user's *electronic mailbox* was developed. Electronic mailboxes were implemented as individual message databases whose contents could be accessed only by the specific user to whom they were assigned (or, in some cases, as databases containing all messages, with specific messages accessible only by the users to whom they were addressed).

At this point, electronic mail was ready for the masses.

Computer-to-Computer Messaging

Those earliest E-mail systems were designed for the use of a limited number of mainframe or minicomputer users who accessed the computers via dedicated terminals (keyboards and video-display and/or printer units designed to access the mainframe or minicomputer in question). However, basic E-mail design and operating principles developed for early computer users are the same as those used by modern computer users. As you will learn in Chapter 6, using a personal computer to access an E-mail system is not unlike using a dedicated terminal to access a mainframe or minicomputer. These computers serve as the hosts for commercial E-mail systems.

With computer-to-computer file-transfer capability available, however, it wasn't long before messages were being shared between computer systems. After all, messages were files, too. With a little modification of the software that handled file transfers, message files could be added to specific databases, rather than be assigned to the status of shared working files and placed under the control of a system's bulletin board or E-mail program. Thus, users on a computer system in, say, New York could exchange public and private messages with a system in Cincinnati—as long as the two systems were connected.

Suddenly, computer messaging was far more than a means of diversion and efficient document delivery for a few people who could access a specific computer. The potential for a virtually limitless E-mail network loomed large on the horizon, even though the personal computer as we know it was yet to be conceived. In the 1960s, the U.S. Department of Defense and various allied research agencies and universities were the first to create E-mail (and bulletin board) networks on a large scale. An experimental network called DARPANET linked scores of computers and eventually evolved to become (and/or include—no one is certain which) USENET and related networks.

Commercial Electronic Messaging

Thanks to DARPANET, computer messaging between computer systems was commonplace for those in the industry by the late 1960s. But the networks were used only for communication among those in the academic and research communities. As far as most people were concerned, direct-dial long-distance telephone service and FAX were the current leading edge in business communications.

As electronic messaging evolved, college students and employees of organizations who had been exposed to large-scale computer-to-computer file transfer filtered into the mainstream business world. They introduced the concept of large-scale electronic data transfer. Before long, corporate computer users were enjoying the benefits of private computer messaging systems, some via their own computers and others via commercial services set up for the purpose of transferring computer data over long distances. Many of the latter services were already established as commercial data processing services (e.g., time-sharing services), which either handled data compiling, storage, and manipulation for businesses or sold time on their computer systems to businesses, who accessed them via terminals, communicating over telephone lines.

By the mid-1970s, computer data transfer had become a big business, not incidentally altering forever the way business, government, and other organizations handled information. Messages accounted for a large portion of the data transferred by such services.

Personal Computer Messaging

As might be expected, the majority of business computer data transfer took place during business hours. The computers handling this data traffic were largely idle for most of the evening and weekend hours. This was regarded as idle time and written off except when used to perform system maintenance or implement software changes.

In the late 1970s, personal computers entered the picture. Management at the larger time-sharing/data-transfer services (most notably, The Source and CompuServe) saw the future—personal computers in every business and most homes—and recognized the commercial potential in linking their users and offering special services such as E-mail. Online services were developed, eventually legitimizing E-mail and putting it within reach of the masses.

Online services didn't catch on instantly, as the initial cost for modems and online service usage was relatively high in those days. After experiencing growing pains throughout the 1980s, online services have attained the status of big business and have become an important part of the personal and business lives of hundreds of thousands of personal computer users. An aggregate total of more than 900,000 personal computer users—business, hobby, and home computer users—have direct access to E-mail on online services. Hundreds of thousands more business computer users can also tap into the vast personal computer E-mail network, via mainframe and minicomputers. Services such as AT&T Mail, BIX, CompuServe, DELPHI, EasyLink, and MCI Mail carry more than two million E-mail messages daily—most are of the type shown in Figure 5.3.

Like personal computer sales, modem sales show no indication of dropping—or even of leveling off. A simple extrapolation will indicate that personal computer messaging will soon be as commonplace as telephone usage was during the 1960s—or FAX in the 1980s.

E-Mail: Gateway to the World

Although online services offer a plethora of services, the services used most often are E-mail and file transfer—the very foundations on which online services are based.

This is not surprising; the most valuable commodity in contemporary society happens to be information, and sharing and gaining information is what E-mail and file transfer are all about. Looking at it from a slightly different perspective, a major and vital segment of our economy

```
** in.3:
Date: Fri Aug 11 09:36:00 EST 1989
From: !lazarus
Subject: Thanks!
To: !banks
Cc: !lazarus
Content-Length: 1590

Mike:

I received the message about data-conversion service.  I guess I
didn't read the fine print enough.  Certainly never intended to
pay to store the files.  Must have cost the company $500.00 or
more in the last year.  The price of ignorance...

The part of New Mexico I'll be working in doesn't have tne same
kind of network nodes I've been using.  I suppose the reasons are
obvious, given the nature of the area.  However, I'm hoping to
find a node at a nearby university, so I can stay in touch with
the net community.

I would indeed appreciate seeing the galleys of PULPHOUSE.
(Easier to read than on the computer screen.)

answer, create, delete, forward, get, help, profile, quit, read, show
Command: .
```

Figure 5.3 An E-mail message.

(and our society) is communication—and E-mail is certainly communication.

As was noted in Chapter 1, standard E-mail consists of text messages delivered to an electronic mailbox on a host system (online service). But E-mail can reach far beyond the electronic mailboxes of users on the online service on which it is sent. Depending on the service one is using, E-mail offers gateways to other kinds of communications services, including:

- FAX. E-mail and specialized modem/FAX services can convert and send text—and in a few cases, graphics—to dedicated FAX machines and computers equipped with PC FAX boards. A minority of such services will also receive text FAX messages and deliver them to your electronic mailbox. (These services are detailed in Chapter 8, and in Chapters 6 through 10.)

- Telex. Before FAX and modem usage became widespread, *Telex*— electronic communications via specialized equipment—was the standard in international communications. It is still a standard in many areas, due to the lack of computer communications nodes or the inertia of its users. It remains an important international communications tool. Most online services offer Telex services, which allow you to send and receive Telex messages worldwide.

- U.S. Mail. Several online services (notable among them is MCI

Mail) provide delivery of hardcopy versions of E-mail messages or documents to postal addresses. E-mail messages are printed out in the city nearest their destination, then sent via First Class mail to the address designated by the sender.

- Courier services. If you need to have hardcopy documents delivered to recipients the next day—or even the same day—that service is available via E-mail as well. Certain E-mail services will print out E-mail in the city nearest its destination, then arrange for courier delivery of the hardcopy.

- Foreign postal services. Computer gateways to Telex services provide all the options available to Telex users—including having a document with a foreign destination printed at the Telex station nearest its destination and sent via the country's postal service.

- Foreign online services. Certain E-mail carriers, among them AT&T Mail and TELEMAIL, offer direct E-mail routing to E-mail services in other countries. Some such foreign services are local versions of the American E-mail system; others are independent systems.

- Other domestic online services. Because they are commercial and competitive enterprises, the majority of online services in the United States do not provide direct E-mail connections with their rivals, even though experiments have been tried in this area. A notable exception is the MCI Mail/CompuServe link. Considering the fact that a significant percentage of modem users employ more than one online service, the lack of direct interconnection is rather silly, but it is a fact that E-mail users have to live with.

Fortunately, some E-mail relay services specialize in carrying E-mail between online services. This is a relatively recent innovation in the online world, and many modem users are unaware of its utility. However, with so many online services extant, such carriers provide an easy alternative to signing up for multiple online services. They also offer E-mail relay service to certain overseas and domestic online services that are not accessible to the average user.

E-Mail Capabilities and Limitations

As you've just learned, E-mail offers a wide range of delivery options. But you may be wondering exactly what kinds of material can be delivered.

Text Documents and Files

Although not every system handles both types, two basic categories of data can be transferred from one computer to another: standard (7-bit) ASCII text and 8-bit or binary text files of the type created by many word processing programs.

All E-mail systems can handle standard (7-bit) ASCII text. If you compose a document online, it will be in 7-bit ASCII format. If you are able to read a document online, it is in 7-bit ASCII format. When you read a document online, it is transmitted to your computer in 7-bit ASCII format—the same format the E-mail system uses to display menus, prompts, help files, and other textual information.

If you *upload* a document prepared with a word processor that stores files in a special format (e.g., WordPerfect or WordStar), it will be in 8-bit or a special binary format and will most likely be unreadable online. To upload it to begin with, you will have to use a special *binary file-transfer protocol*, such as Xmodem, because special formatting and storage characters can be perceived by modems or host computers as commands.

Send E-mail as 7-bit ASCII text, unless you send a large document to someone who uses the same word processing program you use.

If you are using a word processor that stores files in special format to create messages, you will probably want to run a conversion program or perform a "print to disk" operation on a file to convert it to 7-bit ASCII text to transmit it as a regular text file.

Some E-mail systems can transfer specific word processors' files or any 8-bit or binary files, but you won't be able to read them online. You'll have to *download* such files using a binary file-transfer protocol and open or print them with the appropriate word processing program before you can view them.

Nontext Files

E-mail systems that can transfer 8-bit and binary word processing files can also transfer data or graphic files. Here again, you will have to upload and download such files using a binary file-transfer format. You will also be able to view them only with the kind of program used to create them.

Document Format

Most systems limit text messages to a certain line width—the almost universal standard is 80 columns (characters). If you're typing a message while online on most systems, you'll have to press ENTER at the end of each line. For messages prepared offline, most systems require that you have a carriage return at the end of each line.

No word processor formatting codes (8-bit or control characters) can be included in a document prepared offline. If such are included, they may garble or freeze the file transfer.

Document Size

There are no page sizes as such in E-mail, but some E-mail systems place a limit on the number of lines or total file size. Other systems limit a document's size if you select delivery options such as Telex.

E-Mail Channels and Applications

By now you have probably thought of quite a few applications for E-mail. To give you an idea of the full potential of E-mail, here's an overview of E-mail applications, classified by the channels used to carry E-mailed documents.

Document Transfer to Other Modem Users

E-mail's most frequent application is transferring documents between modem users on the same online service. This is a basic service offered by all E-mail systems and the kind of electronic communication with which modem users are most familiar. This kind of transfer requires that both sender and recipient have an account on the service in question.

Such intersystem E-mail is used for sending everything from short memos to long text files by business and personal users alike. Addressing is simple (as shown in Figure 5.3), a wide variety of message-handling options (e.g., filing and carbon-copying), are available, and file upload/download procedures are often streamlined and customized to work with the E-mail systems. Perhaps most important of all (and this is the reason why the lion's share of E-mail traffic consists of intersystem messaging), online service users are most comfortable using such a service within their home systems. The command and menu structures used by online service's E-mail systems (such as the one illustrated in Figure 5.4) are familiar to the online service users and make it easy to send and receive messages.

Intrasystem transfers (those handled by E-mail message-relay services) are used most frequently by those who have only occasional need to send E-mail to users on services where they do not have accounts or cannot gain access. The kind of traffic carried by relay services typically consists of memos and short documents. The newness of such systems and the difficulties inherent in addressing mail to some online services makes for some resistance to using them. But if online

```
EasyPlex   Main Menu

 1 READ mail, 1 message pending

 2 COMPOSE a new message
 3 UPLOAD a message
 4 USE a file from PER area

 5 ADDRESS Book
 6 SET options

 9 Send a CONGRESSgram ($)
Enter choice '
```

Figure 5.4 An E-mail menu.

services continue to avoid direct connection with competitors, relay services are going to "own" a large share of the E-mail market within a few years.

No matter how the E-mail is routed, modem users employ online service E-mail delivery for the following reasons:

- Speed. E-mail is delivered within seconds (or at the most,minutes) of being sent.

- Convenience. Both sender and receiver can access E-mail 24 hours a day, 365 days per year. Outside of the few hours per year when online service computers or communications links are shut down for service or other reasons, the E-mail "post office" is never closed. E-mail can be sent or received any time the user is ready.

Too, with E-mail, there is no need to print a document, no envelope to address, and no trip to make to the post office. Sophisticated message-handling options make it easy to send copies of documents to multiple recipients, forward copies of incoming E-mail to others, and more.

Finally, any document sent via E-mail can be downloaded and stored as a text file on disk, after which it can be edited, printed, resent via E-mail, and otherwise manipulated as needed. This is a boon for those who need to share text with others (e.g., editors and collaborating writers). E-mail document transfer is particularly helpful when the sender and recipient are using different kinds of computers (e.g., Macintosh and IBM), because it frees computer users of the albatross of incompatible disk formats.

Nondocument File Transfer to Other Modem Users

Nondocument file transfer—the transfer of data and program files— from one computer to another via E-mail is a close second to document delivery in terms of application popularity. Systems that enable binary file transfer via E-mail are an eminently preferable alternative to sending copies of files on disk via U.S. Mail or courier. Such transfer is faster and more convenient than either postal or courier delivery. The transfer time, exclusive of uploading, is the same as that of document E-mail.

File transfers are also far less expensive than "next day" courier services. You can, for instance, send a disk containing a 200K data file for about $20 via a courier service; using an online service, the combined cost for sending and receiving a file of that size would be less than $12.

As with documents, data and program files are transferred via E-mail when time is a critical factor.

Nonmodem Electronic Delivery

Nonmodem electronic delivery of text documents alludes to the delivery of E-mail documents to electronic communications devices other than dial-up model-equipped computers—specifically dedicated FAX machines, PC FAX board-equipped computers, and Telex machines.

E-mail documents consigned for FAX or Telex delivery can consist only of text and may be subject to size limitations and special formats.

FAX delivery of computer-generated documents via E-mail is an increasingly important service (covered in detail in Chapter 8). It gives computer users access to millions of FAX machines worldwide, on the same terms as E-mail, which is to say that modem/FAX delivery options are the same as those offered for E-mail by online services. Multiple recipients, delivery receipts, duplicate E-mail and FAX delivery, and other options are available with modem/FAX service. Modem/FAX delivery is used for the same reasons as E-mail or FAX—speed, convenience, and cost savings.

Telex delivery of computer-generated documents via E-mail is less frequently used than E-mail or FAX delivery, mainly because the growth of computer and FAX communications has greatly decreased the importance of Telex. However, where Telex installations are in place (especially in third-world countries), Telex delivery of E-mail is a vital service, indeed. Being able to send and receive Telex messages via E-mail provides rapid communications with virtually any city in the world—without the expense of a Telex machine.

Note: In some areas, brief Telex messages can also be delivered as telegrams, by voice telephone.

Hardcopy Delivery

If someone to whom you wish to send a message doesn't have a modem, FAX, or Telex machine, don't worry. You can still use E-mail to get your message to them via any of several hardcopy delivery options. Hardcopy delivery of electronic mail is the "missing link" that makes E-mail a complete communications system.

With hardcopy delivery of E-mail, you can send messages and longer documents to virtually anyone—anywhere in the world.

The most commonly used hardcopy delivery option is U.S. Mail. Several E-mail services will print a document you've uploaded or entered online in the city nearest the designation, then address and mail it for you. Such documents are typically printed with a laser printer and are mailed in a distinctive envelope. Figure 5.5 shows what a hardcopy document that originated as E-mail looks like.

This letter was electronically transmitted and distributed by **MCI Mail**

August 11, 1989

Michael A. Banks
P.O. Box 312
Milford, OH 45150

Dear Reader:

This is a test/sample of MCI Mail's paper mail (hardcopy) delivery service. This message was entered at 3:00 A.M. via my computer, and I expect to receive it within two days (it will be printed out using a laser printer in a city near my home, then mailed via First Class mail).

As you can see, the printing quality is crisp and clear, and the message is printed with appropriate margins.

MCI Mail's paper mail delivery service is a real convenience for those who have neither the time nor inclination to write a letter, print it out, address an envelope, then stuff it, seal it, and stamp it. MCI Mail does all that for you--all you have to do is type the letter. (And the cost is not only reasonable--it's far less than what you get in return, in terms of convenience, time saved, and the impression the bright orange MCI Mail envelope containing your un-folded message makes!)

Cordially,

Michael A. Banks

Figure 5.5 Hardcopy document from an E-mail service.

Most services that offer hardcopy postal delivery also offer such options as letterhead and signature reproduction on documents and registered delivery.

E-mail services working in conjunction with courier services provide a less common but often vital form of hardcopy delivery. If you specify courier delivery, your document is printed in the city nearest its destination, then delivered via a conventional courier service. Options include overnight or 4-hour delivery and letterhead and signature reproduction.

Note: E-mail hardcopy courier delivery is not restricted to the kinds of deadlines set up for courier services that pick up hardcopy from you. Your document is sent to the destination area instantly, and the physical copy has to be carried a much shorter distance.

Costs

Although hardcopy delivery services are premium services, E-mail is largely more cost effective than other forms of rapid document delivery and communications. Table 5.1 provides some cost comparisons of E-mail with other services.

Table 5.1 E-mail Cost Comparisons

Costs to Send a Half-Page Memo[1]

E-Mail	Postal Delivery	Courier[3] Delivery	Voice or FAX Telephone Call
$.60	$.25	$8.95/$20.00	$.90 to $2.10

Costs to Send a Ten-Page Document[2]

E-Mail	Postal Delivery	Courier[3] Delivery	Voice or FAX Telephone Call
$1.80	$.45	$8.95/$20.00	$4.50 to $7.50

[1] Daytime rates: E-mail and telephone rates are lower during evening and weekend hours.
[2] Daytime rates: assumes 2400-bps modem speed during upload of the document text file to the online service.
[3] Courier delivery refers to next-day delivery service; 4-hour delivery service is five to ten times higher.

What You've Learned

This chapter has taught you the following:

- E-mail originated as internal messaging systems on mainframe computers.

- The advent of computer-to-computer data transfer made true electronic mail possible.

- The first personal computer communications services (networks or online services) were developed as a way to take advantage of mainframe and minicomputer time-sharing services' idle time.

- E-mail delivery is not limited to other modem users. Depending on the system you use, you can have a text document delivered to a FAX machine, a Telex machine, or to a street address (via U.S. Mail or a courier service).

- Data transferred between computers can be divided into two types: 7-bit ASCII and 8-bit or binary data. Straight text documents are typically created and transferred as 7-bit ASCII text; only documents in 7-bit ASCII format can be displayed online.

- Most E-mail systems require that you limit the width of lines in a document to 80 columns or less and that you end each line with a carriage return.

- There are no page sizes as such in E-mail; however, some E-mail systems limit the size of a document that can be delivered. Certain delivery options—mainly, Telex—carry a size limitation, too.

- E-mail channels include document delivery to modem users on the same or different online services, dedicated FAX machines, and computers equipped with PC FAX boards, Telex machines, and postal or courier delivery to street addresses.

- The major advantages of E-mail are its speed and convenience.

- For the most part, E-mail is more cost-effective than conventional delivery and communications services.

That's E-mail in overview. Test your knowledge with the following quiz, then move on to Chapter 6, where we'll delve into some of the more technical details of E-mail.

Quiz

1. E-mail's origins can be found in internal messaging systems developed for:

    a. FAX networks
    b. Personal computers
    c. Mainframe and minicomputers
    d. Voicemail

2. What made long-distance computer file (message) transfer possible?

    a. Printers
    b. Modems
    c. Bulletin boards
    d. Message-handling software

3. What two elements sparked the development of commercial on-line services and E-mail?

    a. Mainframe computers and modems
    b. Minicomputers and telephone lines
    c. The advent of the personal computer and idle time on time-sharing services
    d. The addition of serial ports to computers and the development of the modem

4. Documents for delivery from one modem user to another via text E-mail must be in which of the following formats?

    a. Binary
    b. 8-bit ASCII
    c. 7-bit ASCII
    d. FAX

5. What kinds of services carry E-mail messages from one E-mail system to another?

    a. Modem/FAX
    b. E-mail relay
    c. Telex
    d. Courier

6. Which E-mail delivery channel can be used to deliver messages and documents in hardcopy to anyone, anywhere in the world?

    a. FAX
    b. Telex
    c. Postal delivery
    d. All of the above.

7. E-mail can be used to deliver which of the following kinds of files?

    a. Text documents
    b. Data files and programs
    c. Text and data files
    d. FAX graphics

8. Hardcopy delivery of E-mail services is accomplished by online services working in conjunction with:

    a. Postal and FAX delivery services
    b. Courier and postal delivery services
    c. Intrasystem E-mail relay services
    d. Modem/FAX services

9. Delivery of text E-mail messages to dedicated FAX machines and PC FAX board-equipped computers is called what?

    a. Hardcopy/FAX services
    b. Relay/FAX services
    c. Courier/FAX services
    d. Modem/FAX services

10. Next-day hardcopy delivery service of E-mail messages is:

    a. Less expensive than postal delivery
    b. More expensive than postal delivery but less expensive than courier delivery
    c. More expensive than FAX delivery
    d. More expensive than FAX delivery but less expensive than postal delivery

6 | How E-Mail Works

About This Chapter

This chapter covers the technical side of computer communications—
how computers communicate and what you need to communicate with
computers—as well as a bit of what to expect from an E-mail service.

How Computer Communication Works

To help you understand how E-mail works, let's dive into "the deep
end" first and examine exactly how computer communication works.

Computer communications (also called telecomputing, data communications, and telecommunications) are direct data transfer between
computers. The data, as established in Chapter 5, can be data files
(graphics files, spreadsheet files, etc., used by programs), programs, or
text files. Transferred data may also include control and acknowledg-
ment signals exchanged by the computers transferring data.

Although there are several ways to link computers physically for
data transfer, the kind of link used in accessing E-mail services is a modem link.

A typical modem data transfer sequence goes like this: A computer
transmits binary data (sometimes known as digital data) to its modem, in

119

the form of a sequence of bits. The modem converts to an analog signal. The analog signal is then transmitted over voice-grade telephone lines.

A modem at the receiving end converts the analog signal into a binary signal, then sends the binary signal to its computer, which, at this point, has in its memory a duplicate of the data originally sent.

Unlike FAX communication, this process works in both directions. That is, each computer can send *or* receive data, although data is transmitted in only one direction at a time.

Elements of Data Transfer

Successful data transfer requires four elements: data, data terminal equipment (computers), data communications equipment (modems), and a communications link. Figure 6.1 clearly illustrates those elements and their relationships.

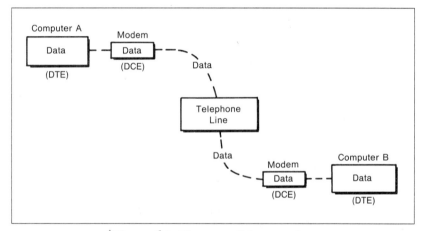

Figure 6.1 Elements of data transfer.

Data and Computer Data Format

The content of documents being transferred by computer has no effect on the transmission. All data looks the same to computers.

Computer data can be information of any kind—business or personal messages, other kinds of documents, program data files such as spreadsheets and data base files, programs themselves, etc.

Data is handled within a computer as *binary* information, using symbolic groups of binary digits (1s and 0s) as described in Chapter 3. The bits are literally represented by low and high voltage levels within the computer. Exactly how the binary numbers these voltage levels represent carry information is described below.

What is Binary Data in Computers? The *patterns* of the groups of binary digits, or bits, within a computer are what actually contain the information used by computers. The actual information is based on a code called ASCII (an acronym for American Standard Code for Information Interchange).

As you may remember from Chapter 3, the groups of bits are called *bytes*. Each byte is a seven- or eight-digit binary number, and each binary number represents an arbitrary character. Among personal computers, the characters represented by each of the first 128 binary numbers (0 through 127 or, in binary terms, 0000000 through 01111111) are shown in Table 6.1.

Table 6.1 ASCII Table

ASCII Number	Character	ASCII Number	Character
0	^@	27	^[
1	^A	28	^\
2	^B	29	^]
3	^C	30	^^
4	^D	31	^_
5	^E	32	SPACE
6	^F	33	!
7	^G	34	"
8	^H	35	#
9	^I	36	$
10	^J	37	%
11	^K	38	&
12	^L	39	'
13	^M	40	(
14	^N	41	)
15	^O	42	*
16	^P	43	+
17	^Q	44	,
18	^R	45	–
19	^S	46	.
20	^T	47	/
21	^U	48	0
22	^V	49	1
23	^W	50	2
24	^X	51	3
25	^Y	52	4
26	^Z	53	5

Table 6.1 (cont.)

ASCII Number	Character	ASCII Number	Character
54	6	89	Y
55	7	90	Z
56	8	91	[
57	9	92	\
58	:	93	]
59	;	94	^
60	<	95	_
61	=	96	`
62	>	97	a
63	?	98	b
64	@	99	c
65	A	100	d
66	B	101	e
67	C	102	f
68	D	103	g
69	E	104	h
70	F	105	i
71	G	106	j
72	H	107	k
73	I	108	l
74	J	109	m
75	K	110	n
76	L	111	o
77	M	112	p
78	N	113	q
79	O	114	r
80	P	115	s
81	Q	116	t
82	R	117	u
83	S	118	v
84	T	119	w
85	U	120	x
86	V	121	y
87	W	122	z
88	X		

Table 6.1 (cont.)

ASCII Number	Character	ASCII Number	Character
123	{	126	[tld]
124	[svb]	127	DELETE
125	}		

Note: A caret (^) preceding a character indicates that the character is a control character.

Table 6.1 displays the ASCII number assignments for each of the 128 characters used in seven-bit transmission, manipulation, and storage by personal computers. A few character assignments (especially numbers 91 through 96 and 123 through 127) may vary from one brand of computer to another, but the control character, letter, number, space, and punctuation mark assignments are consistent in all computers.

Note that many computers use an additional 128 eight-bit binary numbers (all ASCII numbers can be represented by seven-bit numbers) for binary and graphics data storage, as well as for graphics character display. There is, at present, no standard for these additional characters, which is why text intended for data transfer must normally be in seven-bit format, using the ASCII standard.

What Is a Binary Number? In Table 6.1, decimal numbers are used to represent the binary numbers used by computers—a matter of convenience. A true binary number is a string of binary digits, such as 0001010 or 1001001. Only 0s and 1s are used. The values of the numerals themselves (0 and 1) do not determine the total value of a binary number; instead, the *values of the places* marked by a 1 are summed. Each place has a set value. The first place on the right in a binary number has a value of 1, the second place a value of 2, the third place a value of 4, and so on, with the value doubling with each place, as illustrated in Table 6.2 for decimal numbers 1–20.

Table 6.2 Binary Numbering System

Decimal Number	Binary Number
0	0000000
1	0000001
2	0000010
3	0000011
4	0000100
5	0000101
6	0000110
7	0000111

Table 6.2 (cont.)

Decimal Number	Binary Number
8	0001000
9	0001001
10	0001010
11	0001011
12	0001100
13	0001101
14	0001110
15	0001111
16	0010000
17	0010001
18	0010010
19	0010011
20	0010100

Table 6.2 shows that the binary number 000101 is the same as the decimal number 5 (add the values of the places: 4 + 1 = 5). In the same manner, the binary number 0010100 is the same as the decimal number 20 (add the value of the places that contain a 1: 16 + 4 = 20).

Inside a computer, binary data consists of electronic representations of such numbers. A 1 is represented by one voltage level, and a 0 is represented by another voltage level. These voltage levels exist in specified storage areas in a computer's circuitry. When a program reads binary data, it translates it into the appropriate character, per the ASCII code in Table 6.1.

Data Terminal Equipment

Data Terminal Equipment (DTE) consists of the computers or terminals used in telecomputing, which serve as both the ultimate source and destination of data. The use of "terminal" in the phrase alludes to the fact that the computers are the beginning and ending points of data transmission—which is just what a terminal is: a place where a journey begins and ends.

Communications Links

As mentioned earlier, computers may be linked for data transfer in several ways. The majority of data communication, however, takes place via telephone lines.

Data Communications Equipment

While it is the least expensive and most readily available channel of data transfer, the voice-telephone system cannot handle computer data in its native binary format. Thus, a modem must be used to translate data from binary (or digital) format into analog format—a format that *can* be transmitted successfully via ordinary phone lines.

Data Communications Equipment (DCE) performs this task. DCE consists of modems and their associated interfaces, connectors, and cables.

Computer Communications Hardware

Now that you know how data is represented inside a computer and recognize the major hardware elements used in computer data communications, we'll examine those hardware elements more closely.

Computers

At the very least, a personal computer consists of a keyboard, the computer itself (sometimes built into the keyboard), a monitor, and a mass storage device (typically a disk drive), as shown in Figure 6.2.

To this configuration, you will have to add a modem and/or a serial port. As noted earlier, internal modems have a built-in serial port. Modems that do not use a serial port use a parallel port, which, again, you may have to add.

Monitors

Your monitor should have an 80-column display, as the majority of on-line services provide 80-column displays. An 80-column display is more efficient and can save time in the long run, as fewer lines have to be sent to display a block of text. And, an 80-column display is easier to read than a 40-column display.

Most online services do not provide color and graphics. The color combinations you see are an option set from within your program.

If you usc E-mail services (or any computer application, for that matter) a lot, it may be important to have a color monitor. You'll be looking at a lot of scrolling text online, so you need an easy-to-view monitor. If cost forces you to compromise and use a monochrome (single-color) monitor, green is the most commonly used and recommended color for monitors, as it is easy on the eyes. Amber monitors are even easier on the eyes.

Whether you choose a color or monochrome monitor, look for a

Figure 6.2 A personal computer. *Photo courtesy of Radio Shack, a division of Tandy Corporation*

high-resolution monitor—even a nice color display is difficult to look at if the image is grainy.

Storage

Time is often an important factor where E-mail is concerned; many communications programs require exclusive use of your computer. You are, after all, paying for every minute you spend connected to an online service. So, if you intend to do a lot of downloading and uploading, you may want to buy a faster floppy disk drive or a hard disk to speed up read/write access time and thus reduce the amount of time you spend in file-transfer operations.

Printer

A printer is not required for E-mail, but it is a useful accessory—one that most computer users have. You will probably want to make hardcopies of E-mail messages, and this will require a printer. Because most E-mail consists of text documents, you can use pretty much any kind of printer that you want. The exception will be if you are transferring graphics (as data files, of course) that you will wish to print out.

Modems

Computer modems are often called *dial-up* modems, because they use regular or dial-up telephone lines. They may be *external* (Figure 6.3) or *internal* (Figure 6.4).

Figure 6.3 An external modem. *Photo courtesy of Ven-Tel Corporation*

Modem Operations and Functions

A dial-up modem cannot exchange data directly with a FAX modem; the data encoding of FAX is different from that used internally by computers. Such a data exchange would be meaningless.

Computer modems operate in the same way that FAX modems operate (as detailed in Chapter 3). They convert computer data, which is transmitted by the computer to the modem in binary format in the form of negative and positive voltages, into analog signals. As with FAX modems, analog representations of the binary data are superimposed on a telephone-line carrier wave in a process called modulation. The analog signals are then transmitted via voice-telephone lines to a receiving modem, which reverses the modulation process by demodulating the data and converting it back into binary data that the computer can understand.

In addition to converting, sending, and receiving data, a computer's modem is responsible for dialing up, initiating, and maintaining a connection. It may also check data for errors. The error-checking capability of a modem is built-in, but it is not operational unless it is communicating with a modem that has the same kind of error-checking

Figure 6.4 An internal modem. *Photo courtesy of Hayes Microcomputer Systems*

capability. Packet-switching networks, about which you'll learn more later, typically implement modem error checking.

Modem Connections

Unlike a FAX modem, one end of which is preconnected to its FAX machine, a dial-up modem must be connected by the user to both the telephone line and the computer.

Telephone-Line Connections Like a FAX modem, a computer's modem connects directly to a telephone line. Most modems have a jack (receptacle) designed to accommodate a standard telephone line's RJ-11 plug. Modems so-equipped are called *direct-connect* modems. Most direct-connect modems accommodate RJ-14 plugs, and other variations on the RJ-11 plug that are used with office and multiline telephones. All have the same physical configuration, although some have six rather than four conductors.

The only modems that do not accommodate a standard telephone-line plug are *acoustic* modems. Acoustic modems are equipped with microphone and earphone cups that slip over the mouthpiece and earpiece of standard telephone handsets. Acoustic modems were originally devised to circumvent now-defunct prohibitions preventing the connection of any device directly to a telephone line. Acoustic modems send and receive data signals as tones via the cups and the telephone handset's mouthpiece and earpiece. Today, such modems are relegated to being used with pay phones and phone lines that do not use a standard RJ-11-type plug.

Packet-Switching Networks While most FAX traffic is carried via direct telephone calls, connection with the commercial online services that offer E-mail services are via special networks of selected telephone lines and supervisory computers that are used to connect with many online services. These are called *packet-switching networks*, because they transmit by modems in discrete "packets."

Packet-switching networks (e.g., Telenet and Tymnet), enable you to connect with a national commercial online service via a local phone call, thus incurring no long-distance telephone charges. The packet networks are actually service-providers for the online services. Their services include:

- Providing long-distance time for data communications at a rate that is often a tenth of the normal rate (The packet network companies can provide low-cost service because they buy large blocks of long-distance time, and/or use WATS service; they also make extremely efficient use of the data path.)

- Routing data along the fastest possible path, as directed by supervisory computers

- Providing error checking, when a modem with appropriate error-checking capability is used

Several online services—among them GEnie and CompuServe—have their own private packet-switching networks.

As a personal computer user accessing an online service, you do not directly pay for packet-network access charges. The low rates are included in your online service billing.

Computer Connections The standard connection between a computer and a modem is the computer's *serial port*. A serial port may be a D-shaped 9- or 25-pin connector (a standard PC configuration like that shown in Figure 6.5), or it may be circular with four or five pins (e.g., a *DIN plug*—as used with Macintosh computers).

Also called an *RS-232* port, after the standard on which its connections and operation are based, a serial port is connected with a modem via a serial cable—usually a flat, ribbon cable with multiple conductors.

Serial ports do more than just provide a connecting point for a cable. Within a computer, the bits in each byte are manipulated simulta-

Figure 6.5 Serial port connector. *Photo courtesy of Radio Shack, a division of Tandy Corporation*

neously, in a process known as *parallel transmission*. Data signals are sent to some computer peripherals, such as printers, in parallel fashion, too. The modem/telephone link cannot handle the bits in parallel, so the computer's serial port must convert the parallel-bit transmissions to serial order. Depending on the type of connection in use, serial ports may also add and remove bits as a method of error-checking.

> **Note:** An internal modem—a device on a card that is installed inside a computer—usually has its own serial port. An internal modem is installed like any other card and provides an external RJ-11 telephone-line jack.

Modem Options

Many features and options are available with modems. Among the more useful options are:

- Auto-dial (the ability to dial phone numbers)

- Tone- or pulse-dialing capability

- A speaker

- Call status indicator lights

Modems that offer dialing capability and other advanced features are called "intelligent." The number of features that a modem has isn't necessarily an indication of its quality, but the better-quality modems *usually* have more features than the bargain-basement kind.

Computer Communications Software

Unless you use a specialized communications terminal or a computer with built-in communications software, you will need communications software before your computer can talk to a modem. Sometimes called terminal emulation software, or term-soft, communications software routes data and commands to and from the modem and instructs the modem to use proper *protocol* in communicating with another system. Simply put, protocol is an agreed-upon procedure for *how* data are to be transferred.

A typical communications software package includes communications and support programs on disk and an instruction manual, as shown in Figure 6.6.

Figure 6.6 Communications software package. *Photo courtesy of Crosstalk/Digital Communications Associates*

Communications Software Options

At the very least, your communications software should allow you to select communications speed and set basic communications parameters. It should also provide at least one binary file transfer protocol (e.g.,

Xmodem, Kermit, and Ymodem). The better communications software packages offer a variety of features, including:

- The ability to handle multiple uploads and downloads (one after another) automatically

- Auto-dial and redial capability

- Auto-logon capability (This means a program performs all the steps necessary to sign on to another system.)

- Macros, which you can use to send multiple commands to a remote system with one keystroke

The kind of communications software you use and the options available will be limited (or determined) in large part by the type of computer you own and its configuration, the modem you use, and your budget.

E-Mail Channels

Two kinds of commercial online services offer E-mail: E-mail specialty services (e.g., AT&T Mail and MCI Mail) and general online services (e.g., DELPHI and CompuServe).

Most online services are computer friendly—they can communicate with virtually any microcomputer. Accessing another system with your computer should not be a problem, if you have a compatible modem and appropriate software.

E-mail specialty services are concerned primarily with providing E-mail services—intersystem, intrasystem, electronic delivery (FAX and Telex), and hardcopy delivery services. They may offer gateways to other services, like MCI Mail's link to the Dow Jones News/Retrieval Service.

General online services provide varying levels of E-mail services, in addition to such services as news, special-interest groups, software downloads, financial services, and realtime conferencing.

Instead of/in addition to commercial online services, you may find yourself using a computer bulletin board (BBS) for E-mail. A BBS is a personal computer-based messaging system, not unlike those early mainframe and minicomputer messaging systems described in Chapter 5.

Private BBSs are often set up by individuals, groups, or companies to handle E-mail (and public message) traffic. Some public BBSs offer what is called netmail or relay mail to carry E-mail long distances. However, while this kind of service costs little or nothing, it is limited in that only certain BBSs in specified locations can receive E-mail messages. For anything other than hobby or very limited E-mail communication, commercial services are the only way to go. Use these commercial services unless you or someone in your organization has the knowledge and wherewithal to set up a system of private BBSs that are accessible to users and have the capability to relay E-mail.

E-Mail Structure, Features, and Options

At this point, you've looked closely at exactly how computer communications take place. Some more sophisticated equipment and programs than we've discussed here are used on the online service end of a communications link, but these are effectively invisible to you. Suffice it to say that the communication takes place on both ends as described here.

To close out this chapter on how E-mail works, we'll take a look at what awaits you in terms of E-mail features and options. Not all of the features discussed in the following pages are available on all systems.

E-Mail Organization and Structure

The way E-mail messages are stored and handled varies greatly from one system to another. Some systems simply keep track of your new messages for you and delete them once you've read them. Others allow you to keep old messages for later review or download. They may even store groups of related messages in electronic analogs of folders, which are usually called folders.

Generally, the simplest E-mail systems are the straight "read 'em and forget 'em" setups, wherein messages disappear once they've been read or are purged (deleted) automatically after a fixed period of time. Such E-mail systems are not unlike bulletin boards. The difference between E-mail and bulletin board messages on some systems may be fuzzy, beyond the distinction of E-mail being private.

General online services, (e.g., DELPHI and GEnie) along with electronic mail services (e.g., AT&T Mail and MCI Mail) usually offer a plethora of mail-handling options—including many of the features discussed in the following pages.

The E-mail menus shown in Figures 6.7, 6.8, and 6.9 will give you an idea of the range of commands available on various systems.

Message Structure

A typical E-mail message consists of headers and the message itself. The headers (some of which are not used by some systems) are:

- Addressee header—contains the online IDs of those to whom a message is sent (where multiple addressees are specified, the address information may be placed in extra header lines)

- Sender header—contains the online ID of the sender

- Subject header—a line describing the subject in brief

- Date/time header—contains a time/date stamp identifying when the message was sent

```
        * "SPORTS" RT:  Vote for GEnie's TOP *
          20 college football teams listing!

     GEnie              MAIL            Page 200
                        GE Mail

        1. Display Queue of New Letters
        2. List Unread Letters
        3. List All Letters in your Mailbox
        4. List Letters From Specific User
        5. List Letters From Specific Date
        6. Enter a Text Letter Online
        7. Upload a Text Letter
        8. Search GE Mail Directory
        9. GE Mail Command Mode

       10. GEnie Quik-Gram (Paper Mail)
       11. Send (Upload) XMODEM File
       12. Receive (Download) XMODEM File
       13. Send FEEDBACK to GEnie

     Enter #, <P>revious, or <H>elp?
```

Figure 6.7 GEnie mail menu.

```
     MAIL Menu:

     FAX Service              Easylink
     Mail (Electronic)        Translation Services
     Scan for New Messages    Workspace
     SetMail                  HELP
     Telex                    EXIT

     DMAIL>(Mail, FAX, Telex, Trans):
```

Figure 6.8 DELPHI mail commands.

```
        EasyPlex  Main Menu

          *** No mail waiting ***

        2 COMPOSE a new message
        3 UPLOAD a message
        4 USE a file from PER area

        5 ADDRESS Book
        6 SET options

        9 Send a CONGRESSgram ($)
     Enter choice !
```

Figure 6.9 CompuServe EasyPlex menu.

- Folder header—lists the name of the E-mail system folder in which the message is stored

The message is displayed as standard text, which may be captured and stored in a disk file. The width of the lines in the message is determined by display parameters you have specified to the online service. Most services pause when the number of lines you've specified as a screen page (typically 23 to 25) have been displayed; the current screen page is displayed until you signal for the next page to be displayed (usually by pressing ENTER).

Figures 6.10, 6.11, and 6.12 show mail messages from three different online service E-mail systems.

```
EasyPlex

Date:   13-Aug-89 19:24 EDT
From:   Michael A. Banks [72210,3411]
Subj:   NARAM Report

Dear Doug,
        Thanks for the information on NARAM; it sounds like the
meet went off flawlessly--with no little thanks to you and Harry!
        If it's possible, can you do a quick writeup on the "Old-
Timers' Reunion" for the November issue of the magazine?  We'll
need it by the 15th, which is, I realize, a short deadline, so
I'll understand if you can't get it in.


Enter command or <CR> for more !

EasyPlex

        Thanks!
--Mike



Last page.  Enter command or <CR> to continue !
```

Figure 6.10 CompuServe EasyPlex message.

Note that CompuServe offers a message disposition menu, while DELPHI simply provides a command prompt after displaying a message. On GEnie, the system redisplays the mail menu after displaying messages. There is, however, a special command mode to manipulate mail messages.

E-Mail Commands

E-mail can be menu or command driven, or both. Either way, you will find online help available to help you with commands on all commercial E-mail systems.

```
#2               5-AUG-1989 23:48:36
From:    BOS1C::ALECGRAHAM
To:      KZIN
Subj:    Austin

Dear Mike,
         Thanks for the note.  Regarding the ships of Danish
registry, I can recommend the S.S. Konge Knut without
reservation.  We sailed on the vessel to Mazatlan late last year,
and found it to be excellent in all respects, especially where
the staff was concerned.

Alec


MAIL>
```

Figure 6.11 DELPHI mail message.

```
Item     2735062              89/08/11         22:05

From:    JACK.SMITH               Jack Smith

To:      MIKE.BANKS               Michael A. Banks

cc:      J.AMATO                  Jim Amato

Sub: Writing Markets Column

Mike,
         I will be away the first two weeks of September, as I
previously mentioned.  While you're gone, you can transfer the
upcoming "Writing Markets" files to Jim, who will take care of
posting them.
         Any questions, let me know before the end of the month.
Otherwise, I'll see you in mid-September.
         Thanks.

         Jack



=END=



Command?
```

Figure 6.12 GE Mail message from GEnie.

Menu-driven E-mail systems such as CompuServe's menu shown in Figure 6.9, are easiest for new users and those who use several online services.

Most command-driven E-mail systems use commands that are self-explanatory. To read a message, type **READ**; to delete a message, type

DELETE; to reply to a message, type REPLY; to forward a message to another user, type FORWARD, and so forth. Control-key combinations are often used as commands, too.

While commands on most systems are easy to remember, a few E-mail systems have developed some unusual command structures.

Message creation is typically initiated by a command such as CREATE or SEND. When you enter a message-creation command, you are prompted for header information and the message itself (not necessarily in that order). Most systems allow you to type the message after you enter a message-creation command. Uploading a message is typically initiated by a separate command.

E-mail commands may use qualifiers (additional instructions that modify how a command is implemented) to use more advanced features. Various additional commands may be used to address a message and specify text entry mode, as shown in Figure 6.13.

```
create, delete, get, help, profile, quit, read, show
Command: .create
To: !shayes
1: Stan  Hayes <!shayes> Norcross, GA The Ad Works
To:
Cc:
Subject: Photos
** Enter message followed by a .COMMAND or .
Stan,
        Thanks for the product photos, which arrived here on
Friday, Federal Express.  I believe we can use all but one of
them (it is color, but the contrast is such that I think the
color separation won't do it justice.)  But four out of five
```

Figure 6.13 AT&T mail message entry.

Commands may be directed to operate on a specific message, but most systems are set up so that commands operate on the current message.

E-Mail Options

At a minimum, E-mail lets you send, read, reply to, and delete messages. Most online services also provide receipt notification, forwarding capability, and multiple-addressee service, as well as message filing. Such systems usually allow you to send files, and some will extract a mail message to a private online file area, if such is available. What follows is an overview of the options shared by most E-mail systems.

Receipt Notification

Receipt notification means that the system sends a message to you at the time a message is read by the recipient, notifying you that the message has been read. Some systems, such as CompuServe charge a small extra fee for this service.

Message Forwarding

If you wish to send a copy of a mail message you've received to another user on the system where it was received, you can usually do so with a simple command like FORWARD. This will set up a new mail message, the text of which will be the message you've received. You will be asked to fill in the addressee and the topic, which may be a one-line message about the message being forwarded or another message entirely.

A variation on this option allows you to include the header and/or text of a specified message within a new E-mail message.

Multiple Addressees

Most E-mail systems on online services allow you to send the same message to two, a dozen, or even a hundred other users.

This is handled in one of two ways. The first and most frequently used technique requires you to enter multiple user IDs manually in the addressee header and/or to enter more IDs in a Carbon Copy or Courtesy Copy (CC) header, as shown in Figure 6.14.

```
      No more unread messages in this topic
      Hit <RETURN> for next active conf/topic.
      Read: mail
      No unread inbasket messages.
      Mail:to
      To:bozlee jenn gharry jerryp mike_banks pgilster
      Enter subject: 1990 Conference Changes
      Enter text. End with '.<CR>'
      >
```

Figure 6.14 Addressing a BIX mail message to multiple users.

The second way is to use what is sometimes called a distribution file, address file, or mailing list. This is a file that consists solely of user IDs. When you enter the name of the file in the addressee field (or in a special field on some systems), the system creates a copy of the message for each addressee. Examples of this addressing process on DELPHI and MCI Mail are shown in Figures 6.15 and 6.16.

Many E-mail systems also offer a blind carbon copy option, which does not allow recipients to see the IDs of other users who are receiving the same message. Distribution lists do not usually display the names of the recipients in any event.

```
MAIL> SEND

To:     @SFWA.DIS

Subj:   Contract survey results


Enter your message below. Press CTRL/Z when complete, or CTRL/C to quit:
```

Figure 6.15 Addressing a message to a distribution list on DELPHI.

```
Command: CREATE
TO:      BOOKS
         (Address LIST: BOOKS)
TO:
CC:
Subject: Preliminary stock report
Text: (Enter text or transmit file. Type / on a line by itself to end.)

   The current year's inventory is complete, and the final figures
```

Figure 6.16 Addressing a message to an MCI mailing list.

Nonstop Display

Almost all systems allow you to specify that a message be displayed nonstop (i.e., without pausing when a screen page has been displayed). This option is useful when you want to capture a message in a disk file without the system's prompts.

Message Filing

Some E-mail systems offer elaborate filing systems. On DELPHI, for example, you can create named message folders and move messages to and from them. The system creates its own folders for unread, read, and deleted messages, too. When you use folders, you move from one to another, and commands operate only on the messages in that folder. AT&T Mail, MCI Mail, and other online services offer similar filing systems.

Sending Files

Files currently stored in an online personal file area can be sent as E-mail messages on some services. The operation may require using the file name with the system's send command or with a specialized command such as READ FILE or SEND FILE. Or you may be able to merge a file into a message. This is an option restricted mainly to general online services.

Extracting Files

If an online service offers a personal file area, you may be able to copy or move mail messages to a designated file in the area. Typical commands for this operation are COPY, EXTRACT, and FILE, used with or without a file name. Again, this is an option that is found mainly on general online services.

Uploading Messages

I've referred to uploading files several times, and you're probably curious about it. How you upload a file for use as E-mail messages depends on the configuration of the online service you're using. If the service offers no personal file area, you'll have to upload your message directly into an "open" message under creation. If the system offers a personal file area, you can probably upload your file to that and send the file from the system's mail menu.

Downloading Messages

Downloading messages follows the same rules for uploading messages.

Binary File Transfer

Binary file transfer is an option that is not available on all E-mail systems—especially on E-mail specialty online services. Where offered, it may be implemented by transferring binary files addressed to a user to that user's personal online file-storage area. Or, it may be a special mail operation, as with items 11 and 12 on the GEnie Mail menu in Figure 6.7.

What You've Learned

This chapter has taught you the following:

- Most computer communication is carried via telephone lines.

- In a typical computer communications sequence, a computer sends data to its modem, and the modem converts the data from binary to analog format and transmits it to a receiving modem at the other end of a telephone link. Then the receiving modem translates the analog data to binary data and sends it to the computer to which it is connected.

- Unlike most FAX communication, computer communication is two-way.

- Data is handled within a computer as groups of binary digits, called bytes. Each byte represents a character.

- An optimum configuration for computer communication would include a computer with a color monitor, a hard disk drive, and a printer.

- A computer modem (also referred to as a dial-up modem) is categorized as external or internal by whether it is a stand-alone device or mounted inside a computer. Almost all internal modems are equipped with a serial port.

- Computer modems cannot communicate directly with FAX modems without extremely expensive and complex software.

- Most commercial online services are accessed via packet-switching networks, which allow computer users to connect with a service via a local telephone call.

- A serial port is required to translate binary data from parallel to serial form before it can be used by a modem.

- Most dial-up modems have auto-dialing capability, as well as other intelligent features.

- The communications software you can use with your computer, as well as the options included with the software, are determined and, in some cases, limited by the kind of computer you use.

- The major channels of E-mail communications are E-mail specialty services and general online services. Computer BBSs provide access to only a limited number of E-mail addresses.

- An E-mail message consists of headers and the message itself. The headers may include such information as the ID of the sender, the ID(s) of addressee(s), the subject of the message, the date and time the message was sent, and the folder in which the message is currently stored.

- E-mail systems may be menu driven, command driven, or both.

- E-mail messages are normally displayed as standard seven-bit text.

- E-mail message-sending and -handling options include (but are not limited to) automatic receipt notification, forwarding messages, filing messages online, sending and receiving binary files, uploading and downloading text documents as files, and multiple addressees.

Now you understand how E-mail works. Take the following quiz, then move on to Chapter 7 for a closer look at how to use E-mail to send FAX messages.

Quiz

1. Successful computer communication requires data, data terminal equipment (computers), data communications equipment (modems), and:

    a. A bulletin board
    b. A communications link
    c. Error checking
    d. Binary file transfer

2. What is a more common name for Data Communications Equipment?

    a. Computers
    b. Telephone lines
    c. Modems
    d. Ports

3. Most computers use what to store data?

    a. Cassette recorders
    b. Magnetic tape
    c. Disk drives
    d. Serial ports

4. What is another name for a modem used with a computer?

    a. FAX modem
    b. Dial-up modem
    c. Digital modem
    d. Serial modem

5. The major channels for E-mail communication are:

    a. BBSs and E-mail specialty services
    b. Telex and BBSs
    c. E-mail specialty and general online services
    d. All of the above

6. An E-mail message consists of what two elements?

    a. The message itself and one or more headers
    b. A message and a binary file
    c. A binary number and a subject header
    d. A subject header and a date/time stamp

7. E-mail messages are displayed in what format?

    a. Seven-bit ASCII
    b. Eight-bit ASCII
    c. Binary data
    d. ASCII code numbers

8. In addition to text messages or documents, many E-mail services allow you to send what?

    a. Instant messages
    b. Binary data files
    c. FAX modem output
    d. Encrypted data

9. Uploading consists of what?

    a. Sending a prepared text or binary file from disk
    b. Sending a voice mail message
    c. Typing a message online
    d. Including a copy of a previously received message in a new message

10. What are often used in conjunction with commands to use advanced features?

    a. Files
    b. Menu selections
    c. Qualifiers
    d. Headers

7 | The Modem/FAX Connection

About This Chapter

This chapter provides an overview of modem/FAX services. Modem/FAX services enable sending and receiving FAX messages without a FAX machine or PC FAX board—via a computer equipped with a modem using any of several online services as an intermediary.

You'll also learn about *FAX network services*—networks that carry messages from both FAX machines and modem-equipped computers to other FAX machines *and* to modem-equipped computers.

Finally, you'll find advice on deciding whether a dedicated FAX machine or a computer and modem will meet your FAX needs.

> **Note:** For the purposes of this and later chapters, "dedicated FAX machine" refers to both dedicated FAX machines and computers equipped with PC FAX boards. When "message creation" is used, it may allude to typing a message online and/or uploading a message or document.

FAX Without a FAX Machine

When FAX exploded onto the business and personal communications scene in 1987, the development of modem/FAX services was almost

145

inevitable. There were more than seven million computer users assessing commercial online services via modem at that time. Seven million computer- *and* communications-literate individuals were a potential market for FAX service via the electronics communication medium with which they were most familiar: online services.

Various online services recognized the potential for modem/FAX service and developed software that translated from seven-bit ASCII to FAX formats, much in the way that PC FAX boards perform computer-to-FAX data translation. Additional software, working with special hardware, handled dialing up, and transmitting data to designated FAX machines, along with such chores as interpreting FAX addresses (telephone numbers), generating cover sheets, and providing verification of delivery.

As complex as this sounds, using the end product was not that different from using electronic mail. FAX messages could be entered, addressed, and sent in pretty much the same manner as E-mail. As illustrated in Figures 7.1 and 7.2, sending a message by E-mail requires almost the same steps as sending one by FAX; the major difference is how the message is addressed. Figures 7.1 and 7.2 illustrate an E-mail message and a FAX message, respectively, after addressing and message entry on MCI Mail.

```
Command: create
TO:         carrabis
            344-6700 Joseph-David Carrabis       Joseph-David Ca Nashua, N

TO:
CC:
Subject: New book
Text: (Enter text or transmit file. Type / on a line by itself to end.)

JD,
        I don't know if I mentioned it with the other information I
sent to you, but you will want to know that UNDERSTANDING FAX AND
E-MAIL will be available from Howard W. Sams & Co. by the end of
the year.  No ISBN# yet, but you should be able to locate it by
title.
--MAB
/
Handling:
Send? y
One moment please; your message is being posted.

Your message was posted: Sun Aug 13, 1989  7:29 pm  EST.
There is a copy in your OUTBOX.

Command:
```

Figure 7.1 Sending an E-mail message via MCI mail.

All online services integrate FAX services with their E-mail systems. Some services require users to select FAX via a special menu selection, while others require a special addressing format to send a message

```
Command: create
TO:        Jack Cunkelman (EMS)
Enter name of mail system.

EMS:        FAX
      EMS        354-8235 FAX              Fax Dispatch      MCI Mail

Enter recipient's mailbox information.
If additional mailbox lines are not needed press RETURN.

MBX: PHONE: 555-555-1212

MBX:
TO:        Jack Cunkelman
           EMS: FAX / MCI ID: 354-8235
           MBX: 555-555-1212

Is this address correct (Yes or No)? y
TO:
CC:
Subject: MCI FAX
Text: (Enter text or transmit file. Type / on a line by itself to end.)

Jack,
      We're trying out MCI Mail's FAX delivery service here, as
an alternative to printing out computer-generated documents and
scanning them with the dedicated FAX machine.
      You may want to try the same at your end; cutting out the
printing and scanning steps saves time and paper.

---Mike

/
Handing:
Send? y
One moment please; your message is being posted.

Your message was posted: Wed Mar 21, 1990  7:20 am  EST.
There is a copy in your OUTBOX

Command:
```

Figure 7.2 Sending a FAX message via MCI mail.

via FAX. But, again, sending a message or document to a FAX machine was similar enough to sending it to an electronic mail box that users quickly adapted to it. The same was true when Telex and hardcopy mail delivery were added to online services' E-mail systems.

Being able to send and receive FAX in the same manner as E-mail offered a number of attractions and advantages for modem users. Modem users could send (and, in some few instances, receive) FAX messages without having to invest in expensive specialized equipment. What's more, they could send computer-generated documents without having to print them out. Messages and documents could be transmitted at any time of the day or night, and the cost was reasonable. In short, FAX by E-mail offered all the advantages of E-mail *and* FAX, with few disadvantages.

The same online service you use to deliver FAX messages can also be used to deliver E-mail to thousands of other modem users, to Telex machines, and to street addresses.

Today, most of the major online services offer at least outgoing FAX service (the ability to *send* text messages and documents to designated FAX machines). These include AT&T Mail, CompuServe, DELPHI, EasyLink, GEnie, MCI Mail, PAN, TELEMAIL, and UNISON. DASnet, an E-mail relay service, also offers FAX service.

As you'll learn, several of the services offer enhancements to their FAX services, such as:

- The ability to receive FAX messages

- Translation to FAX format and FAX transmission of computer-generated graphics files and documents created with certain word processors.

Note: Limitations inherent to the OCR software used to convert computer-generated text and/or graphics documents may result in a small number of errors in a large document.

Various delivery options are also available, including cover sheets. Figure 7.3 shows a FAX message that originated as a computer text file, was sent to a dedicated FAX machine, and includes a cover sheet.

How It Works

When you create a message online or upload a document to an online service's E-mail system and specify FAX delivery, the message is either translated to FAX format by the service's main computer or transmitted to a computer that is dedicated to handling FAX messages, which then translates the message.

After translation to the binary format required by FAX machines, the online service's computer calls the number you gave it when you addressed the message as a FAX message. The time between when you send the message and when the online service's computer dials up the receiving FAX machine may be a few minutes, or an hour or two, depending on the service you are using and the amount of FAX and other communications traffic it is currently handling.

When contact is made with the receiving FAX machine, the online service's computer transmits your message, then disconnects. If the number you specified is busy or if there is no answer, the online service's computer will call back. The number and interval of the retries are either system defaults or specified by you. This gives you, in effect, store-and-forward capability.

Most systems (but not all) provide an automatic confirmation of delivery, like that shown in Figure 7.4. Confirmations of delivery are in the form of E-mail messages to you.

```
Mail FAX                                          page   1
         .AT&T  MAIL
Customer Assistance: 1-800-MAIL672
Mon Aug 14 21:19:42 GMT 1989 page count   2 including cover sheet

   ATTENTION:  H. Feltner


DESTINATION FAX NUMBER: +13172985604
From: !banks (Michael A Banks )
Phone: +1 513 722 1969
Date: Mon Aug 14 21:20:40 GMT 1989
Subject: PC Power Protection
MTS-Message-ID: banks2262120410

To: fax!+13172985604 ( /H. Feltner )


                                                  page   2
Dear Mr. Feltner:

     Per our previous conversation about personal computer
power requirements, I can refer you to the book, PC Power Protection,
by Mark Waller, as an excellent source of information on all
aspects of PC power needs.
     Waller covers both theoretical and practical requirements
of computer power supplies, and provides "hands-on" information
about devices such as surge protectors, uninterruptable power
supplies, etc.  (Waller is an acknowledged expert in the industry,
by the way.)
     The publisher is Howard W. Sams & Co., and you should
be able to find or order the book through any local bookstore.


Sincerely,

Michael A. Banks
```

Figure 7.3 FAX message and cover sheet sent via AT&T mail.

Systems that do not provide automatic confirmation of delivery may offer it as an option, sometimes at an extra cost.

Systems that receive FAX messages for you deliver them as E-mail messages. The party sending a FAX message to you via an online service must put some kind of identifier (usually on the first line) indicating your ID on the system. The computer handling incoming FAX messages

```
From:     BOS1A::MAILTHRU     25-JUL-1989 23:01
To:       PHILLIPET
Subj:     FAX/Telex Receipt (Delivery) Notification

FROM: EASYLINK

TO:     62918703

DELIVERY NOTIFICATION:

RE MESSAGE NUMBER: 4204612C001
CUSTOMER REFERENCE NUMBER: PHILLIPET
INPUT ADDRESS:      6174916642
DELIVERED TO:       (FAX)   GROUPIII 6174916642
DELIVERED AT:       21JUL89 18:05 EST



MAIL>
```

Figure 7.4 Confirmation from DELPHI of FAX delivery.

must have this information so it knows to whom to deliver it. The incoming FAX message is converted from FAX format to seven-bit ASCII, after which it is E-mailed to you.

What You Need

To send and/or receive FAX messages via an online service's E-mail system, you will need a computer, communications software, a modem, and a telephone line. You may also need a word processor to generate longer messages and a file-conversion program if your word processor is not capable of storing text in seven-bit ASCII format. These requirements are detailed in Chapter 6.

Using E-mail FAX Services

As indicated earlier (and as illustrated in Figures 7.1 and 7.2), using an E-mail service to send a FAX message differs little from sending a message to an E-mail service. On some systems, you must use a special menu selection to specify FAX delivery, as shown in Figure 7.5, while on others you specify FAX delivery when addressing the message, as shown in Figure 7.6. The latter option typically moves you to a special FAX subsystem.

You may also be asked to specify certain delivery options before or after message creation or upload, as shown in Figure 7.7.

After addressing and creating the message and specifying any options, you issue the system's SEND command (or select it from a menu), and the message will be sent.

```
MAIL Menu:

FAX Service              Easylink
Mail (Electronic)        Translation Services
Scan for New Messages    Workspace
SetMail                  HELP
Telex                    EXIT


DMAIL>(Mail, FAX, Telex, Trans): FAX

Welcome to the FAX interface.
Enter Control-C to terminate your request at any time.
```

Figure 7.5 Selecting a menu item to initiate a FAX message.

```
create, delete, get, help, profile, quit, read, show
Command: .create
To: FAX!3175551212
Attention To: Cmdr. Aaron Sheffield
To:
Cc:
Subject: Test Report
** Enter message followed by a .COMMAND or .
        The preliminary returns from the testing of the XJM-6
are encouraging.  Throughput was 19.2KB, with a .001% error
benchmark.  Cadigan will present a thorough analysis tomorrow,
but at this point, intuition says "Go!"
delete, edit, get, help, profile, quit, read, send, show
Command: .
```

Figure 7.6 Specifying FAX delivery in a message's address header.

Remember: Messages or documents intended for FAX delivery via an online service must meet the same requirements as E-mail messages. Depending on how your word processing program stores files, you may have to convert documents to seven-bit ASCII files before the online service will accept them.

Options

When selecting an online service, remember that sending a FAX via an online service affords you the same features and options as sending E-mail via that service.

Some of the options you may specify on various systems are:

- The number and interval of retries if the specified FAX number is busy or if there is no answer the first time delivery is attempted

- A confirmation of delivery receipt (sent to your E-mail box)

- A copy of the message (sent to your E-mail box)

- Multiple FAX recipients (either entered one at a time or via a distribution list), which is the same as broadcast FAX capability with a dedicated machine

```
Command: create
TO:       Rosa L. Banks (EMS)
Enter name of mail system.

EMS:      FAX
    EMS    354-8235 FAX                    Fax Dispatch     MCI Mail

Enter recipient's mailbox information.
If additional mailbox lines are not needed press RETURN.

MBX: PHONE: 704-555-1212


MBX: RETRY: 2.5
TO:       Rosa L. Banks
          EMS: FAX / MCI ID: 354-8235
          MBX: 704-555-1212

Is this address correct (Yes or No)? y
TO:
CC:
Subject: MCI FAX
Text: (Enter text or transmit file. Type / on a line by itself to end.)
```

Figure 7.7 Specifying FAX options.

- Simultaneous delivery to both E-mail boxes and FAX machines and, on some systems, hardcopy delivery

- Priority delivery (guaranteed delivery time)

- Various filing options for outgoing and incoming FAX messages

- Page breaks (specified *during* message entry)

- Review, edit, or cancel a message after entering it

E-mail FAX systems usually prompt you through the steps required to address and enter a message and request that you specify options at appropriate times during the message-creation process.

Modem/FAX Connections

Online services allow you to send FAX messages to dedicated FAX machines and those who use online services that receive FAX.

As noted earlier, almost all online services offer some kind of FAX service or are contemplating it. Details on the FAX services offered by several of the major online services listed a few pages back will be presented in Chapters 9 and 10.

Dedicated FAX Machines and Online Services

While a dedicated FAX machine can receive messages from any online service that offers modem/FAX service, not every online service is set up to receive messages from dedicated FAX machines. Sending a FAX from a dedicated FAX machine to those services that do accept incoming messages is, however, the same as sending a message to any other FAX machine. The only exception is that you will rarely get a busy signal. Receiving modem/FAX services are typically equipped with multiple modems and multiplexing devices that allow them to take more than one call at a time, in the same manner that online services can take more than one call at a time from computer users.

FAX Networks

FAX networks and online services are open 24 hours a day and provide for multiple incoming calls.

FAX networks provide the ultimate in modem/FAX connection, being capable of communicating with both dedicated FAX machines and modem-equipped computers. Such networks offer computer users full access to FAX services on a two-way basis. Dedicated FAX machine users are able to communicate with E-mail users. Both computer and dedicated FAX machine owners enjoy such benefits as store-and-forward, broadcast FAX, and many of the modem/FAX features described earlier in this chapter. In addition, they also use a few other unique features, such as automatic telephone notification of an incoming FAX message and E-mail relay service to specific online services.

Some FAX network services will translate graphic images created with popular PC graphics software, as well as eight-bit or binary text files created with certain word processing programs. This eliminates having to scan graphics to be sent and having to convert word processor files to seven-bit ASCII before sending them.

FAX or Modem/FAX?

By now, you may be wondering if you really need a dedicated FAX machine, since you can handle almost any kind of FAX traffic via modem. Before you decide to buy a computer and modem (or, if you are already a computer and modem user), consider the advantages and disadvantages of modem/FAX.

Modem/FAX Advantages

- Ease of message creation—online or off (You don't have to print and scan a document.)

- Store-and-forward, multiple-recipient, and broadcast FAX capability

- Time savings (Retries and multiple FAXes are handled for you; you have to go through the sending process only once.)

- Simultaneous E-mail/FAX/hardcopy delivery

- Convenience (You can send and receive FAX messages whenever you wish.)

- Access to most E-mail features

- Access to services other than FAX

Modem/FAX Disadvantages

- The cost of a computer, software, and modem may exceed that of a full-featured FAX machine

- The cost of sending a FAX via an online service may be higher than a direct-dial FAX transmission, when the per-minute charges imposed by some online services are added to the per-page FAX charge

- Setting up to access an online service via modem is more complex than using a dedicated FAX machine (Once you've learned the ropes, using a modem is easy, but you will have to invest some time learning how to use a computer/modem/communications software package.)

- Sending a lengthy document usually requires some kind of preparation—conversion to seven-bit ASCII, modifying margins, etc.

If you already have a computer and modem, you should sign up for one or more online services and experiment with modem/FAX to see if it will satisfy your FAX needs. The investment will be small, compared with buying a dedicated FAX machine.

If you have neither FAX nor modem, think about what your FAX needs will be. If you'll be sending text documents only, a computer and modem are probably a better investment in the long run, because of the other applications you'll find for the computer. If you need to send scanned text and documents, however, you will probably find it simpler to do so via a dedicated FAX machine. Using a computer scanner and a modem to FAX graphics can be a fairly complex process. In fact, even if you have a computer, you should consider a dedicated FAX machine for sending material that has to be scanned. The cost of a scanner and software is close to that of many low-end FAX machines. And the time you'll save with a dedicated FAX machine's "plug-in-and-go" technology can also make it worthwhile.

If you will be receiving a lot of text documents, you'll probably find receiving modem/FAX services to be more than adequate for your needs. Incoming graphics are another matter. If you require precise transmission of detailed graphics, you may find that a quality dedicated FAX machine meets your needs better than modem/FAX.

You should also consider the comparative costs of sending documents, convenience (if most of your messages are created on a computer, modem/FAX is a time-saver), and the access to alternate modes of delivery that modem/FAX offers.

> **Note:** If you can't decide between a dedicated FAX machine and a modem/FAX service, you may require some of the features of each. In that case, a FAX network—accessible via either FAX machine or computer—is probably the answer. Using such a service costs more than using a FAX machine or modem/FAX service.

What You've Learned

This chapter has taught you:

- Online services integrate FAX services with their E-mail services.

- Most of the same options available for E-mail (described in Chapter 6) are available when you send a FAX message via an online service. Special FAX options are also available.

- A major advantage of modem/FAX is that access to an online service includes access to other communications and information services.

- Most online services allow you to send FAX messages, but only a minority allow you to receive FAX messages.

- Some online services offer translation of binary text and graphics files to FAX format.

- FAX cover sheets and confirmations of receipts are generated by some online services automatically. On other services, they are an extra-cost option.

- If a FAX machine is busy or unavailable when an online service's computer dials it up, the computer will usually redial until the FAX message is delivered.

- Incoming FAX messages for delivery via an online service must contain your user ID.

- To use an online service to deliver FAX messages, you need the same hardware and software required to access any online service (as described in Chapter 6).

- Documents intended for FAX transmission via an online service must meet the same requirements as E-mail messages.

- During and after FAX message entry/creation, you may be able to specify such options as the number and interval of retries, multiple recipients, priority delivery, and simultaneous delivery to E-mail or hardcopy addresses.

- On some systems, you can specify page breaks while entering a FAX message online. You may also be able to display and edit messages after entering or uploading them.

- Most online service E-mail systems guide you through the process of entering and sending a FAX message using prompts.

- Sending a FAX message from a dedicated FAX machine to an online service that is capable of receiving FAX messages is no different to the person sending the message from sending a message to another dedicated FAX machine.

- FAX networks provide the ultimate in FAX communication, being able to send and receive FAX messages to and from dedicated FAX machines and modem-equipped computers.

- Some FAX networks offer translation of binary text and graphics files to FAX format.

- The major factors involved in deciding whether you should use a dedicated FAX machine or modem/FAX are your applications and cost.

- In general, a dedicated FAX machine is preferable to a computer/modem/scanner if you plan to transmit a large number of scanned documents (especially where graphics are concerned).

Those are the basics of modem/FAX and FAX network service. Test your knowledge with the following quiz before moving on to Chapter 8 for a hands-on look at using online services.

Quiz

1. What two ways can messages be consigned to FAX delivery?

    a. By uploading or creating online
    b. By menu selection or address header specification
    c. By including the FAX number in the message or by including the online ID of the recipient in the message
    d. All of the above

2. In most cases, the same online service used to deliver FAX messages can also deliver which of the following?

    a. E-mail
    b. Telex
    c. Hardcopy
    d. All of the above

3. Cover sheets and confirmation of receipt notices are included with modem/FAX service on what basis?

    a. Automatically
    b. As an extra-cost option
    c. Either a or b, depending on the system
    d. None of the above

4. How do online services require that you format text messages?

    a. As eight-bit ASCII text
    b. As seven-bit ASCII text
    c. In the binary format used by dedicated FAX machines
    d. No special format is required

5. When are FAX delivery and other options specified?

    a. During message creation
    b. After message creation
    c. Before message creation
    d. Before or after message creation, depending on the system

6. After creating a message for FAX delivery, you can send it, or:

    a. Review it online
    b. Edit it online
    c. Cancel it
    d. All of the above

7. FAX networks can communicate in what ways with dedicated FAX machines and modem-equipped computers?

    a. Send messages to each
    b. Receive messages from each

    c. Send and receive messages to and from computers, but only send messages to dedicated FAX machines

    d. a and b

8. If your FAX requirements include sending a large number of scanned documents, which system is probably your best choice?

    a. A dedicated FAX machine

    b. A computer, modem, and scanner

    c. A FAX network

    d. A flatbed scanner

8 | Using E-Mail and Modem/FAX Services

About This Chapter

This chapter shows you what it's like to use an online service, by description and example. You'll learn how to connect with online services and how to send and receive E-mail, as well as how to use some special features offered by online services.

Getting Started

As you know, you will need a computer equipped with a serial port and communications software, a modem and connecting cable, any necessary power supplies, and a telephone line to access an online service.

You will also need an account on an online service that hosts an E-mail system and the service's local telephone number.

Online Service Accounts

Online services are, as previously established, commercial enterprises. Thus, you cannot simply dial one up, log on, and gain full access after a waiting period, as is the case with a computer bulletin board (BBS). You must go through a sign-up process that requires you to provide a credit card number or some other method of guaranteeing payment (e.g., automatic checking account deductions or direct-billing/credit information).

Most services offer online sign-ups to speed up the process of getting online, but you may still have to wait a day or so before your account becomes active. Such sign-ups are frequently offered in promotional material that accompanies modems or communications software and usually include some sort of discount or free time offer.

For more information on specific online services, their costs, and sign-up offers (online or offline), you can contact them via the telephone numbers in Appendix A or the addresses in Appendix C.

Online IDs and Passwords

An online service account is more than just a billing agreement. The number or word by which your account is identified is also your online ID—also called a username, PPN, address, etc., depending on which service you're using. Your online ID is also your E-mail address.

Try to use the same ID on all online services that allow you to specify your ID.

Some systems will assign you a number as an ID (as is the case on CompuServe, where everyone is assigned a five-digit number, followed by a comma and another number of either three or four digits). Others, such as MCI Mail, assign you numbers and assign or allow you to choose from a list of mnemonic names. Still other systems such as BIX, DELPHI, and GEnie allow you to specify your online ID, which may consist of any combination of characters up to a certain limit.

Keep your password secure. Never give it to anyone—online or off. Change it monthly.

Along with your account will come a password, which you can (and should) change periodically. Your password is your key to the online service. Anyone can *try* to sign on to an online service as you (using your ID). If no one knows your password, it can't be used to get on the system. If, however, someone knows your password, this intruder has complete access to all of your mail and can run up an enormous bill for which you will be responsible. This is why you should change your password periodically—just in case someone learns it.

Online Service Account Options Most online services provide one level of service—which is to say, one kind of account. Some offer special enhanced accounts with additional services—among them CompuServe's Executive Option, for example, which provides streamlined access to certain services, among other benefits; DELPHI's minimum monthly billing in exchange for receiving a discount access rate; or MCI Mail's Advanced User option. Almost all of these cost extra in one way or another.

Online Service Telephone Numbers

As explained in Chapter 6, access to online services is typically via a packet-switching network. If you sign up for an online service, you will receive some kind of manual that contains all the dial-up phone numbers for the public and/or private packet-switching networks used to access that service. You can also obtain such numbers by calling the online service's customer service number or—where public packet-switching networks are involved—calling the packet-switching network's customer service telephone number. Furthermore, all services provide an online listing of telephone numbers, usually searchable by area code or city.

> **Note:** Customer service telephone numbers are always for voice communication—not modem calls.

A few online services provide access via a WATS (toll-free) telephone number instead of or in addition to packet-switching networks. Such numbers are provided when you sign up for a service.

The Basics of Using Online Services

We'll focus more on specific online services in Chapters 8, 9, and 10, but here are some general guidelines for using an online service.

Dialing Up and Signing On

If you've never used a modem, practice connecting with and using another computer by accessing public BBSs in your area.

There are three steps involved in connecting with and signing on to an online service:

1. Setting up your computer system to make the call

2. Dialing the service's phone number

3. Identifying yourself to a packet-switching network and entering the address of the online service with which you wish to be connected (This is not always a part of the sign-on process.)

4. Identifying yourself to the online service

Setting Up to Make a Call

Before you can make a call, you must, of course, turn on your computer and modem and run your communications software. This done, you must set up communications parameters. Communications parameters are typically set with communications software, via commands or menu selections, and include these elements:

- Duplex or echo (set to Full or No echo; if you get online and can't see what you're typing, change the duplex setting to Half or Echo)

- Communications speed (in bits per second, usually misstated as baud)

- Data bits—the number of bits per byte transmitted (7 or 8)

- The setting for parity checking (usually even or none)

- The number of stop bits (usually one)

How you set these will vary with the software you are using, but typical communications settings are:

- Full duplex (no echo)

- Either 1200 or 2400 bits per second (bps)

- Either seven data bits, even parity, and one stop bit (a.k.a. 7E1) or eight data bits, no parity, and one stop bit (e.g. 8N1).

Almost all online services will communicate with your computer system if you set your parameters to 7E1 or 8N1. If one doesn't work, the other one will.

Most communications software packages allow you to create what are called script files or autologon files, which are programs or data files that automate dialing up and signing on to online services. Script files handle all four of the steps described here, including setting parameters, making a call, requesting a specific online service via a packet-switching network, and providing your user ID and password to the online service.

For more detailed information on setting parameters, creating and using script files, and other elements of using communications software, see your communications software's manual.

Making a Call

Assuming you're signing on manually, rather than with a script file, once you've set the proper communication parameters, you must tell your software or modem the number to dial. Do this through commands to the software or by sending the correct command sequence to the modem while in terminal mode (usually **ATDT** followed by the number).

Packet-Switching Network Identification and Service Request

As explained in Chapter 6, most online services are accessed via packet-switching networks. These are computer-supervised telephone networks that use the worldwide voice-telephone network.

Packet-switching networks typically require some identification that a personal computer (as opposed to, say, a terminal) is calling before they will allow you to enter a request for connection with an online service (the online service's address). This is accomplished by sending a signal at connect (when a packet-switching network's modem answers and establishes a communication link with your modem).

Telenet, for example, requires that you press ENTER two or three times at connect when calling at 300 or 1200 bps. If you're calling at 2400 bps, you must type **@D** at connect. Tymnet requires that you press **A**. GEnie's private packet-switching network requires that you type **HHH**, and CompuServe's network requires that you enter a **^C** to identify your call as a computer and to request connection with CompuServe.

After identifying your call, a public packet-switching network (e.g., Telenet and Tymnet) will prompt you to enter the network address of the service you wish to access. When so prompted (by **@** on Telenet and **Please log in:** on Tymnet), you type the address, and the packet-switching network connects you with the online service in question.

Here are some sample online service addresses on public packet-switching networks:

- BIX—via Tymnet, **BIX**

- DELPHI—via Telenet, **C DELPHI**
  via Tymnet, **DELPHI**

- UNISON—via Tymnet, **UNISON**

With private packet-switching networks, you are usually connected with the service in question immediately. This is also the case with online services that offer direct-dial numbers (e.g., AT&T Mail and MCI Mail).

As with local dial-up numbers, you can obtain the network address and any required sign-on commands or sequences from the online service in question before signing up.

Once you've entered the online service's network address or otherwise reached it, you'll receive a message to the effect that you are connected with the service. From there on, the packet-switching network link will be invisible to you.

Identifying Yourself to the Online Service

An online service requires two things from you when you connect with it: your user ID and your password. (The significance of these were explained in Chapter 6, and earlier in this chapter.)

You'll first be prompted to enter your online ID. The prompt will be a word such as "Name:" "Username:" "ID" or something equally obvious. Type your online ID at this prompt.

Next you'll be prompted for your password, usually by the word "Password." Type your password at this prompt, and you're in!

Note: On most services, your password will not be displayed—echoed—as you type it. This is an additional security measure, to protect your password from anyone who may be looking over your shoulder.

Figure 8.1 illustrates the steps just described, including network identification and online service address-entry, for sign-on to DELPHI via Telenet.

Navigating a Service

Okay, so you've signed on to an online service—now what? The first thing you'll see on most services is a menu—called the Main Menu or Top Menu—similar to those shown in Figure 8.2.

A few services provide only a prompt or a line with the main commands. On such services, you can view normally a menu and/or a summary of available commands by typing **MENU**, **HELP**, or a question mark.

To navigate a menu-based system, you simply type the name or number of the menu item you wish to select. At the GEnie menu shown in Figure 8.2, you would type **4** to select Mail. At the DELPHI menu, you would type **Mail** to select mail services.

Menu-based online services are organized in pyramid fashion, which means that each selection on a menu leads either to a submenu with more selections, or to a command prompt. You can go through several layers of menus before you get to what you need. To backtrack, all you have to do is type **EXIT** and **P** for Previous Menu, or a similar command.

As just explained, selecting an item from a menu either takes you to a more specialized submenu (e.g., GEnie's COMMUNICATE menu or DELPHI's MAIL menu as shown in Figure 8.3) or to a prompt at which you are expected to enter commands.

Most online services offer alternate short-cut commands for getting to a specific service area from anywhere on a service. These usually involve typing a mnemonic (e.g., **MAIL** to reach GEnie's mail menu) or issuing a command with a mnemonic or identifying number. A nice alternative to wading through several levels of menus, these are available despite whether menus are displayed (or even available).

Getting Help

If HELP doesn't provide a list of commands, try typing a question mark.

After reading the preceding, you may wonder how you're supposed to know what to type at prompts. If you have the manual for the online service in question, you can look up the commands for the area you're in. But if you don't have the manual (or, sometimes, even if you do), you

```
CONNECT 2400/ARQ
@d
TELENET
513 10B

TERMINAL=

@C DELPHI


DELPHI CONNECTED


Username: KZIN
Password:


Hello KZIN

Welcome to DELPHI
Copyright (c) 1989
General Videotex Corporation


Logon at   : 13-AUG-1989 18:45:20
Last Logon : 13-AUG-1989 18:19:35



MAIN Menu:

Business & Finance      News-Weather-Sports
Conference              People on DELPHI
DELPHI/Regional         Travel
Entertainment           Workspace
Groups and Clubs        Using DELPHI
Library                 HELP
Mail                    EXIT
Merchants' Row

MAIN>What do you want to do?
```

Figure 8.1 Signing on to DELPHI via Telenet.

can find out more quickly by typing **HELP**. This command accesses the service's online help system and usually produces a listing or summary of commands and/or detailed information on the area you're accessing. Typing **HELP** with the name of a command will usually produce more detailed information on the command.

Figure 8.4 shows a portion of MCI Mail's online help system.

Another source of help with an online service is its customer service number. Customer service numbers (numbers for most major services are listed in Appendix A) are usually WATS lines, staffed during business hours and often throughout the evening hours.

```
GEnie              TOP              Page   1
       GE Information Services

   1. GEnie Users' RT   2. Index - Info
   3. Billing/Setup     4. GE Mail & Chat
   5. Computing         6. Travel
   7. Finance           8. Shopping
   9. News             10. Games
  11. Professional      12. Leisure
  13. Reference         14. Logoff

Enter #, or <H>elp?




                      MAIN Menu:

                      Business & Finance    News-Weather-Sports
                      Conference            People on DELPHI
                      DELPHI/Regional       Travel
                      Entertainment         Workspace
                      Groups and Clubs      Using DELPHI
                      Library               HELP
                      Mail                  EXIT
                      Merchants' Row

                      MAIN>What do you want to do?
```

Figure 8.2 GEnie and DELPHI main menus.

Using E-Mail

It's safe to say that the main business of online services (with the exception of information/research/news services, such as Dialog and Dow Jones News/Retrieval Service) is communication. And most of that communication is via E-mail. That being the case and since our primary topic of interest here is using E-mail services, we'll take a closer look at what online services have to offer in the way of E-mail features and options and how to use them.

Sending Messages

Sending an E-mail message involves three steps:

- Addressing the message (or, as it is referred to on some services, creating the "electronic envelope")

- Creating the message

- Sending the message

```
GEnie        COMMUNICATE       Page 235
     GEnie Communcations Products

1. About Communications Products

2. GE Mail - Electronic Mail
3. QuikGram Paper Mail

4. LiveWire CB Simulator
5. This Week In History
6. National RealTime Conference
7. The Grand Hall

Enter #, <P>revious, or <H>elp?
```

```
                      MAIL Menu:

                      FAX Service              Easylink
                      Mail (Electronic)        Translation Services
                      Scan for New Messages    Workspace
                      SetMail                  HELP
                      Telex                    EXIT

                      DMAIL>(Mail, FAX, Telex, Trans):
```

Figure 8.3 GEnie and DELPHI submenus.

Message creation is initiated by typing a command e.g., **CREATE**, **SEND**, **TO**, or **UPLOAD**, or by selecting a menu item (e.g., **6** or **7** on the GEnie Mail menu in Figure 8.3). This "opens" a message for text input.

Depending on the system you're using, you will be prompted either to address the message or to enter or upload the message (explained in a few paragraphs) first, after which you'll address it.

Addressing Messages

The first step in addressing a message is to enter the online ID of the recipient. If the message is to be delivered via FAX or Telex, or to a street address, you will have to enter the delivery specification instead of the recipient's online ID. The system will then prompt you to enter specific information about the delivery (a FAX or Telex number or a street address), and perhaps some other delivery options (e.g., postal or courier delivery for street addresses).

For multiple recipients or carbon copies, you may be able to enter

```
Command: HELP


----------------------------------------
¦          Command:   HELP
----------------------------------------
¦
¦      Welcome to MCI Mail for
¦        Advanced Users!
¦
¦ Type HELP MAILBOX for information on
¦ your MCI Mailbox.
¦
¦ Type HELP GLOSSARY for a reference
¦ guide to the MCI Mail commands.
¦
¦ Type HELP INDEX for a complete list-
¦ ing of all topics that are available
¦ to you.
¦
¦ Type HELP REQUEST for information on
¦ MCI Mail manuals and reference guides.
¦

Press RETURN for more; type NO to stop:
¦ Type EXIT to leave MCI Mail.
¦
¦ Help is available to you at any
¦ prompt.  When you're not sure what
¦ to do next just type HELP and an ex-
¦ planation will appear.
¦
¦ If you need further assistance call
¦ Customer Support at 1-800-444-6245
¦ (Washington D.C. call 833-8484) or
¦ send a message TO: MCI HELP.
¦
------------ End of Help ------------

Command:
```

Figure 8.4 MCI mail online help system.

multiple IDs on one address line, or you may be prompted to enter the IDs/addresses separately.

After entering all requested address and delivery option information, you will usually be prompted for a subject line, after which the actual message is opened for entry.

As noted earlier, a few systems will prompt you to enter your message first. Either way, the addressing process is the same.

Creating and Uploading Messages

Before you can send a message on an E-mail system (be it to another user's electronic mail box, to a FAX or Telex machine, or to a street address), the message must be on the E-mail system's host computer. You can either create it online, using the system's editor or upload it.

> **Note:** Type short notes or memos online. Prepare documents of more than a page in length offline. This will not only save you time and money online, but it will also afford you the opportunity to spell-check and edit the documents before you send them.

Creating Messages Online The majority of online editors (or, if you prefer, word processors) are basic text-entry systems called *line editors*. A line editor lets you enter text one line at a time. The only frills available are backspacing to delete characters, inserting spaces or a tab character (^I) by pressing the Tab key, and, on a very few systems, word wrap. Otherwise, an online line editor is as basic as you can get. You type a line at a time, backspace to erase mistakes on the current line, and press ENTER at the end of each line. Message entry is terminated by any of several commands, depending on the online service you're using. A message-termination command is typically entered on a line by itself. (Some message-termination commands are **.**, **/**, **/EXIT**, **^Z**.)

After a message has been entered, some more sophisticated commands are usually available (e.g., search-and-replace), as shown in Figure 8.5.

```
  1 CHANGE characters in line
  2 REPLACE line
  3 DELETE line
  4 INSERT new line(s)
  5 TYPE all lines
  6 POST message on board
  7 MAIL via EasyPlex
Enter choice !1

Which line #: 3
Current line:
3: track the sales figures against the ranking and keep you posted

Text to replace : track
Replacement text: compare
compare the sales figures against the ranking and keep you posted
Okay? y
```

Figure 8.5 Editing options with an online editor.

Online message entry is best used for creating brief messages and replies.

Uploading Messages If you have to send a lengthy document via E-mail, it is easiest to prepare it offline using your favorite word processor, then upload it to the E-mail system.

There are two ways to upload messages: via ASCII transfer and via binary file-transfer protocol. In each case, you must tell the remote system with a command or menu selection that you wish to upload a file, before you initiate the upload from your end.

When available, uploading a document using a binary file-transfer protocol is preferable to uploading via ASCII transfer because of the error-checking built into binary protocols.

In an ASCII transfer, your communications software reads a text file, then it is transmitted to the online service's computer just like keyboard input. Such a transfer is many times faster than you can type a message, of course. Most online services allow you to upload via an ASCII transfer, but some (e.g., GEnie) have to go into a special receive mode before you can send a message (hence selection number 7 on the GEnie mail menu). In general, unless there's a special selection for uploading a message, you can upload text via ASCII transfer into an open message.

How you initiate sending a file with your communications software will vary, depending on the software package, but starting an ASCII upload typically requires that you type a command such as **SEND** or **UPLOAD** followed by the name of the file to be uploaded. When a file is sent via ASCII transfer, it is *echoed* to your screen, which means you'll see each line of the file on your screen as it is sent. After the file has been sent, you can type additional lines. Message-entry termination is the same as when you are entering a message online.

In a binary file-transfer protocol upload, your communications software reads the file to be transferred, then places it into data packets, which are sent to the remote system. The use of a binary file-transfer protocol (e.g., Xmodem, Ymodem, or Kermit) ensures almost error-free transfer.

All systems must go into a binary file-transfer mode before they can receive a file using a binary file protocol. This is accomplished via a command (e.g., **XUPLOAD** or **KUPLOAD**) or a menu selection. How you initiate a binary file transfer with your software depends on the software you are using, but it typically requires that you type a command specifying the type of protocol to be used, followed by the name of the file to be uploaded.

A few systems (typically general online services) that provide online file storage do not accept binary file uploads as messages directly. Instead, you must first upload the file to the file-storage area, after which you must use a Send File command in the E-mail system to send the file as an E-mail message.

The binary file is not displayed as it is uploaded. Instead, most communications software displays the status of the transfer (e.g., number of bytes transferred). When the transfer is complete, your computer sends an end-of-transfer signal to the remote system, which then returns to command mode or prompts you to address your message, as appropriate.

Sending Messages

Sending a message to a FAX machine via an

After you have addressed and created your message, it is ready to send. Some systems automatically send a message after the message-entry ter-

online service E-mail system differs very little from sending an E-mail message to an electronic mail box.

mination command; others require that you type a Send Message command at a prompt or that you select a Send Message option from a menu. At this point, you also have the option of canceling the message. Some systems will prompt you to enter delivery specifications (e.g., FAX, Telex, or street address) or other options after terminating message entry.

On all but a small minority of E-mail systems, you cannot recall a message once it is sent.

Sending FAX Messages

Sending a FAX message via an online service is almost the same as sending an E-mail message. On most systems, the major difference is in addressing the message. As shown in Figure 8.6, you need only include a FAX specification and phone number when entering the address header.

```
create, delete, get, help, profile, quit, read, show
Command: .create
To: FAX!3175551212
Attention To:
```

Figure 8.6 Specifying FAX delivery in a message address header.

Systems that use a special menu selection require that you enter addressing information in a similar manner, as shown later in this chapter.

Reading and Downloading Messages

Being able to view a directory of messages helps you identify messages. This helps you find a message when you have a lot of messages and a little time.

Most E-mail systems notify you automatically at sign-on when you have E-mail messages waiting. A few move you to their E-mail menus or prompts automatically when you have mail waiting.

New mail (or mail in any folder, as explained later) can be initially dealt with in one of three ways: You can view a list (directory) of waiting messages, read messages, or download messages.

Seeing What's There

Before you read messages, you can see a list of waiting messages, if you wish, by typing a Directory command—typically **DIR**, **SCAN**, or something similar. This displays a list of waiting messages, as shown in Figure 8.7.

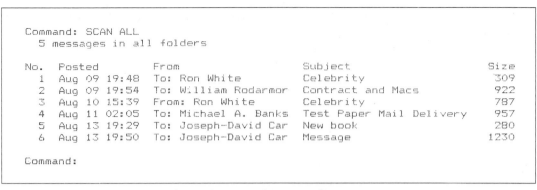

```
Command: SCAN ALL
  5 messages in all folders

No.  Posted          From                 Subject                   Size
  1  Aug 09 19:48    To: Ron White        Celebrity                  309
  2  Aug 09 19:54    To: William Rodarmor Contract and Macs          922
  3  Aug 10 15:39    From: Ron White      Celebrity                  787
  4  Aug 11 02:05    To: Michael A. Banks Test Paper Mail Delivery    957
  5  Aug 13 19:29    To: Joseph-David Car New book                    280
  6  Aug 13 19:50    To: Joseph-David Car Message                    1230

Command:
```

Figure 8.7 E-mail message directory.

A typical message directory displays the ID of the sender, the date and time the message was sent, and the subject line.

Some E-mail systems provide an automatic directory listing of new messages in menu form.

Reading Messages

To read a message, you either make a selection from a menu or—more frequently—type a command such as **READ** or **READ NEW** at a command prompt. The message is then displayed in seven-bit ASCII format. Most systems display messages one screen page at a time. A few such as GEnie display all messages nonstop (although you can review messages with the appropriate commands). Systems that display one screen page at a time usually provide a way for you to display the message nonstop. This is important if you wish to download the message by capturing it, as explained in the next section.

Downloading Messages

Some systems provide special commands to download messages via binary file-transfer protocol or as ASCII downloads. Others such as DELPHI do not provide these options, but they do allow you to copy a message to your online file storage area and download them from there.

If binary file-transfer is available, the process of downloading a message is similar to that of uploading a message using a binary file-transfer protocol. You tell the remote system that you wish to download the file using a specific binary protocol, then type the commands your communications software requires to receive a file using that protocol. If available, binary protocol downloading is preferable to ASCII downloads for long messages or documents.

An ASCII download is more easily implemented, since it is nothing more than a "file capture" operation, from your communications software's viewpoint. A file capture (also called turning on the capture buffer) consists of the communications software opening a disk file and saving all incoming text (i.e., an E-mail message) in the disk file. To capture text, all you have to do is initiate the capture (turn on your software's capture buffer), which requires assigning a file name to the text to be captured, then issue the appropriate Read command to the online service. After the system displays the message(s) you wish to capture, you issue the command to turn off the file capture, and the file is saved.

Folders

Capturing E-mail messages to disk is more practical than storing messages online.

Almost all E-mail systems offer an online filing system that you can use to store related messages that you want to save in groups. These groups are called folders, because they are electronic analogs of file folders. One or two folders are created for you, as explained below. All available commands the E-mail system offers operate in all folders.

New, unread messages are typically stored in an online folder reserved for new messages. This folder is usually called New, Newmail, Inbox, or something similarly appropriate. After they are read, they are automatically moved to a folder that contains old messages (unless you delete them or file them in a specific folder). Old mail is kept in a folder called Mail, or any other appropriate name. Some systems retain copies of messages you've sent, as well, in a folder with a name like Sent or Outbox.

Reviewing messages on disk is quick and easy.

To access messages in a folder other than the current folder, you type a Mail Read or Directory command followed by the name of the folder (e.g., **READ NEW**, **DIR OUTBOX**, and **SCAN INBOX**).

Message-Handling Options

After you've read a message, you have these basic options on almost all online services:

- Reread it (useful if you want to capture it)

- Download it

- Delete it (some systems allow you to recover a message if you accidentally delete it or if you change your mind after deleting it, but only during the current online session)

- Forward it to another user (with a subject header or as a part of a message, depending on the service)

- File it in a folder with related messages (you create the folder name)

Note: Many E-mail systems automatically delete messages after a certain period of time, which may not be determined by you. Systems that do not delete messages automatically typically charge you for storage space if the messages take up more than a specified minimum amount of space.

Reading, Downloading, and Filing FAX Messages

Because incoming FAX messages are handled just like any other E-mail message, all of the commands and options just described for handling incoming E-mail apply to incoming FAX messages.

A Sample E-Mail Session

To better illustrate what I've just described, the following groups of figures show how to address, enter, and send a message on MCI Mail and how to view a directory of waiting messages and read a message on CompuServe.

In Figure 8.8, I've issued MCI Mail's Create command to open a message, and I've filled in the online ID of the recipient. Note that the system offers the opportunity to specify more than one addressee.

```
Command: create
TO:      ron white
There is more than one:

No.       MCI ID   Name                 Organization     Location
  0 NOT LISTED BELOW. DELETE.
  1 NOT LISTED BELOW. ENTER AN ADDRESS.
  2        329-1704 Ron White           FAX/Comp Press   Cincinnati, OH
  3        318-6750 Ron X. White        Roberts Press    Asheville, NC

Please enter the number: 2
         329-1704 Ron White             FAX/Comp Press   Cincinnati, OH
TO:
CC:
```

Figure 8.8 Opening and addressing a message on MCI Mail.

In Figure 8.9, I'm entering the message (could be uploading it via an ASCII transfer). In Figure 8.10, I've terminated message-entry by typing **/** on a line by itself and responded to the prompts to send the message.

Now, let's take a look at the message directory and reading procedures. In Figure 8.11, I'm in DELPHI's E-mail area and have typed **DIR** to see a directory of waiting messages.

```
Command: create
TO:      ron white
There is more than one:

No.       MCI ID   Name             Organization    Location
  0 NOT LISTED BELOW. DELETE.
  1 NOT LISTED BELOW. ENTER AN ADDRESS.
  2        329-1704 Ron White       FAX/Comp Press  Cincinnati, OH
  3        318-6750 Ron X. White    Roberts Press   Asheville, NC

Please enter the number: 2
         329-1704 Ron White         FAX/Comp Press  Cincinnati, OH
TO:
CC:
Subject: January deadlines
Text: (Enter text or transmit file. Type / on a line by itself to end.)

Ron,
     Regarding the January 10th deadlines for the reviews, I
think that may be cutting it a bit tight.  We have to obtain the
products, which is going to require a month or more; then we have
to test them, which---if we're going to be fair---will take another
```

Figure 8.9 Entering a message on MCI Mail.

In Figure 8.12, I've typed **READ 3**, selecting message number 3 from the directory list. The system displays the first page of the message.

A Sample Online FAX Session

As previously indicated, sending and receiving a message via FAX on an online service is not much different from sending and receiving a message via E-mail. On systems that do not offer a separate FAX selection but instead allow you to specify FAX delivery in an address header, the FAX process is almost indistinguishable from E-mail.

I've selected a system (DELPHI) that implements FAX as a separate menu selection on its E-mail menu to illustrate the steps and some of the options involved in sending FAX via E-mail. Figures 8.13 through 8.15 show the process of addressing, creating, and sending a FAX message via E-mail.

Figures 8.16 and 8.17 show a previously uploaded text file being sent as a FAX message.

Figure 8.18 shows the FAX message sent in the preceding two figures as it was printed by the receiving dedicated FAX machine.

What You've Learned

This chapter has taught you the following:

- An online service account carries an identifying number, name, or alphanumeric string that is also your E-mail address.

- A password is your key to signing on to an online service. You should change it frequently and never reveal it to others.

- Most online services are accessed via packet-switching networks. The remainder are accessed via direct-dial telephone numbers.

```
Command: create
TO:        ron white
There is more than one:

No.        MCI ID   Name              Organization      Location
   0 NOT LISTED BELOW. DELETE.
   1 NOT LISTED BELOW. ENTER AN ADDRESS.
   2        329-1704 Ron White        FAX/Comp Press    Cincinnati, OH
   3        318-6750 Ron X. White     Roberts Press     Asheville, NC

Please enter the number: 2
           329-1704 Ron White         FAX/Comp Press    Cincinnati, OH
TO:
CC:
Subject: January deadlines
Text: (Enter text or transmit file. Type / on a line by itself to end.)

Ron,
        Regarding the January 10th deadlines for the reviews, I
think that may be cutting it a bit tight.  We have to obtain the
products, which is going to require a month or more; then we have
to test them, which---if we're going to be fair---will take another
month.  That doesn't leave much time for preparing the reviews
and verifying them.  What do you think?  Any chance of pushing
the deadline to the second week of February?
        Thanks.

-MB
/
Handling:
Send? y
One moment please; your message is being posted.

Your message was posted: Wed Mar 21, 1990  11:51 am  EST.
There is a copy in your OUTBOX

Command:
```

Figure 8.10 Sending a message on MCI Mail.

- The first step in accessing an online service is to set up your computer to communicate. This process includes setting modem speed and communications parameters.

- Communications parameters include data bits, stop bits, and parity.

```
MAIL> DIR

# From                    Date              Subject

  1 BOS1B::MONTE          24-MAY-1990       MANUAL
  2 BOS1B::JOHNMYSELF     24-MAY-1990       The Official Guide
  3 BOS1C::WWSMITH        24-MAY-1990       RE: Competition
  4 BOS1B::PARRISHJ       25-MAY-1990       Delphi: The Official Guide
  5 BOS1A::JIMSB          25-MAY-1990       Re: Mutual Funds
  6 BOS1B::PAG             3-JUN-1990       Thanks for the advice!
  7 BOS1A::AUDREY          9-AUG-1990       FAX Files
  8 BOS1B::ELLISCO        11-AUG-1990       RE: Book Update
  9 BOS1A::BUSSIGMGR      11-AUG-1990       Upload
 10 BOS1B::KIP            12-AUG-1990       RE: Need to know
 11 BOS1A::PKC            12-AUG-1990       Agents
 12 BOS1B::AKIRAJAPAN     12-AUG-1990       Network Guide

MAIL>
```

Figure 8.11 An E-mail message directory.

```
MAIL> READ

#3              24-MAY-1990  12:04:06                      MAIL

From:   BOS1C::WWSMITH
To:     BOS1A::KZIN
Subj:   RE: Competition

Mike,

     The margins are fairly slim as is, and we're already losing
money on the shipping operation, thanks to the high percentage of
credits we have to give dissatisfied customers.  It's silly for
us to try to compete, time- and price-wise, with Roberts.
     I honestly believe that the only way our group can be
successful is to get some open-ended contracts with some solid
customers who are interested in quality rather than speed.
     What you you think?  If we can come up with a good angle on

Press RETURN for more...

MAIL>
```

Figure 8.12 Reading an E-mail message.

- After setting up the system to make a call, you must dial a packet-switching network's number or the direct-dial number for the on-line service with which you wish to connect.

- If you use a packet-switching network to access an online service, you must enter a network address for the online service at the packet-switching network's prompt.

- Once you are connected with an online service, two things will be required before you can sign on: your online ID and your password.

```
MAIL Menu:

FAX Service              Easylink
Mail (Electronic)        Translation Services
Scan for New Messages    Workspace
SetMail                  HELP
Telex                    EXIT

DMAIL>(Mail, FAX, Telex, Trans): FAX

Welcome to the FAX interface.
Enter Control-C to terminate your request at any time.


Would you like to read the help (includes rates) for this service
(Y/N)? [n]y


MAIL

FAX

Sending text messages to Group III facsimile machines is easy.
All you need to know is the area code and phone number of the FAX
machine that you are calling for messages destined to the United
States, Canada and the Caribbean.  For international FAX, you
need to know the country code, city code and phone number of the
destination terminal.

A FAX message can be created in Workspace and sent at the
filename prompt, or it can be typed live.  The same message can
be sent to multiple FAX machines by simply entering each
destination number when prompted.

Should you wish to include page breaks in your FAX, enter /PAGE
by itself as the first line of text, and then /PAGE at each place
in the message that you wish the break to occur.

The rates for sending FAX messages are as follows:

Press Return.
```

Figure 8.13 DELPHI FAX menu selection and information.

- Many communications programs can perform automated dial-up and sign-on procedures using program or information files called script files.

- After you sign on to an online service, you can select the service you wish to access by selecting items from a menu or by issuing navigation commands.

```
The rates for sending FAX messages are as follows:

Press Return.


The rates for sending FAX messages are as follows:

                       First       Additional
    Destination        Page        Half Pages
    -----------        ------      -----------
    United States      $1.25       $0.50
    Canada             $2.00       $1.00
    International      $7.00       $2.00


A page is defined as 2500 characters and a half page is defined
as 1250 characters.  Each FAX message sent to multiple numbers
will be billed at the above rates.

To abort sending a FAX, use Control-C.  To send the FAX, use
Control-Z. FAX messages are sent throughout the day, generally
within minutes of when they are entered.

Receipt notification: You will get a message if your FAX could
NOT be sent.  Notification with date/time of delivery for SENT
messages costs $0.40 per message.


Enter the 3-digit FAX area code below (even if it is you local
area code).  If you are sending to a country other than the US,
Canada, or the Caribbean, enter "I".


Area Code or I> 913

Enter the rest of the Number> 491-6642


Do you want your message to go to 913/491-6642 (Y/N)? [y] Y

/NOTE: You can enter R here to enable Receipt Notification.

Will there be any more phone numbers for this message (Y/N)? [n] R
```

Figure 8.14 FAX pricing information and addressing.

- Online help is available on all online services, to one degree or another. To get help while online, type **HELP** or **?**.

- Sending a message via E-mail involves three steps: addressing the message, creating the message, and sending the message.

```
Enter the name of the file that will be the body of the message,
and press RETURN to enter the message now.  No line should be
longer than 90 characters.

Filename or RETURN?

7/21/89
                                              Buenos Aires
Dear Les,

Sr. Gorge Valaqueza and his children are planning a trip to
Southern California next summer.  He is a long-time friend whom
we have spent numerous vacations with here in Argentina.  While
there they are planning a visit to Southern California's great
sights.  They'll see Hollywood, Disneyland, and as many beaches
as they can.  They have accomodations for their visit to
Disneyland but would enjoy spending some time with an American
family.

As I will be in the area, I would love to stop by and see you as
well.  It has been far too long since our last visit.

Sr. Valasquez is 40 years old and his wife is about the same age.
Their children are Anita, 3, Gorge, 8, and Gabr ielle, 14.  I
think that your family would get along very well with these
children and a week together would bring fun and much cultural
exchange.

Maria Valasquez has a recipie for a traditional South American
barbeque that she woul d like to prepare.  She will require a
large pig for roasting and some chicken.  I have had these dishes
on my last visit to their home and they are delicious.  She will
bring her own authentic spices. I know that you are interested in
South America and I look forward to telling Sr. Valasquez that I
can meet him at your home in July.

Best Regards,
Phillippe
^Z

1681 characters will be sent to 1 phone number(s)

The approximate total charge for this message in $1.25

OK to send (Y/N) [y] Y

One moment...

Thank You.
```

Figure 8.15 FAX message entry and sending.

- Delivery options (e.g., FAX and hardcopy delivery) and multiple recipients are often specified when addressing a message.

- E-mail (or modem/FAX) messages can be entered online or uploaded.

- Handling options for incoming E-mail or FAX messages include deleting, filing (in a system of groups of related messages called folders), forwarding, and downloading.

- Procedures for sending and reading E-mail and FAX messages on-line differ very little.

Test your knowledge of what it's like to use E-mail on online services with the following quiz, then move on to Chapter 9, where you'll be able to preview specific E-mail specialty services.

```
MAIL Menu:

FAX Service              Easylink
Mail (Electronic)        Translation Services
Scan for New Messages    Workspace
SetMail                  HELP
Telex                    EXIT

DMAIL>(Mail, FAX, Telex, Trans): workspace
Enter ? for list of commands.


WORKSPACE Menu:

APPEND to File      HELP
CATALOG Files       LIST File
COPY File           PURGE Old Versions
COUNT Words         RENAME File
CREATE File         SETTINGS
DELETE File         UNPROTECT File
DOWNLOAD File       UPLOAD File
EDIT File           KERMIT-Server
EXIT                Other Commands


WS> (Please Select a Command) EDIT

Name of file for EDIT ? ORTIZ.LETTER
```

Figure 8.16 Editing an uploaded file for FAX transmission (first page).

```
FAX TO: Mr. Les Ortiz              IMPORTANT MESSAGE CONCERNING
        CBA Co.                    INTERNATIONAL VISITORS ! !
        10 Upton Street
        Los Angeles, CA 90026      DELIVER IMMEDIATELY
        12260 Plaza de Ninos
        Buenos Aires, Argentina
-----------------------------------------------------------------

7/21/89
                                            Buenos Aires

Dear Les,

Sr. Gorge Valaqueza and his children are planning a trip to
Southern California next summer.  He is a long-time friend whom
we have spent numerous vacations with here in Argentina.  While
there they are planning a visit to Southern California's great
sights.  They'll see Hollywood, Disneyland, and as many beaches
as they can.  They have accomodations for their visit to
Disneyland but would enjoy spending some time with an American
family.

As I will be in the area, I would love to stop by and see you as
well.  It has been far too long since our last visit.

Sr. Valasquez is 40 years old and his wife is about the same age.
Their children are Anita, 3, Gorge, 8, and Gabr ielle, 14. I
think that your family would get along very well with these
children and a week together would bring fun and much cultural
exchange.

Maria Valasquez has a recipie for a traditional South American
barbeque that she woul d like to prepare.  She will require a
large pig for roasting and some chicken.  I have had these dishes
on my last visit to their home and they are delicious.  She will
bring her own authentic spices. I know that you are interested in
South America and I look forward to telling Sr. Valasquez that I
can meet him at your home in July.

Best Regards,
Phillippe
*ex
```

Figure 8.16 Editing an uploaded file for FAX transmission (second page).

```
MAIL Menu:

FAX Service              Easylink
Mail (Electronic)        Translation Services
Scan for New Messages    Workspace
SetMail                  HELP
Telex                    EXIT

DMAIL>(Mail, FAX, Telex, Trans): fax

Welcome to the FAX interface.
Enter Control-C to terminate your request at any time.

Would you like to read the help (includes rates) for this service
(Y/N)? [Y]n

Enter the 3-digit FAX area code below (even if it is you local
area code).  If you are sending to a country other than the US,
Canada, or the Caribbean, enter "I".

Area Code or I> 913

Enter the rest of the Number> 491-6642

Do you want your message to go to 913/491-6642 (Y/N)? [y] Y

/NOTE: You can enter R here to enable Receipt Notification.

Will there be any more phone numbers for this message (Y/N)? [n] R

You'll receive notification when the FAX has been sent.  This is
40c extra per message.  (Type NR here to turn this off.)

Will there be any more phone numbers for this message (Y/N)? [n] N

Enter the name of the file that will be the body of the message,
or press RETURN to enter the message now.  No line should be
longer than 90 characters.

Filename or RETURN? ORTIZ.LETTER

1681 characters will be sent to 1 phone number(s).

The approximate total charge for this message is $1.65

(Of that, $.40 is for Receipt Notification.)

Ok to send (Y/N)? [y] Y

One moment...

Thank you.
```

Figure 8.17 Specifying a file to be sent as a FAX message.

```
Sent via DELPHI on 25-JUL-1989 at 16:25 ET.

FAX TO:      Mr. Les Ortiz            IMPORTANT MESSAGE CONCERNING
             CBA Co.                  INTERNATIONAL VISITORS !!
             10 Upton Street
             Los Angeles, CA 90026    DELIVER IMMEDIATELY

FAX FROM:    Phillipe Torez
             12260 Plaza de Ninos
             Buenos Aires, Argentina


--------------------------------------------------------------------

                                     7/21/89
                                     Buenos Aires
        Dear Les,


        Sr. Gorge Valaqueza and his children are planning a trip to Southern
        California next summer.  He is a long-time friend whom we have spent
        numerous vacations with in Argentina.  While there they are planning a
        visit to Southern California's great sights.  They'll see Hollywood,
        Disneyland, and as many beaches as they can.  They have accomodations for
        their visit to Disneyland but would enjoy spending some time with an
        American family.  I know that this interests you.

        Sr. Valasquez is 40 years old and his wife is about the same age. Their
        children are Anita, 3, Gorge, 8, and Gabrielle, 14.  I think that your
        family would get along very well with these children and a week together
        would bring fun and much cultural exchange.

        Maria Valasquez has a recipie for a traditional South American
        barbeque that she would like to prepare.  She will require a large pig
        for roasting and some chicken.  I have had these dishes on my last visit
        and they are delicious.  She will bring her own authentic spices.

        I know that you are interested in South America and I look forward to
        telling Sr. Valasquez that I can meet him at your home in July.

        Best Regards,
        Phillippe
```

Figure 8.18 FAX message received from an online service.

Quiz

1. What serves as your E-mail address on an online service?

    a. Your password
    b. Your online ID
    c. Your credit card number
    d. Your telephone number

2. Most online services are accessed by which means?

    a. Direct-dial telephone numbers
    b. FAX networks
    c. Packet-switching networks
    d. Modem networks

3. If you are not using a script file, what do you do after preparing your computer, modem, and communications software to communicate?

    a. Sign on
    b. Enter an online service's address
    c. Dial a packet-switching network or online service's direct-dial telephone number
    d. Enter a password

4. In addition to your user ID, what does an online service require of you to sign on?

    a. A password
    b. An online service address
    c. A computer ID
    d. A command

5. After you have signed on to an online service, you can access specific services or areas by issuing specific commands or:

    a. Typing **HELP**
    b. Typing your password
    c. Navigating
    d. Selecting items from a menu

6. How can you view a summary listing of available commands and/ or get detailed help online?

    a. By typing **HELP** or **?**
    b. By calling the online service's customer service department
    c. By exiting to another menu
    d. By typing your password

7. Creating an electronic envelope is usually the first step in sending an E-mail or E-mail/FAX message. Of what does this consist?

  a. Entering a message
  b. Entering an online ID or other address for the message
  c. Entering a page break
  d. Uploading a message

8. E-mail and E-mail/FAX messages can be entered online. They can also be prepared offline, then transmitted to the online service in a process called what?

  a. Downloading
  b. Scanning
  c. Uploading
  d. Filing

9. After reading an E-mail or FAX message online, you can, among other options, file it with related messages. What are such groups of related messages called?

  a. Files
  b. Folders
  c. Documents
  d. Directories

10. On most systems, sending a FAX message is virtually the same as sending an E-mail message, because the FAX delivery specification and phone number are entered in the address header. On systems that aren't set up this way, how is a FAX message initiated?

  a. By scanning a document
  b. By uploading the message
  c. By selecting an item on an E-mail menu
  d. By typing a Send command

Part 2 | Online FAX and E-Mail

The emphasis in this section is on computer communication. The chapters that follow detail the E-mail, FAX, and general online services described in the latter half of Part 1. This section also provides help in evaluating and selecting an online service.

Chapter 9, entitled "E-Mail Services," describes the E-mail, FAX, and other delivery services and options provided by the major E-mail specialty services: AT&T Mail, DASnet, MCI Mail, and TELEMAIL. Telex is also covered. Costs are discussed on a comparative basis.

Chapter 10, entitled "General Online Services," covers general, or full-service, online services, including such major players as CompuServe, DELPHI, and GEnie. As with the E-mail services covered in Chapter 9, you'll learn the kinds of services, features, and options these services offer, as well as how they compare in terms of cost.

Chapter 11, entitled "Choosing the Service That's Right for You," helps you define your online service needs and applications and shows you how to evaluate online services in terms of cost, accessibility, and other important factors.

Chapter **9** | E-Mail Services

About This Chapter

The purpose of this chapter is to give you an idea of what each of the major E-mail specialty services has to offer. In this chapter, you'll learn about the services, features, options, and costs of using AT&T Mail, DASnet, MCI Mail, and TELEMAIL. You'll also learn something about Telex—the original electronic mail system.

> **Note:** Chapter 10 provides a similar survey of general online services.

AT&T Mail

AT&T Mail is an E-mail-only service whose apparent target market consists of medium- and large-size corporations that need to integrate their computing and telecommunications operations. AT&T sells complete computer communications packages consisting of AT&T microcomputers, modems, communications software, and AT&T Mail access.

AT&T Mail is particularly well suited to this market. It provides almost every E-mail service imaginable, and its pricing structure is favorable to large-volume users. AT&T's ability to provide a complete

191

hardware-software-service package is particularly appealing to corporate users, and the AT&T name wields some power in the marketplace.

AT&T Mail serves as AT&T's internal mail system, as well as that of a number of other readily recognizable corporate entities (browsing its online subscriber directory will demonstrate this fact). This is not to say that there are no individuals or small companies using AT&T Mail. Many of the services it offers are ideally suited to those who need to send E-mail to other systems, and for FAX, Telex, and hardcopy delivery. And, of course, individuals and small companies that need to communicate electronically with other AT&T Mail users find the service indispensable.

E-Mail Services and Options

AT&T Mail's involvement in setting up and implementing international communications standards puts it at the forefront of electronic communications technology.

AT&T Mail offers virtually all the options available for electronic mail, including receipt notification, COD delivery, multiple addressee and mailing lists, forms to set up automatic querying and response return, and a fairly sophisticated filing system.

Xmodem is available for message upload/download, and you can review and edit a message online before sending it.

In addition to sending E-mail to users on the AT&T Mail system, you can send messages via UNIX system gateways, via LAN gateways, and to other E-mail systems with which AT&T Mail is linked.

FAX Delivery and Options

AT&T Mail delivers text messages to any Group 3 or Group 4 FAX machine, anywhere in the world. It generates a cover sheet at no charge for each FAX message you send and makes multiple delivery attempts.

Optional features include receipt of delivery notification, and an "Attention" line to specify the person to whom the FAX should be delivered after it is received.

AT&T Mail is currently the only E-mail service that offers Group 4 delivery.

FAX delivery is specified on the AT&T Mail address line, along with the required telephone number. The typical format is to enter **FAX!** followed by the receiving FAX machine's area code and phone number, plus optional additional information at the **To:** prompt. If you omit any necessary information, the system will prompt you for it. This makes sending a message to a FAX machine the same as sending an E-mail message.

Other Delivery Options

For urgent document delivery, AT&T Mail

AT&T Mail will deliver hardcopies of messages and documents by U.S. Mail or courier. Courier options include overnight, 4-hour delivery,

provides the only 4-hour hardcopy delivery service.

COD, and confirmation of receipt. Hardcopy messages can include a company or personal logo and/or your signature.

AT&T Mail also provides two-way domestic and international Telex service. Incoming Telex messages are delivered to you as E-mail.

Address conventions for hardcopy and Telex delivery are similar to those for FAX.

Special Services and Features

Additional AT&T Mail services include E-mail enhancements, a subscriber directory, a voice-delivery system for retrieving your messages via voice telephone, and project billing.

E-Mail Enhancements In addition to the features already mentioned, AT&T Mail offers these E-mail enhancements:

- Autoresponse—This feature enables you to create a message that will be sent as an automatic reply to incoming messages, a useful feature when you are going to be offline for an extended period.

- Automatic command execution—This optional setting causes a command to be executed automatically when you sign on. For example, you might have the system display all new messages automatically whenever you sign on.

- Secondary password—You can set a secondary password that allows only you to access your mail services. If someone else signs on as you but doesn't know the password, or the secondary password, the intruder cannot read your mail.

Subscriber Directory AT&T Mail's subscriber directory can be searched, but by user name only. This makes searching difficult, as you have to know at least some part of the user name. Fortunately, AT&T user names are usually based on last names or company names.

AT&T Mail Talk Voice Mail Delivery AT&T Mail Talk heads the list of unique offerings on AT&T Mail (and indeed on online services anywhere). As the name implies, AT&T Mail Talk is a service that allows you to retrieve your electronic mail by voice phone. The service is based on an extremely sophisticated and intelligent speech synthesizer, which not only reads your messages to you but also provides introductory information and online help. The only messages you can retrieve with Mail Talk are those from other AT&T Mail subscribers or incoming Telex messages. If your entire company or important business associates use AT&T Mail, you're ahead of the game.

Project billing AT&T Mail provides a special feature for businesses that need to track expenses on a project basis. Individual messages can be assigned to a particular project via a special command, which results in their being itemized and subtotaled in a separate group on your monthly bill.

> **Note:** AT&T Mail's services are ideally suited to those who need both electronic and voice communication capabilities. The structure of the service is especially well suited to large organizations with heavy E-mail traffic among many users.

Using AT&T Mail

Using AT&T Mail is fairly simple. There are very few menus (the main menu is shown in Figure 9.1), and prompts guide you through most operations. Once you're familiar with the system, you can turn off menus, which speeds up the system.

```
ORIGIN: NODE D1 MODULE 22 PORT 5

Welcome
Enter User Name: banks
Password:
** Welcome to the AT&T Mail Service.
Last logged in: Sun Aug 13 02:49:29 GMT 1989

HELP NEWS contains important information
regarding new AT&T Mail NEWS features.

For Customer Assistance send a free
message to !atthelp or call 1800MAIL672.

create, delete, get, help, profile, quit, read, show
Command: .
```

Figure 9.1 AT&T Mail welcome message and menu.

Getting Help

AT&T Mail provides a very detailed and comprehensive online help system. Typing **HELP** at the main menu displays an overview of the help system. Typing **HELP** or **?** at a prompt will usually (though not always) bring up a help file dealing with the current operation. Help with specific commands and topics is available, too. Typing **HELP INDEX** will display a comprehensive, cross-referenced listing of help topics.

AT&T Mail customer service can be reached via a WATS voice-telephone line, or free E-mail messages.

Access

From most regions of the United States, access to AT&T Mail and AT&T Mail Talk is via special WATS numbers (which is exactly what one might expect, since AT&T is the originator and provider of WATS service). International access is available via a direct-dial number with a 201 area code.

AT&T Mail communicates at 300, 1200, or 2400 bps.

Individual message costs can vary tremendously, as several volume-usage discounts are offered.

DASnet

DASnet is the first ripple of what may be a wave of the future (depending on whether commercial online services decide that E-mail that interconnects with other services is viable): total interconnectivity of all online services. Simply described, DASnet delivers electronic mail between a number of online services, as illustrated in Figure 9.2.

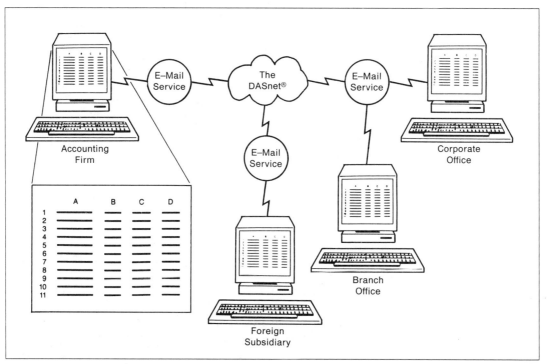

Figure 9.2 DASnet organization and connections. *Courtesy of DA Systems, Inc.*

DASnet provides links with almost all major E-mail specialty and online services.

Through various subsystems and other services not shown on the chart in Figure 9.2, DASnet actually provides access to more than two dozen individual services. (More will be added in the near future.) It also gives you access to more than three million E-mail subscribers.

How DASnet Operates

The starting point of a DASnet message is the E-mail system of a host online service. The message must first be addressed to DASnet's online ID for that system. This is done by entering the DASnet ID in the message's To: field or, on some systems, using a special inter system mail area set up by the host system.

Once a message has been addressed to DASnet, the system and the recipient's online ID must be entered in the message's Subject: (or similar) field. The user then enters the text of the message and sends it in the usual manner.

When the DASnet computer signs on to the online service in question (it signs on to each system on its route several times daily), it collects all messages addressed to the DASnet ID. Offline, it sorts these messages by the information in the subject header and prepares them for delivery on the appropriate systems.

When the DASnet computer signs on to a system for which it is holding messages for delivery, it sends these messages to their recipients' E-mail boxes automatically, using the host system's E-mail commands and the information it has extracted from each message's Subject: field.

No humans handle or read messages.

All this is accomplished using the existing commands on each system and the DASnet computer's special capabilities.

DASnet can even use certain special delivery options offered by some systems, which means you don't have to leave your favorite or "home" online service just to access features that your system doesn't offer.

FAX Delivery

DASnet offers delivery of E-mail messages to any Group 3 FAX machine in the world. A simple addressing procedure specifies FAX delivery of a message that you enter or upload to one of the systems that offers DASnet connections, and the FAX message is delivered as soon as possible after you send it.

DASnet FAX delivery provides FAX service on many systems that otherwise do not offer it. In other words, if DASnet is available on your favorite online service, you don't have to go to the trouble and expense of signing up for another online service just to have modem/FAX capability.

Other Delivery Options

DASnet also offers hardcopy delivery via U.S. Mail and worldwide Telex delivery.

Access and Costs

Access to DASnet is via the systems on which DASnet maintains accounts and service agreements.

Depending on the system to which you are sending mail via DASnet and the direction it is traveling, a 1K message costs anywhere from 59¢ (to systems such as ARPAnet and UUCP) to over $5 (Telex to England). Other sample prices for a 1K message include: $2.18 for a message via TELEMAIL to or from Japan and $1.85 for a message to or from AT&T Mail.

DASnet has a small minimum monthly membership fee, but some systems such as UNISON provide DASnet membership free of charge to their subscribers.

MCI Mail

MCI Mail has the distinction of being the first successful commercial E-mail service to be marketed as a *communications* service, as opposed to just a computer service. An operating unit of MCI Telecommunications Corp., MCI Mail was introduced to the general public (not just computer users) in 1983 through multimedia advertising. MCI Mail's target market appears to be business and personal computer users, as well as computer hobbyists—basically, anyone with a computer and modem.

MCI Mail's offerings are fairly straightforward, as evidenced by the service's main menu (Figure 9.3). This menu doesn't show all of MCI Mail's services, however.

```
You may enter:

SCAN           for a summary of your mail
READ           to READ messages or LISTS
PRINT          to display messages nonstop
CREATE         to write an MCI Letter
CREATE LIST    to make a distribution list
DOWJONES       to Dow Jones News/Retrieval
ACCOUNT        to adjust terminal display
HELP           for assistance

Command (or MENU or EXIT):
```

Figure 9.3 MCI Mail main menu.

MCI Mail is probably the most efficient E-mail specialty service for individual and small-business users, both because of its rate structure and its links with CompuServe and TELEMAIL and because of the fact that so many individuals and professionals use it. MCI Mail also hosts a number of large corporate communications networks.

E-Mail Services and Options

E-mail message delivery to overseas subscribers via MCI Mail is the same as message delivery to U.S. subscribers.

MCI Mail offers virtually all the options available for electronic mail, including receipt notification, multiple addressee and mailing lists (shared or individual), forms (called scripts), and a fairly complex filing system.

Messages and mailing lists can be uploaded or downloaded via ASCII transfer. MCI Mail offers standard E-mail addressing options, including multiple addressees and courtesy copy (CC) options.

FAX Delivery and Options

FAX delivery is implemented on MCI Mail by entering a special character sequence **MHS** (which stands for "Message-Handling System") in the address header and **FAX** in the prompt that follows. The system prompts you through the FAX addressing, message creation, and sending processes afterwards. MCI Mail offers communication with Group 3 FAX machines only, and you can send a maximum of 50 pages per document.

Other Delivery Options

MCI Mail offers hardcopy message delivery via U.S. Mail. Options include confirmation of receipt.

You can send and receive Telex messages via MCI Mail, as well. Telex messages are delivered as E-mail messages.

Additional Services and Features

MCI Mail offers several E-mail enhancements, a subscriber directory, gateways to other services, bulletin boards, and project codes.

E-Mail Enhancements A unique E-mail enhancement on MCI Mail is the system's use of a subscriber directory to help address a message. Simply type in the name of the company or individual to whom you wish the message sent, and MCI Mail automatically finds and fills in the proper MCI Mail user ID. If there is more than one ID whose name contains the string you enter, the system will display a menu, from which you can select the desired address.

Toll-free mail boxes are another unique E-mail enhancement. MCI mail boxes can be set up to pay the charges for all incoming messages. This is useful if you have set up, for instance, a customer support or field rep reporting system on MCI Mail. You receive one bill for all related services, while offering customers the courtesy of free messaging.

> **Note:** MCI Mail's bulletin board and toll-free mail box services are useful for corporate internal mail and communications between sales organizations and customers.

Subscriber Directory MCI Mail's subscriber directory is fairly intelligent. It can be searched by entering a name or portion of an individual or company name, after which the system will find and list all addresses that contain the entered string.

Service Gateways MCI Mail offers a gateway to the full Dow Jones News/Retrieval Service and displays noteworthy news headlines at sign on.

You can send and receive messages to and from CompuServe subscribers and send messages to users of several other E-mail systems that are connected to MCI Mail. The other systems include DASnet, which offers E-mail relay service to more than two dozen online services.

> **Note:** If you need E-mail with FAX, Telex, and/or hardcopy delivery options, but would like to have occasional access to news, business, and financial information, MCI Mail may fill the bill. You can access news and information via MCI's gateway to Dow Jones News/Retrieval Service.

Bulletin Boards There are a variety of public and private read-only bulletin boards on MCI Mail, most offering products or product information. Individual users can set up their own bulletin boards, for an extra fee.

Project Codes Individual MCI Mail messages can be assigned a special project code. Such messages are then itemized and subtotaled in groups on your monthly bill. This aids in tracking expenses related to a specific project.

Using MCI Mail

Using MCI Mail is fairly simple. There are very few menus (the main menu is shown in Figure 9.3), and these appear only when needed. Prompts guide you through most operations.

Menus cannot be turned off by Basic Service users. MCI Mail Advanced Service users see no menus at all, except on request.

Note: Many of MCI Mail's special features are available only to Advanced Service users. In any event, the streamlined nature of MCI Mail makes Advanced Service the way to go on MCI Mail.

Getting Help

MCI Mail provides a fairly comprehensive online help system. Typing **HELP** at the main menu displays an overview of the help system. Detailed help can be available by combining HELP with the command or topic of interest (up to three levels of topics can be used in one help request). Typing **HELP INDEX** provides a brief description of areas in which help is available.

Customer service can be reached via a toll-free voice help line or an E-mail message.

Access

MCI Mail is accessible from most areas of the United States via a WATS number. For areas where WATS service is not available, direct-dial and/ or Tymnet access are available. Tymnet charges are billed to the user. Canadian users can connect with MCI Mail via Datapac (a packet-switching network that incurs additional charges). International access is via special arrangement.

Access is at 300, 1200, or 2400 bps.

TELEMAIL

Telenet is one of the two major public packet-switching networks in the United States.

TELEMAIL is Telenet's E-mail service. Overall, it's a business-oriented system, designed to serve the specialized and general telecommunications needs of businesses of all sizes.

TELEMAIL is strictly command driven. Most commands are issued at the main command prompt (shown in Figure 9.4), and other prompts are supplied for text entry or specialized commands. Virtually any operation can be suspended or aborted with an appropriate command or a true break signal.

Thanks in part to the fact that it is command driven, TELEMAIL is an unusually fast and responsive system.

E-Mail Services and Options

TELEMAIL offers most of the more popular electronic mail options, including receipt notification, multiple addressee and mailing list ad-

```
CONNECT 2400/ARQ

TELENET
513 10A

TERMINAL=

@TELEMAIL

User name?  MBANKS
Organization?
Password?



Welcome to Telenet's TELEMAIL messaging service!
TELEMAIL is registered in the U.S. Patent and Trademark Office.
Copyright Telenet 1980-1989

Your last access was Saturday, Aug 12, 1989   3:34 PM EDT
Today is Sunday, Aug 13, 1989   7:18 PM EDT

  No new mail.

Command?
```

Figure 9.4 TELEMAIL sign-on greeting and command prompt.

dressing, courtesy copies, and forms. Commands related to reading and otherwise handling messages are particularly powerful, as they can be directed to operate on specific sets of messages by date or other criteria. You can also recall a message after sending it.

Messages can be either created and edited online or created offline and uploaded. A simple online file storage area is provided for each user. Messages can be uploaded via ASCII or binary Xmodem file transfer. ASCII and binary downloads are also available.

Note: TELEMAIL's unique status as a worldwide packet-switching network *and* custom E-mail service, combined with its powerful E-mail options, bulletin boards, and other features, makes it an ideal base for large corporate electronic communications networks.

FAX Delivery and Options

TELEMAIL'S FAX delivery service allows you to send an E-mail message to any Group 3 FAX machine in the world. FAX delivery features these TELEMAIL sending and delivery options:

- Return receipt
- Confirmation of delivery
- Timed delivery (delivery at a specified time)

- Auto-delivery

- The use of online nicknames in a message header

TELEMAIL FAX messages are delivered with a cover sheet, which is generated automatically. If the first FAX message delivery attempt fails, the system retries up to ten times over the ensuing 2 hours. If delivery cannot be made within 2 hours, the system advises sender that the message was undelivered.

Other Delivery Options

TELEMAIL messages can be delivered in hardcopy form via U.S. Mail. Letterheads, logos, and signatures can be digitized for reproduction via TELEMAIL's laser printer output.

Like AT&T Mail and MCI Mail, TELEMAIL provides two-way Telex service. TELEMAIL also provides a direct link with MCI Mail.

Additional Services

TELEMAIL offers some unique E-mail enhancements, a subscriber directory, user-to-user binary file transfer, scripting capability, bulletin boards, and direct international E-mail service.

E-Mail Enhancements TELEMAIL provides an interesting set of options for sending messages. In addition to the more common options such as return receipt, the following options can be specified when an E-mail message is sent:

- Urgent—Places a message at the top of the recipient's message directory, with an "Urgent" flag.

- Private—Requires the recipient to enter personal password before the message can be read.

- Registered—Requires the recipient to acknowledge receipt of a message before being allowed to read it.

- Saved—Files a copy of a sent message in your online file area.

- On—Specifies a date and time for message delivery.

- After—Specifies a date and time *after* which a message is to be sent.

- Every—Causes a message to be sent repeatedly at specified periods (any number of hours, days, weeks, months, or years).

Subscriber Directory TELEMAIL's subscriber directory allows you to search by user ID, online address, or character string (which returns a list of all names containing the entered string). Other search options can be specified, as well.

User-to-User Binary File Transfer Binary files can be transferred between users, a feature that is unusual on electronic mail-only services.

Scripts A special set of editing tools, in the form of dot commands, enables you to embed forms within messages as you are creating them. The forms system is an especially powerful one that enables you to specify prompts for input, rules for proper responses, system responses to improper responses, the layout of the message, and more.

Bulletin Boards TELEMAIL hosts an impressive number of private bulletin boards, created for the use of various companies and organizations who use the service. Bulletin boards are especially powerful and feature-rich.

International Service Because Telenet is an international network, TELEMAIL can be used to send E-mail messages directly to many parts of the world that other services may not serve. Other countries tied in with Telenet include Australia, Canada, England, Italy, Japan, Mexico, Sweden, and Taiwan (ROC). (The recipient must be a TELEMAIL user, of course.) The international E-mail standard "X.400" E-mail service is implemented on TELEMAIL, which makes for easier international communications.

Using TELEMAIL

As already noted, TELEMAIL is a command-driven system that supplies only prompts. This makes using TELEMAIL fast and simple, once you learn the system. The system prompts you through virtually every step of any operation, after you initiate the operation with the appropriate command.

Getting Help

TELEMAIL'S online help is comprehensive and makes good use of examples. Typing **HELP** at TELEMAIL's **Command?** prompt displays an overview of the system, as shown in Figure 9.5. Typing **HELP** or **?** followed by a command or topic will bring up a help file dealing with the specified command or topic. Context-sensitive help is available at some prompts (e.g., at the **To:** prompt during message composition).

```
HELP
                      COMMANDS AND TOPICS
                      -------------------

When the system issues the Command? prompt, it is waiting for
instructions from you.  The system commands are as follows:

ADMINS [OF]     ALTER          ANSWER          BOARDS [OF]
BYE             CALL           CANCEL          CHECK
COMPOSE         COPY           DELETE          DIRECTORY
DISPLAY         DOWNLOAD       EDIT            ENCODE
EXIT            FILE           FORWARD         GOTO
HOSTS [OF]      INQUIRE        INSERT          LIST
LISTS [OF]      MEMBERS [OF]   MODIFY          NICKNAMES
NODES [OF]      NUMBER         PASSKEYS        PURGE
READ            RECOVER        REGISTER        REMOVE
SAVE            SCAN           SCRIPTS [OF]    SEND
SET             STATIONS [OF]  STATUS          SYSTEMS
TALLY           TOKEN          TRANSFER        TRY
UNPURGE         UNREAD         UPLOAD          USERS [OF]

Do you wish to see more on commands and topics? [YES/NO]

Some of the most frequently used commands for basic use
of the system are the following:

READ        ANSWER      SCAN          CHECK
FORWARD     FILE        COMPOSE
PURGE       UNPURGE     DIRECTORY

The system also provides several features that are described by
the following topics:


BATCH            FILE.TRANSFER      NICKNAMES
BULLETIN.BOARDS  HARDCOPY           OAG (OFFICIAL AIRLINE GUIDE)
DIRECT.DELIVERY  HOTLINE            TELEX
DOCUMENTATION    INTERCONNECTION    UPI
DJ (DOW JONES)   INFORM.SCRIPTS     XPRESS
EDITING          MARKET             X.400
FAX              NEWS

Do you wish to see more on commands and topics? [YES/NO] NO

Command?
```

Figure 9.5 TELEMAIL help system.

Customer service is available via a WATS voice number or by E-mail.

Access

TELEMAIL can be accessed via any Telenet node, which means that there are more than 18,000 local numbers for TELEMAIL. Access is at 300, 1200, or 2400 bps, depending upon the local node you use.

Telex

Telex is the original electronic mail system. The direct successor to the telegraph, it was established in the 1920s to transmit textual data via a network of teletypewriters (TTY) or teleprinters (printing terminals) using a five-bit system of character coding called the BAUDOT code, rather than the seven- or eight-bit ASCII systems used by computers.

You may have been exposed to Telex systems in the military or in the news media, where for many years weather and news bulletins were commonly received via Telex. Telex is often referred to as teletype, a common designation derived from the name of the company that was once the largest manufacturer of teleprinters in the United States—the Teletype Corporation.

Early Telex systems were electromechanical in nature and operated at extremely slow speeds, typically 50 or 110 bps (as slow as ten characters per second). Data transmission required a human operator, and the machines were by nature cranky and difficult to use.

Modern Telex

Improvements in technology eventually brought automation and faster, more reliable transmission to the Telex network. Computer technology enabled such features as store-and-forward.

Along with TWX, a similar system, Telex was the world's major media for nonvoice communication for almost 50 years and continues to play an important role in domestic and international communications today.

E-mail and FAX have far from replaced Telex, for several reasons. First, Telex offers certain kinds of access and services that E-mail services cannot equal, which is why E-mail services provide Telex access. Too, the Telex system is firmly entrenched; nearly two million Telex terminals are in use around the world.

Public Telex carriers in the United States—among them ITT, Western Union, and RCA—are thus carrying a major chunk of the world's electronic communications traffic. Major corporations and other organizations maintain their own private domestic and international Telex networks, as well (some facilitated by the major carriers).

Telex Access

Until the late 1970s, you had to have a teletypewriter or teleprinter to use Telex. By then, however, the microcomputer was perceived as something more than a hobbyist's toy, and the Telex networks moved to accommodate personal computer users.

Computer access to Telex services is typically via direct-dial phone numbers in local cities. As already explained, some Telex services are accessible via online services such as AT&T Mail, CompuServe, DEL-PHI, MCI Mail, and TELEMAIL.

Unless you handle a lot of Telex traffic (especially incoming Telexes), you probably won't need an account with a Telex carrier. Online service Telex capability should meet your needs. I recommend this, because, in using an online service to access Telex, you avoid the monthly service charges that some Telex carriers charge, plus you have access to conventional E-mail. Too, E-mail services are usually easier to use than direct Telex connections.

Telex costs vary but are usually based on message transmission time and the distance the message is transmitted.

What Does It Cost?

By now you're wondering exactly how much sending and receiving E-mail, FAX, Telex, and hardcopy messages is going to cost you. There's no easy answer to that question; costs depend upon many variables, including:

- The online service you use

- The length of messages or documents

- Subscriber options

- Delivery options you select

- Your volume of message traffic

However, I can provide a basis for cost comparisons, based on prices currently extant for E-mail services. (Keep in mind that these prices are subject to change.) Tables 9.1 and 9.2 show base costs and per-message costs, respectively.

Table 9.1 E-Mail Service Base Charges

Service	Minimum Charges	Enhanced Service
AT&T Mail—There are no surcharges for access at 1200 or 2400 bps.	$30.00 per year basic user registration fee $10.00 per month for FORMS/FILES users $12.00 per year fee for entry in the AT&T Mail Directory of an off-net user	$12.00 per year per graphic for signature or letterhead for use with hardcopy delivery Discounts of 10 to 25% for $2000 or $8000 monthly usage volume Storage fees for shared files/folders, and for large numbers of messages $.50 per minute charge for using Mail Talk
DASnet—Access costs include the cost of using the online service you use to access DASnet.	Varies, depending on the optional services you use; certain online services provide DASnet membership for subscribers at no extra charge	Options include private Telex number ($8.40 per month + 16% surcharge); DASnet directory; DASnet directory listings; auto transfer of all E-mail and specified conference activity from BIX, CompuServe, TWICS, UNISON, NWI, or NEWSNET ($6.83 per month, each)
MCI Mail—There are no surcharges for access at 1200 or 2400 bps, unless the access is via Tymnet.	Advanced Service (brief prompts, chained commands, and other benefits) is now offered to all subscribers at no extra cost (Basic subscribers are provided with menus) $25.00 annual mail box fee (waived for those who sign up for the Preferred Pricing Option) $10.00 per month minimum billing for Preferred Pricing Option	Preferred Pricing Option allows user to send 40 message pages per month at no charge (beyond the minimum billing) and additional message pages at the discount rate of $.25 per page (this includes domestic FAX) Per-minute surcharge for access Tymnet $20.00 per year per graphic for signature or letterhead for use with hardcopy delivery Delivery receipt (E-mail only): $.25 per message

Table 9.1 (cont.)

Service	Minimum Charges	Enhanced Service
		"Mail Alert" voice-phone notification of E-mail waiting: $1.00 per message
		Dow Jones News/Retrieval Service: Surcharged at normal DJNS rates

Table 9.2 E-Mail Service Per-Message Charges

Service and E-mail Rates	FAX Rates	Telex Rates	Hardcopy Rates
AT&T Mail+ User-to-user E-mail: Notes (400 or fewer characters): $.20 to create Messages (401 characters or more): $.45 to create and $.80 per recipient $.80 for each additional 7500 characters or less	Send FAX: $.55 for the first half page (1500 characters) and $.40 for each additional half page Receive FAX: N/A	Send Telex: $.95 per "Telex minute" (approximately 400 characters) Receive Telex: N/A	U.S. Mail: $.20 per recipient for the first 7500 characters or less Overnight: $7.50 per recipient for the first 7500 characters or less Urgent (same day courier delivery): $27.50 per recipient for the first 7500 characters or less $.80 for each additional 7500 characters or less
MCI Mail User-to-user E-mail: Up to 500 characters: $.45 501 to 2500 characters: $.75 2501 to 7500 characters: $1.00 Each additional 7500 characters: $1.00	Send FAX: $.50 for the first half page and $.30 for each additional half page (a half page is 28 lines of no more than 80 characters per line) Receive FAX N/A	Send Telex: $.55 for each "Telex minute" to MCI, and $.75 for each "Telex minute" to other carriers Receive Telex N/C	U.S. Mail: $2.00 (up to three pages; $1.00 for each additional three pages or fraction thereof) Overnight letter: $6.00 (up to six pages; $1.00 for each additional three pages or fraction thereof)

Table 9.2 (cont.)

Service and E-mail Rates	FAX Rates	Telex Rates	Hardcopy Rates
DASnet User-to-user E-mail: limited to public conferences, N/C Rates for relaying mail between systems vary, depending on the system	Send FAX: Per MCI Mail FAX rates	Telex: Monthly Telex mail box rate per Table 9.1	(Per MCI Mail rates)

FAX and Telex rates quoted are for U.S. delivery only. Rates to other countries are higher and vary by country.

10 | General Online Services

About This Chapter

Just as Chapter 9 gave you an idea of the capabilities of the major E-mail specialty services, this chapter will show you what several of the more popular general online services have to offer in the way of E-mail services. Specifically, you'll learn about CompuServe, DELPHI, and GEnie.

Note that, while the services covered in this chapter aren't the only commercial online services available to dial-up modem users, they are among the largest and most popular and are generally representative of how online services operate and what they have to offer. These services were selected for inclusion here based on the following criteria:

- Availability of FAX delivery of E-mail messages
- Availability of hardcopy and/or Telex delivery of E-mail messages
- Accessibility
- Range of services offered
- Cost effectiveness

CompuServe

CompuServe is among the world's largest public online services. It is also one of the first commercial online services to cater to computer hobbyists. Established in 1979, CompuServe today has more than 300,000 subscribers.

In addition to its public services, CompuServe provides communications, database, and private network services for a variety of businesses and government agencies.

> **Note:** The large number of CompuServe subscribers, combined with its link to MCI Mail, make it a logical choice for heavy E-mail users who want to stick with one service. The chances are good that anyone with whom you might want to exchange E-mail is already a CompuServe or an MCI Mail subscriber.

Service Overview and Features

As with any other online service, providing a detailed listing of CompuServe's offerings here would be impossible. A complete survey of CompuServe would fill a book (and, indeed, several have been written). However, I'll provide at least an overview of CompuServe's plethora of services, focusing on electronic communications.

We'll begin at the beginning, with CompuServe's main menu, called the TOP menu (Figure 10.1).

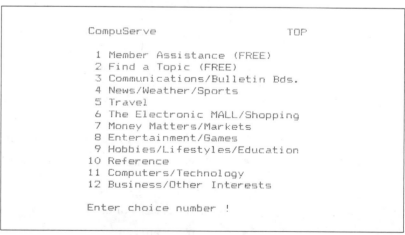

```
CompuServe                          TOP

    1  Member Assistance (FREE)
    2  Find a Topic (FREE)
    3  Communications/Bulletin Bds.
    4  News/Weather/Sports
    5  Travel
    6  The Electronic MALL/Shopping
    7  Money Matters/Markets
    8  Entertainment/Games
    9  Hobbies/Lifestyles/Education
   10  Reference
   11  Computers/Technology
   12  Business/Other Interests

   Enter choice number !
```

Figure 10.1 CompuServe's TOP menu.

CompuServe's TOP menu is like the tip of an iceberg. While it shows us in general what is there, there is much, much more than the TOP menu even implies. Literally hundreds of services exist on CompuServe—among them some extremely useful electronics communications. Beyond this menu lie general and specialized news and information services; special-interest groups for computerists, professionals, hobbyists, and others (called Forums on CompuServe); online games and other entertainment; sophisticated research services; a free online tutorial; and much, much more.

CompuServe is particularly strong in online research facilities, which include Grolier's Academic American Encyclopedia and gateways to Dow Jones News/Retrieval Service and several specialized services—including IQUEST, a collection of more than 700 specialized research databases.

For more information on the specific services CompuServe offers, contact CompuServe via one of the telephone numbers in Appendix A.

Now, let's take a closer look at CompuServe's E-mail service, EasyPlex.

EasyPlex E-Mail

Selection 3 ("Communications/Bulletin Bds.") leads to all sorts of communications services, including CompuServe's CB Simulator (realtime conference), a complete listing of CompuServe Forums (SIGs), the Access public file area, and CompuServe's EasyPlex Electronic Mail service.

Our main area of interest here is, of course, CompuServe's EasyPlex mail service. As you can see by looking at the EasyPlex menu in Figure 10.2, EasyPlex is a menu-driven service that requires no knowledge of commands to use. You can use direct commands if you wish, however.

```
EasyPlex   Main Menu

   *** No mail waiting ***

2 COMPOSE a new message
3 UPLOAD a message
4 USE a file from PER area

5 ADDRESS Book
6 SET options

9 Send a CONGRESSgram ($)
Enter choice !
```

Figure 10.2 CompuServe's EasyPlex menu.

Simply select the item on the menu that corresponds to what you want to do, and prompts will guide you through the necessary steps.

For example, if you select Item 2, "COMPOSE a new message", you will be asked to enter your message.

After you have terminated message entry (by typing /EXIT at the beginning of a line), you will be prompted to enter an address and a subject header. At this point, you can enter the online ID of the recipient or an MCI Mail ID, FAX telephone number, or Telex number. Each of these delivery options—MCI Mail, FAX, and Telex—must be preceded by a delivery specifier on the address line.

> **Note:** CompuServe provides a unique gateway service that enables you to send messages to and receive messages from MCI Mail users. You have to know the MCI ID of the addressee. The gateway doesn't give you direct access to MCI Mail services; it only transfers mail. Telex service is available via a similar setup.

After you terminate message entry, the menu shown in Figure 10.3 will present you the options of sending, editing, reviewing, filing a copy of, or requesting a return receipt of your message.

```
            EasyPlex   Send Menu

            For current message

              1 SEND
              2 EDIT
              3 TYPE
              4 FILE DRAFT copy
              5 SEND with /RECEIPT   ($)


            Enter choice !
```

Figure 10.3 CompuServe's EasyPlex Send menu.

E-Mail Enhancements Selection 3 on the EasyPlex menu, "UPLOAD a message", initiates a process whereby you can upload a message or other document using your choice of Xmodem, ASCII, or other protocols. Selection 4 lets you send a file that you've previously uploaded to your personal online file-storage area. Selection 5 involves the maintenance of a distribution list. Selection 6 leads to a menu that allows you to set any of several options that determine how you use EasyPlex, including whether the EasyPlex menu is displayed. Selection 9 opens input for a message to be sent to the U.S. Congress.

Other EasyPlex enhancements include multiple addressing via a carbon copy option and message forwarding. You can also transfer binary files (up to 8K in size) directly to another user with EasyPlex.

Using CompuServe

Navigating CompuServe

You've already seen how you can navigate CompuServe using menus. But this isn't the only way to get around. You can also move directly to a specific service's menu—or to a database section of that service—using the GO command with specific words or page numbers that identify a service.

CompuServe is set up so that each menu, prompt, or screen display has two unique identifiers. The main menus of specific services are referred to by mnemonic names, called quick reference words, such as EASYPLEX and TRAVEL. Thus, to access the EasyPlex or Travel menu, you would type **GO EASYPLEX** or **GO TRAVEL**, respectively.

To move to a specific selection within a service, you would use a page number with GO. A page identifies a specific page (screen display) service name and page number, as in **GO HOM10**. The database name by itself identifies the first page of a database (e.g., GO HOM is the same as GO HOM1). Once you're in the area, you can go to another page in the current service by using the page number alone with GO.

Other commands enable you to move to previous selections or to the TOP menu, and perform other functions. See Table 10.1 for a summary of CompuServe's major commands.

Table 10.1 CompuServe Command Summary

Systemwide Commands

Systemwide Commands Operate at any Prompt or Menu

ENTER	Implement a menu selection or typed command.
BYE or OFF	Sign off and disconnect.
FIND <keyword>	Find and/or access all services that are related to the keyword used.
GO<mnemonic> or <page nnn>	Move to the indicated menu or display page number.
HELP or ?	View context-sensitive or general help.
M	Move to the menu immediately preceding the current menu.
TOP	Move to CompuServe's TOP menu.

Control-Key Commands

^C	Abort the current activity and operation or program (text display, etc.).

Table 10.1 (cont.)

Control-Key Commands

^O	Abort the display of text without aborting the current operation or program.
^Q	Resume text display after pausing with ^S.
^S	Pause text or menu display.
^U	Erase a line you are currently typing (can only be used before you press ENTER).

Finding What's Where

You may have noticed that some services are available via more than one menu. This is one of the more convenient features of CompuServe for those who like to navigate with menus. Rather than restrict a service to one menu, CompuServe gives you access to each service via whatever menus contain related services. This way you don't miss a thing. However, this can be confusing, as CompuServe's menus are numerous and complex.

Fortunately, CompuServe makes it easy to find what you're looking for. The Find a Topic selection on the TOP menu leads to an online index you can use to locate a service by keyword or by scanning a list. The keyword search feature is also accessible from almost any prompt on the system; just type **FIND**, with or without a keyword. If services related to the keyword you type (e.g., BUSINESS or FISH) exist, you'll be presented with a custom temporary menu from which you can select the service of your choice.

Getting Help

CompuServe offers more than a little online help, in the form of Q&A areas, references on specific topics, and other features—like a context-sensitive help system (accessible by typing **HELP**). You'll also find the Sysops who manage CompuServe's Forums to be especially helpful.

CompuServe customer service can be contacted via voice WATS phone outside Ohio (direct-dial inside Ohio) or by E-mail or special Feedback areas.

Access

CompuServe can be accessed via Telenet, Tymnet, DataPac (from Canada only), ConnNet (from Connecticut only), and its own national packet-switching network.

DELPHI

DELPHI is operated by General Videotex Corporation (GVC). Established in 1982 as an online encyclopedia (the first of its kind), DELPHI has evolved into a full-service network, providing products and services of all types.

In addition to its public consumer and business services, DELPHI provides private network services for businesses and smaller, special-interest networks.

An especially friendly system with a real sense of community, DELPHI is a good place to meet others who share your interests, in computing and other areas.

As is the case with CompuServe, DELPHI offers enough features to fill a book, which, also like CompuServe, it has. If you intend to become a DELPHI member, I highly (and modestly) recommend that you buy a copy of *DELPHI: The Official Guide* by Michael A. Banks (published by Brady Books).

If you join DELPHI, this section can serve as a helpful quick reference.

Service Overview and Features

We'll start with DELPHI's MAIN Menu (Figure 10.4), which will give you an idea of the extent of DELPHI's products and services.

```
MAIN>

MAIN Menu:

Business & Finance      News-Weather-Sports
Conference              People on DELPHI
DELPHI/Regional         Travel
Entertainment           Workspace
Groups and Clubs        Using DELPHI
Library                 HELP
Mail                    EXIT
Merchants' Row

MAIN>What do you want to do?
```

Figure 10.4 DELPHI's MAIN Menu.

As I said of CompuServe's TOP menu, DELPHI's MAIN menu is like the tip of an iceberg. It shows what's available only in a general sense. Like CompuServe, DELPHI sports a variety of general and topical news and information services, online entertainment and games, special-interest groups, two online encyclopedias (Grolier's and the original Kussmaul Encyclopedia), a unique gateway to the Dialog information service, and more. DELPHI's special-interest groups are particularly noteworthy, both for the BBS-style communication facilities they provide and for the information available for downloads. Also of note on DELPHI are weekly online realtime "poker" and trivia tournaments.

> **Note:** DELPHI's gateways to Dialog and EasyPlex, combined with a variety of other online reference sources, make DELPHI an especially useful research tool.

For more information on the specific services DELPHI offers, contact DELPHI via one of the telephone numbers in Appendix A.

And now, let's take a closer look at DELPHI's Mail menu and the E-mail services it offers.

The DELPHI Mail Menu

The Mail selection on DELPHI's MAIN Menu leads to the DELPHI Mail menu, which offers several special communications services.

The FAX selection leads to a FAX service that you can use to send a message entered online (or one previously uploaded) to a dedicated FAX machine. (This selection was used as an example at the end of Chapter 8.) In addition to creating a file online or sending a previously uploaded file, you can review and edit an uploaded file before you send it and get a confirmation of delivery of the FAX message.

The Mail (Electronic) selection leads to DELPHI's command-based E-mail system, an extremely powerful and full-featured service.

The Telex selection initiates a process whereby you can send a Telex message to any Telex machine in the world. (The process is similar to that of sending a FAX message.) You can also receive Telex messages via DELPHI's Telex link (Telex messages are delivered as E-mail messages).

The Easylink selection is a gateway to Easylink, Western Union's Telex, E-mail, and information service.

Translation Services provides translation of documents from English into any of several languages.

Other selections include mail utilities and access to a personal online file area.

The DELPHI Mail menu can be accessed by direct command from within DELPHI's special-interest groups.

E-Mail Enhancements In addition to allowing you to send and receive E-mail messages DELPHI's E-mail system (the Mail selection on the DELPHI Mail menu) offers multiple addressing and distribution lists, message forwarding, and direct ASCII upload and download. You can also search incoming or stored messages for specific text.

A multifaceted filing system lets you move or copy messages among folders and files and retrieve deleted messages.

DELPHI's E-mail system interfaces with Workspace, the personal online file storage area, in several ways. You can send files previously uploaded to Workspace to other users. You can also copy a message to a new or existing file in Workspace, for later review, editing, or download via any of several binary file-transfer protocols. You can also reply to a message with a file from your Workspace area.

DELPHI's E-mail system can be customized in a number of ways. Your name, title, or any phrase can be entered following your membername in a message header's From: field. The system can be set up to send automatic carbon copies, and you can even have all your mail forwarded to another DELPHI member if you aren't going to be online for a while.

DELPHI's E-mail system is accessible from the DELPHI Mail menu, from any realtime conference area, and from other areas online, including SIGs. Special features enable sending copies of online bulletin board messages to other members and sending one-line E-mail messages from within a realtime conference. You can also reply to a bulletin board message or to a database posting via E-mail.

> **Note:** DELPHI's powerful message-handling features and links among its online file-storage area, E-mail, and FAX make for a flexible and extremely powerful message management system.

Using DELPHI

Commands

Overall, DELPHI's commands are fairly simple and straightforward, as illustrated in Table 10.2.

Table 10.2 DELPHI Command Summary

Systemwide Commands

Systemwide Commands Operate at Any Prompt or Menu

ENTER	Implement a menu selection or typed command.
BYE	Sign off and disconnect.
EXIT	Exit a menu or service and move to the immediately preceding menu or prompt.
GO <menu name>	Move to the indicated menu.
HELP or ?	View context-sensitive or general help.

Table 10.2 (cont.)

Systemwide Commands	
MENU	Display or redisplay the current menu.
Control-Key Commands	
^C	Abort or cancel the current activity or operation.
^O	Abort a text display.
^Q	Resume text display after pausing with ^S.
^S	Pause text or menu display.
^U or ^X	Erase a line you are currently typing (can only be used before you press ENTER).

Navigation

DELPHI is obviously navigable by menus, but you can also chain commands and selections in logical order (i.e., the order in which you would enter them if you were typing them individually) to move directly from a menu to any selection on that menu—and to ensuing selections. For instance, if you were at the DELPHI MAIN menu and wanted to enter the Science Fiction SIG, you might type GROUPS to get to the Groups and Clubs menu, and then SCIENCE to enter the Science Fiction SIG. With chained commands, all you would have to type would be GROUPS SCIENCE (or, in abbreviated form, GR SC). If you wished to go to the Science Fiction SIG's General database, you could take a shortcut by chaining the database access command/selection with the SIG access command, like this: GROUPS SCIENCE DATABASE GENERAL.

A GO command is also available to move directly to any menu on the service. When used with chained selection commands, it operates as if you had typed the chained commands from DELPHI's MAIN menu. You could, for example type GO GR SC DA GEN at the DELPHI Mail and move directly to the aforementioned database prompt.

Finding What's Where

DELPHI is not quite as complex as CompuServe; therefore, you can find what you want fairly easily by selecting the obvious items on menus. The Using DELPHI selection on the DELPHI MAIN menu, however, does offer an indexed listing of DELPHI services. The index is not keyword-searchable like CompuServe's. The Using DELPHI area also offers an online tutorial.

Getting Help

Like most other services, DELPHI provides an online, context-sensitive help system that you can access for information on a current activity or for information on any other aspect of DELPHI. Special help files are available in SIG databases; you'll see brief articles on using DELPHI if you type **HELP** at a SIG main menu. DELPHI SIG managers and other members are especially helpful, too.

DELPHI customer service is available via voice WATS line and E-mail.

Access

DELPHI can be accessed via Telenet, Tymnet, DataPac (from Canada only), or its direct-dial numbers in Boston. Regional versions of DELPHI in Boston, Kansas City, Miami, and Buenos Aires offer gateways to the national DELPHI service.

GEnie

GEnie (General Electric Network for Information Exchange) is a consumer network operated by General Electric Information Services. GEnie offers services for home and business microcomputer users, professionals, and computer hobbyists.

Established in 1985, GEnie is the fastest-growing service of its kind. It enjoys a tremendous growth rate, thanks to its services, an aggressive advertising campaign, and a friendly price structure.

Service Overview and Features

GEnie's TOP menu (Figure 10.5) provides an overview of service categories.

```
   GEnie                TOP              Page   1
            GE Information Services

      1. GEnie Users' RT   2. Index - Info
      3. Billing/Setup     4. GE Mail & Chat
      5. Computing         6. Travel
      7. Finance           8. Shopping
      9. News             10. Games
     11. Professional     12. Leisure
     13. Reference        14. Logoff

     Enter #, or <H>elp?
```

Figure 10.5 GEnie's TOP menu.

GEnie offers the same categories of services as CompuServe and DELPHI. News, weather, sports, and travel information are particularly strong areas for GEnie, as are GEnie's versions of special-interest groups, called RoundTables. Online research facilities include Grolier's Academic Encyclopedia and a gateway to Dow Jones News/Retrieval Service. GEnie's news offerings include searchable headline news and columns by a number of well-known writers in the computer field.

E-Mail

GE Mail is GEnie's E-mail service, which you can use to send and receive letters from other GEnie users and to send paper mail.

GEnie's E-mail is a straightforward user-to-user E-mail system with some extras. In addition to multiple addresses and mailing lists, carbon copies, message forwarding, editing, and replying, GE Mail offers a separate mail utility section that provides search capability of a sort, along with other tools. You can also send paper mail using GE Mail's Quik-Gram service.

Because GEnie has no personal file system as such, you must upload messages to be sent using a special utility (listed on the GE MAIL menu in Figure 10.6).

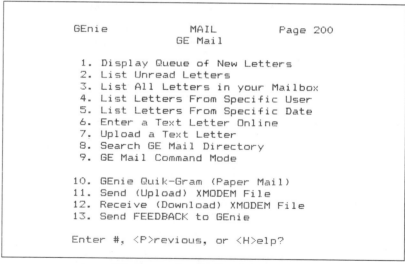

```
GEnie               MAIL            Page 200
                    GE Mail

        1. Display Queue of New Letters
        2. List Unread Letters
        3. List All Letters in your Mailbox
        4. List Letters From Specific User
        5. List Letters From Specific Date
        6. Enter a Text Letter Online
        7. Upload a Text Letter
        8. Search GE Mail Directory
        9. GE Mail Command Mode

       10. GEnie Quik-Gram (Paper Mail)
       11. Send (Upload) XMODEM File
       12. Receive (Download) XMODEM File
       13. Send FEEDBACK to GEnie

    Enter #, <P>revious, or <H>elp?
```

Figure 10.6 GEnie MAIL menu.

A unique GE Mail command enables you to cancel a message that you've already sent, removing it from the recipient's online mailbox. You can use GE Mail to send a binary file to another user, too. (Uploads and downloads are via Xmodem.) Simply select the appropriate option on the GE MAIL menu and follow the prompts. The addressee will receive the file with notification that it is an Xmodem file, after which it can be downloaded.

GEnie's mail address file is located here, too. It features a flexible search system that you can use to find both GE Mail addresses and the names of people online.

> **Note:** If E-mail cost is an issue but you still need access to a full-service online service, consider subscriptions to GEnie for yourself and for those with whom you need to exchange E-mail. GEnie's per-minute rates are among the lowest offered by any online service.

Other Delivery Options In addition to electronic and paper mail, you can send FAX and Telex messages. Telex is two-way messaging. GEnie offers a unique feature in an option by which GEnie users may have their own Telex numbers, at an extra fee. Other online services offer incoming Telex service via one Telex number, identifying the user to whom a Telex message is to be sent by the inclusion of the user's online ID in the first line of a message.

Using GEnie

Navigating GEnie

Each GEnie menu and screen has a unique page number assigned to it (somewhat similar to CompuServe's system). In addition, main menus for services have mnemonics attached to them. Both pages and mnemonics can be used to move around GEnie. Mnemonics can also be used in conjunction with certain special commands.

You can navigate GEnie in three ways:

1. Select items at menus.

2. Use the Move command in conjunction with a GEnie page number to move to *any* menu or prompt in a service. Move commands can be issued at almost any prompt. (For example, to move to the GE Mail menu, you would type **MOVE 200**.)

3. Use mnemonic commands to get to a service's main menu or prompt (e.g., **MAIL** for the GE Mail menu).

Commands GEnie offers several basic commands that can be used at almost any prompt. These are listed in Table 10.3.

Table 10.3 GEnie Command Summary

Systemwide Commands

Systemwide Commands Operate at Any Prompt or Menu

ENTER	Implement a menu selection or typed command.
BYE	Sign off and disconnect.
HELP	View context-sensitive help.
INDEX	Access Genie's online index, for lists of system navigation mnemonics or keyword search for specific services.
LOCATE \<ID\>	Find out if user xxxx is online, and where.
M \<nnn\>	Move to the menu or prompt at the indicated GEnie page number.
NOT \<ID\>	Send an online message to the indicated user.
P	Move to the menu immediately preceding the current menu.
READ	Enter mail system and read waiting mail from any menu prompt.
SEND	Enter mail systems and send mail from any menu prompt.
T	Move to GEnie's TOP menu.
US	See a list of users online in the current area; or use with a system mnemonic to display a list of users in the indicated area; or use with ALL to see a list of all users currently online.

Control-Key Commands

^C	Abort the current activity and operation or program (text display, etc.). This is the default BREAK key.
^Q	Resume text display after pausing with ^S.
^S	Pause text or menu display.

Finding What's Where

Like CompuServe, GEnie offers a comprehensive index of services. Type INDEX at any prompt, and you will be presented with a menu offering options such as lists of services organized in different ways and a keyword-searchable index. Select the searchable index, enter a keyword, and GEnie will create a custom menu of services related to that keyword. Select a service from the menu, and GEnie will display a description of the service and ask if you want to move to that service.

Getting Help

Typing **H** at most GEnie prompts displays a list of basic commands. Some prompts feature context-sensitive help, accessed by typing **H** or **HELP**. An online manual is available at the GEnie Help & Information menu, along with a number of other informational aids.

GEnie also provides an online manual, and GEnie customer service is available via a voice WATS line.

Access

GEnie offers 300, 1200, and 2400 baud access, via its own national network of direct-dial, local numbers in several hundred U.S. cities.

> **Note:** GEnie differs from the vast majority of online services in that it expects your computer to operate at half duplex and, thus, does not echo what you input. This can be changed once you're online, but be sure to set your software or modem to half duplex operation the first time you dial up GEnie.)

What Does It Cost?

The cost of using a general online service to send or receive E-mail, FAX, Telex, and hardcopy messages includes the online service's basic per-minute rate plus any additional charges for delivery options (including confirmation of delivery, and sending FAX, Telex, and hardcopy messages).

Restrict your use of online services to evening and weekend hours to reduce your total cost.

Unlike E-mail specialty services, online services charge a per-minute rate for every minute you are online. The charge is higher during what are known as prime time hours—between 7 A.M. and 6 P.M., weekdays, for almost all services. The per-minute charge during non-prime time (also known as off-peak or evening hours) can be as much as 70% less than prime-time charges. Note that non-prime time also includes all day on weekends and most national holidays.

In general, there is no charge for *reading* messages, whatever their source, beyond the online service's per-minute charges. There is typically no extra charge for sending E-mail messages to other users on the same service, either. However, as already noted, surcharged services include special delivery options and charges for sending FAX, Telex, and hardcopy messages. Surcharges are based on message length and on any special options (e.g., overnight delivery rather than U.S. Mail delivery for hardcopy messages).

Other variables that affect cost include:

- The specific online service you're using

- How you access the service in question

- Service options or enhancements

Tables 10.4 and 10.5 provide a basis for comparing the costs of using the three services examined in this chapter, based on their current prices. (As with the costs quoted for the E-mail specialty services in Chapter 9, please keep in mind that these prices are subject to change.) Tables 10.4 and 10.5 show per-minute access rates and message surcharges, respectively.

Table 10.4 Online Service Connect Charges

Service	Time Period	Prime Time	Non-Prime Time
CompuServe[1]	300 bps	$ 6.00 per hour	$ 6.00 per hour
	1200 bps	$12.50 per hour	$12.50 per hour
DELPHI[2]	(all speeds)		
	Network access	$17.40 per hour	$ 7.20 per hour
	Direct-dial	$ 9.60 per hour	$ 6.20 per hour
	Advantage plan[3]	$ 8.40 per hour	$ 4.80 per hour
GEnie[4]	300 bps	$18.00 per hour	$ 5.00 per hour
	1200 bps	$18.00 per hour	$ 6.00 per hour
	2400 bps	$18.00 per hour	$10.00 per hour

There may be extra charges for enhanced services (like CompuServe's "Executive Option"), and for specific services.

[1]Billed in 1-minute increments. Does not include CompuServe Network surcharge of 30 cents per hour. Telenet, Tymnet, or other network access, carries an extra per-minute surcharge, as does overseas access.
[2]Billed in 1-minute increments. Access from Canada, Alaska, and most other countries and U.S. possessions higher.
[3]Requires four-hour minimum monthly billing.
[4]Bill in 1-second increments. Prices for Alaska, Hawaii, and Puerto Rico. Some cities may carry network surcharges.

Table 10.5 Online Service Message Surcharges

Message Type	FAX	Telex	Hardcopy
CompuServe User-to-user E-Mail: N/C Mailthru to MCI Mail: Variable surcharge based on message size Mailthru to InterNet and Infoplex: N/C Surcharges for delivery receipt and for multiple addressees	Send FAX: $.75/first 1000 characters, and $.25/ additional 1000 characters Receive FAX: N/A	Send Telex: $1.15 per 300 characters or portion thereof Receive Telex:N/C	"CONGRESSgram" only: $1.00 per message (sent via U.S. Mail)
DELPHI User-to-user E-mail: N/C Mailthru to EasyPlex carries a surcharge of $.85 per 200 characters or portion thereof	Send FAX: $1.25 first page and $.50 for each additional half page (a page is 2500 characters; a half page is 1250 characters) Receive FAX: N/A	Send Telex: $.85 per 200 characters or portion thereof Receive Telex: N/A Private Telex Mailbox: $15.00 per month	N/A
GENie+ User-to-user E-mail: N/C	Send FAX: Not yet set Receive FAX: N/A	Send Telex: Not yet set Receive Telex: N/C Private Telex Mailbox: Monthly fee	$2.00/first page (40 lines) $.75/for each additional page (50 lines) Five-page limit

FAX and Telex rates quoted are for U.S. delivery only. Rates to other countries are higher, and vary by country.

11 | Choosing the Service That's Right for You

About This Chapter

This chapter will help you decide which online service(s) can best meet your electronic communications needs. While it is not unusual to use more than one online service, you should sign up for one service initially and use that one for a month or so, or until you have a good feel for and understanding of using an online service, before trying another online service.

The advice in this chapter is geared toward helping you select services on an individual basis—with the basic criterion being how an online service meets *your* needs. We'll cover these considerations:

- Your online service needs, interests, and applications
- The cost of using online services
- Online service accessibility
- Ease of use

Defining Needs and Applications

The first step in determining your online service needs is to decide exactly what you will be doing online. Consider your communications needs first; these may well dictate a specific service or services to use.

E-Mail Applications

If you will be sending primarily E-mail, you will have to use the service(s) used by your E-mail correspondents—or use a service that is connected with or relays E-mail between the other service(s) and the service you prefer to use.

If E-mail is your main concern, ask yourself these questions in evaluating a specific online service:

- Are the people with whom I need to exchange E-mail using, or likely to use, online service x?

- What other services is online service x linked with? Are people with whom I need to exchange messages using those services?

Note: Links and gateways between services, as well as message relay services, may make it possible for you to do everything you need to do via one online service. Bear in mind, however, that using links, gateways, and message relay adds to the cost of using an online service.

E-Mail Features, Options, and Enhancements

If E-mail is a primary application for you, you'll want to consider the enhancements an online service provides for its E-mail service. These were described in detail in Chapters 5, 6, 9, and 10, but here is a list of what most E-mail users find to be the more important E-mail features and options:

- Message upload and download capability (ASCII and/or binary file-transfer protocols)

- Incoming message-filing systems

- Online file storage

- Multiple-recipient or carbon-copy capability

- Distribution lists

- Message review and editing prior to sending

- User-to-user binary file transfer capability

Other Electronic Communications Applications and Alternate Delivery Options

If E-mail is not your primary modem communications application (or even if it is), the kinds of electronic delivery services and options you will need to use will be major criteria for selecting a service. In evaluating your online communications needs, ask yourself these questions:

- Will I need to send FAX?

- Will I need to receive FAX?

- Will I be sending FAX to Group 3 machines only?

- Will I be sending long or short FAX documents?

- Will I need to send Telex messages?

- Will I need to receive Telex messages?

- Is hardcopy delivery important?

- Will I use overnight or 4-hour hardcopy delivery?

Think these through carefully, taking into consideration possible future communications needs, as well. The questions to which you answer "Yes" will define your requirements for an online service's communications services.

Other Applications for Online Services

After you define your communications needs, you will probably find that more than one service qualifies. You can narrow your choices by thinking about what other applications you will have online. Decide which of these services you are likely to need or find interesting:

- Business news

- General news and sports information

- Financial information

- Weather information

- Travel info and reservations

- General research and reference sources

- Specialized research and reference sources

- Contact with professional, hobby, or personal special-interest groups

- Online file-storage and editing capability

- Realtime conferencing

- Online entertainment

Remember that some of these services (e.g., news and information services) are available via gateways that some online services provide to other services (e.g., DELPHI's gateway to the Dialog Information Service).

If none of these services are important or of interest to you, your online service needs can be met by an E-mail specialty service (provided, of course, the system in question is used by your E-mail correspondents and/or has E-mail links or relay capability to other online services). If you have only occasional need for, say, news and information services, you might consider an E-mail specialty service that offers a gateway to such a service (e.g., MCI Mail's gateway to Dow Jones News/Retrieval Service). If several of these services are important to you but you still need E-mail service with or without various delivery options, consider a full-service online service that offers a gateway to an E-mail specialty service (e.g., CompuServe, with its link to MCI Mail).

Cost

Although most of us would rather not have to think about it, the cost of using an online service is an important issue, whether our online applications are business or personal in nature.

Sample costs for using E-mail specialty services and general online services were provided at the ends of Chapters 9 and 10, respectively. Although some specific costs may change, in general the *ratio* of costs of one service to another are likely to remain the same, so you can use those cost charts as the basis for comparison, anyway.

Here are some basic rules that may help you decide between an E-mail specialty service and a general online service:

- E-mail specialty services generally charge by the number and length of messages sent, with extra charges for special delivery options (FAX, Telex, and hardcopy). There is no charge for reading messages. If, however, the standard means of accessing an E-mail service is not available, you may be subject to per-minute surcharges for using a packet-switching network.

- Online services charge a per-minute rate for all services. They do not charge you for reading or sending E-mail to users on the same system, but there are message-size and/or per-minute surcharges for sending E-mail to other systems (if such links are available). There are also surcharges for special delivery options.

Actually, comparing the costs of online services is a good way to narrow your choices. If service A and service B, in general, meet your requirements, you'll probably be better off selecting the less costly of the two. You may sacrifice one or two E-mail enhancements by selecting the lower-cost service, but, on reflection, you may realize that you don't need those enhancements in any event.

Costs are also useful in helping you determine just how useful a specific service or option will be. You may, for instance, decide that, all other things being equal, access to certain noncommunication services on a general online service doesn't justify the per-minute rates you have to pay and that an E-mail specialty service is good enough for your needs.

> **Note:** Some online services have hidden costs that are not imme-
> diately obvious (e.g., minimum monthly charges despite whether
> you use a service and surcharges for certain kinds of access). Look
> for such costs when you sign up for an online service, so you
> won't be surprised by your online service billing.

In comparing costs, be sure to look at the details—including extra costs, called surcharges, levied for the use of certain features. These price factors can cost or save you money:

- The cost of enhanced service or access (including custom menus or prompts and extra-feature access)

- The size of a message page (E-mail on E-mail specialty services and on all services where sending FAX, Telex, or E-mail relay messages are concerned) versus the cost per page

- The cost for the first message page *and* the cost for ensuing message pages

- Monthly minimum charges

- Per-session surcharges

- Surcharges for higher-speed access (1200 and/or 2400 bps)

- Surcharges for network access

- Surcharges for access to gateways to other online services

- Discounts for volume usage (either number of messages sent or amount of time spent online)

Accessibility

The accessibility of an online service is important. There are, for instance, areas in the United States where no public packet-switching networks maintain local dial-up numbers (nodes). This means that, unless the service in question operates a private packet-switching network with a node in your area, you may have to make a long-distance telephone call to a nearby city to reach a packet-switching number.

Or an online service that offers local dial-up numbers via its private packet-switching network may not have a number in your area—in which case you'll have to use a public packet-switching network at an extra cost. In extreme cases, you may live in an area where there are no public or private packet-switching network nodes, which means you'll have to pay for that long-distance call.

Too, adding an extra link in the telecommunications chain between you and the packet-switching network or the service itself may erode or eliminate the error-checking capability of some online services.

Make sure the online service you wish to use is accessible via a local number in your area, either via a public or private packet-switching network, or look for a service that offers toll-free WATS service. If none of these options is available (e.g., you need to use DELPHI because the individuals with whom you need to exchange E-mail use DELPHI, and there are no Telenet or Tymnet nodes in your area), you will have to live with the extra long-distance charges.

Note: If you must dial long-distance to access a packet-switching network node, compare the costs of calling all the nodes within several hundred miles. It may be less costly to call a node in another state than to call a node within your state.

Note: Instead of using a long-distance packet-switching network to dial an online service, consider dialing the online service's direct-dial number. This will be a local number in the city in which the online service is located. The cost may be more, but you may spend less time online, since transmission speed is faster via a service's own direct-dial number.

Ease of Use

How easy an online service is to use is important for more reasons than just avoiding headaches. The easier an online service is to use, the less likely you are to make mistakes, and the less time you'll spend online. Both of these benefits can save you money. Most modem users consider an online service to be a tool, and this is as it should be. Using an online service should be a means to an end rather than an end in itself. The snazzy features and options offered by an online service are useless if the service is so user belligerent that you can't access those features.

When evaluating an online service for ease of use, look for these features:

- Menus. These are valuable for learning the system and for making a system easier to use if you're not online for a while. You should be able to turn the display of menus off, of course, once you're proficient in using the system.

- Optional Menu Selection or Command Entry. Being able to use your choice of menus or commands is important. Entering commands can speed up your use of the system, while selecting menu items can enable you to use a system without having to learn a lot about it. The option should be available on most systems.

- Alternate Means of Navigation (General Online Services). A well-structured online service offers a choice of moving from one service to another. You'll find that, when multiple navigation systems are available, you will be a more efficient user. An online index of services that helps you locate what you need quickly is a plus, too.

- Online Help Systems. Online help is an invaluable aid to learning to use a system and to facilitating efficient access of services or features you don't use frequently enough to have memorized their structure and commands. At the very least, an online service should have a *topic-based help system*—a system that displays a list of topics with which you can get help and which provides that help. The better services offer context-sensitive help, which displays information about the service or operation you are currently using when you type **HELP**, in addition to topic-based help. Ideally, an online service will offer both kinds of help systems, as well as an online service index *and* an online tutorial/tour.

- Customer Service. The availability of real people (customer service representatives) to help you with problems online is important because online help systems don't cover everything. At the very least, an online service should have a customer service section that will respond to your questions by E-mail. The norm, however, is to offer customer service by E-mail and by voice telephone. (Voice-telephone customer service for most online services is via a toll-free WATS number.)

- User Guide. Ideally, an online service will provide you with a comprehensive user guide when you sign up. The guide should be a part of your sign-up; you should not have to pay extra for it. There are very few services that don't provide such guides.

What You've Learned

- The major criterion in selecting which online service(s) you use is what you will use the online service(s) for.

- When defining your applications, you should examine your communications applications first.

- The most important consideration regarding E-mail applications is whether those with whom you need to exchange E-mail are available via the online service(s) you intend to use.

- Accessibility of other services via E-mail links or message relay services can make the difference in whether an online service will meet your needs.

- If E-mail is an important application for you, the enhancements an online service provides for its E-mail system will be a determining factor in whether you use that service.

- When evaluating message delivery options other than E-mail (i.e., FAX, Telex, and hardcopy message/document delivery), you should take into consideration not only your current needs but also potential future needs.

- You should consider noncommunication services offered by online services carefully when deciding whether to use a general online service. If you really don't have a need for or an interest in online news, research, entertainment, and other services, an E-mail specialty service will probably be best for your communications applications.

- Cost comparison of online services is a good way to determine whether you really need or have enough interest in the noncommunication services offered by an online service to use that service.

- You should compare *all* charges and surcharges of the online services you are considering using before making a decision. These costs include hidden costs such as network and modem-speed surcharges, restrictions on message size, and session and monthly minimum charges.

- The accessibility of an online service is very important. If there is no local node for an online service in your area, you will have to spend money on long-distance charges to access a node, and you may lose the advantage of quality data transmission afforded by packet-switching networks.

- An online service should be as easy to use as possible. Features that contribute to ease of use include optional menus, optional direct command entry, multiple means of system navigation, on-line help systems, customer service, and a user guide or manual for the online service.

Now you're prepared to evaluate online services and their E-mail systems. Be sure to look for free or discount sign-up offers in magazine advertising and in communications software and modem packages. Such offers usually include an hour or two of free time online, enough time for you to test drive an online service and find out if it's for you.

Quiz

1. How many online services should you sign up for initially?

    a. 1
    b. 2
    c. 3
    d. 4

2. What is the most important criterion in selecting an online service?

    a. Your modem's maximum speed
    b. Your applications
    c. The online service's E-mail enhancements
    d. Cost

3. Which of your potential online applications should you evaluate first?

    a. Research
    b. Ability to make contacts with others who share your interests
    c. Online file storage
    d. Communications

4. E-mail specialty services generally charge how?

    a. By the minute
    b. By the number and length of messages sent
    c. By the hour
    d. By access speed

5. Extra charges levied by an online service for special delivery options, enhanced services or access, the use of gateways to other services, and the like are called what?

    a. Enhancements
    b. Per-minute charges
    c. Surcharges
    d. Billing errors

6. Some online services offer a discount for:

    a. Not signing on
    b. Higher modem speeds
    c. Volume usage
    d. Packet-switching network access

7. The accessibility of an online service is based primarily on what criterion?

    a. Hours of operation

    b. Services offered

    c. Availability of local packet-switching network nodes

    d. Links with or gateways to other online services

8. Not having a local node available for an online service means that you will have to spend extra money on long-distance charges to access the service and that you may lose what?

    a. Data transmission speed

    b. The benefit of error-checking afforded by some packet-switching networks

    c. Access to certain noncommunication services offered by the online service

    d. Volume-usage discounts

9. What feature contributes greatly to learning to use an online service?

    a. Menus

    b. Online help

    c. Customer service representatives

    d. All of the above

10. There are two kinds of online help systems. What are they called?

    a. Topic-based and user guides

    b. Online tutorials and topic-based systems

    c. Toll-free and context-sensitive systems

    d. Context-sensitive and topic-based systems

Part **3** | Reference

This section contains sources for more information (online service providers, equipment manufacturers, and books), as well as an informative glossary.

Appendix Online Service Contact Information

Use these voice numbers to obtain sign-up and other information about online services.

Online Service	Customer Service & Information Numbers	
AT&T Mail	800-624-5672	800-367-7225
BIX	800-227-2983	603-924-9281
CompuServe	800-848-8990	800-848-8199
	614-457-8650 (Ohio)	614-457-0802
DASnet	408-558-7434	
DELPHI	800-544-4005	617-491-3393
Dialog	800-334-2564	415-858-3810
Dow Jones News/Retrieval	609-452-1511	609-452-1511
EasyLink	800-527-5184	201-825-5000
GEnie	800-638-9636	800-638-9636
MCI Mail	800-424-6677	201-833-8484
TELEMAIL	800-835-3638	703-689-5700
UNISON	800-334-6122	513-731-2800

Appendix B | Bibliography

For a more comprehensive understanding of the technical aspects of electronics communications and computers in general, these books are recommended:

Banks, Michael A., *The Modem Reference* (Brady Books, New York), 1988

Cannon and Luecke, *Understanding Communications Systems* (Howard W. Sams & Co., Indianapolis)

Held, Gilbert, *Understanding Data Communications* (Howard W. Sams & Co., Indianapolis), 1989

Mims, Forrest M., III, *Understanding Digital Computers* (Radio Shack, Fort Worth), 1989

Waller, Mark, *PC Power Protection* (Howard W. Sams & Co., Indianapolis), 1989

C | Equipment Manufacturers and Vendors

For more specific information about what's available in dedicated FAX machines, PC FAX Boards, and modems, contact the manufacturers in this listing.

Dedicated FAX Machine Manufacturers and Vendors

AT&T
99 Jefferson Road
Parsippany, NJ 07054

Brother International
Corporation
8 Corporate Plce
Piscataway, NJ 08855

Canon U.S.A., Inc.
P.O. Box 3900
Peoria, IL 61614

Citifax
3667 Woodhead Drive
Northbrook, IL 60062

Citizen/CBM America
Corporation
2999 Overland Drive
Los Angeles, CA 90064

Fujitsu Imaging Systems
Commerce Park
Corporate Drive
Danbury, CT 06810

Gestetner Corporation
Gestetner Park
Yonkers, NY 10703

Harris/3M Corporation
23000 Park Lake Drive
N.E. Atlanta, GA 30345

Hitachi America
50 Prospect Avenue
Tarrytown, NY 10591-4698

Konica Business Machines USA,
Inc.
500 Day Hill Road
Windsor, CT 06095

Minolta Corporation
101 Williams Drive
Ramsey, NJ 07446

Mitsubishi Corporation
P.O. Box 6008
Cypress, CA 90630

Monroe Systems for Business
The American Way
Morris Plains, NJ 07950

Murata Business Systems, Inc.
4801 Spring Valley, Suite 108B
Dallas, TX 75244

NEC Information Systems, Inc.
8 Old Sod Farm Road
Melville, NY 11747

Olivetti U.S.A.
765 U.S. Highway 202
Somerville, NJ 08876

Olympia USA, Inc.
Box 22, Route 22
Somerville, NJ 08876

Panasonic/Panafax
10 Melville Road.
Melville, NY 11747

Pitney-Bowes, Inc.
3191 Broadbridge Avenue
Stratford, CT 06497

Ricoh Corporation
5 Dedrick Place
West Caldwell, NJ 07006

Sanyo Business Systems
51 Joseph Street
Moonachie, NJ 07074

Savin Corporation
9 West Broad Street
Stamford, CT 06904

Sharp Electronics Corporation
Sharp Plaza
Mahwah, NJ 07430

Tandy Corporation
One Tandy Center
Fort Worth, TX 76102

Toshiba America, Inc.
Telecommunication Systems
Division
9740 Irvine Boulevard
Irvine, CA 92718

Xerox Corporation
P.O. Box 24
Rochester, NY 14692

PC FAX Board Manufacturers and Vendors

American Data Technology, Inc.
44 W. Bellvue Drive, #6
Pasadena, CA 91105

AT&T
1 Speedwell Avenue
Morristown, NJ 07920

Brooktrout Technology, Inc.
110 Cedar Street
Wellesley Hills, MA 02181

Brother International Corporation
8 Corporate Place
Piscataway, NJ 08855

DEST Corporation
1201 Cadillac Court
Milpitas, CA 95035

GammaLink
2452 Embarcadeo Way
Palo Alto, CA 94303

Hayes Microcomputer Products, Inc.
P.O. Box 105203
Atlanta, GA 30348

Intel PCEO
Mail Stop CO3-07
5200 NE Elam Young Parkway
Hillsboro, OR 97124

Microlink International, Inc.
4064 McConnel Drive
Burady, British Columbia V5A 3A8
Canada

Omnium Corporation
1911 Curve Crest Boulevard
Stillwater, MN 55082

Panasonic Corporation/ Panasonic Industrial Company
2 Panasonic Way
Secaucus, NJ 07094

Quadram
One Quad Way
Norcross, GA 30093

Ricoh Corporation
5 Dedrick Place
West Caldwell, NJ 07006

Xerox Imaging Systems
1215 Terra Bella Avenue
Mountain View, CA 94043

Modem Manufacturers and Vendors

Anderson Jacobson, Inc.
521 Charcot Avenue
San Jose, CA 95131

AT&T
1 Speedwell Avenue
Morristown, NJ 07920

Hayes Microcomputer Products, Inc.
P.O. Box 105203
Atlanta, GA 30348

Radio Shack
300 One Tandy Center
Fort Worth, TX 76102

USRobotics
800 McCormick Boulevard
Skokie, IL 60076

Ven-Tel Modems
2121 Zanker Road
San Jose, CA 95131

Glossary

Analog Signal A signal that varies in a continuous manner (e.g., music or tones carried over telephone lines). Analog signals can vary amplitude (strength) or frequency to carry information.

ASCII Acronym for American Standard Code for Information Interchange. ASCII is a standard numeric code used by most computers for transmitting data. There are 128 standard ASCII code numbers (0 through 127), each of which is assigned to an alphanumeric character, control character, or special character.

Auto-Answer The capability of a modem to detect an incoming call and answer the phone by responding with a tone that is recognizable by the calling computer all without the use of a telephone set.

Auto-Dial The capability of a modem to dial telephone numbers, as opposed to the user dialing the telephone manually. It is used to describe a modem that is capable of generating pulse-dial and/or touch tone signals without a telephone set.

Auto-Logon A sign-on process whereby a computer's terminal software communicates with another computer system in a prearranged sign-on sequence.

Auto-Logon File A special disk file containing instructions for a computer communications program to follow in dialing up and connecting with another computer. Auto-logon files can usually be edited to include user IDs, passwords, etc. Also called a script file.

Background Operation The ability of a PC FAX board and its software to operate unattended while other computer software and peripherals are in use.

Backup Dialing A FAX feature that, when in effect, dials a preassigned secondary, or backup, number if a number it dials is busy.

Binary A number system that uses only two digits: 1 and 0. Binary also refers to a data format that uses only two states (off/on, high/low, negative/positive, etc.) to represent information.

Binary File-Transfer Protocol A computer file-transfer procedure in which data is transmitted in sets or groups of characters, called blocks, packets, or frames, rather than one character at a time. For the purpose of error checking, information from which the receiving system can calculate the number of bytes in each block transmitted is sent along with the block. If there is a difference between the number of bytes received and the number of bytes specified with the block, most error-checking protocol systems will cause the block to be retransmitted. Examples of transmission systems using error-checking protocol include KERMIT, Xmodem, and Ymodem.

Bit Contraction of BInary digiT. The smallest unit of computer information; a bit's value is either 0 or 1.

Bits Per Second (bps) A measure of the rate of data transmission expressed as the number of data bits sent in one second. This is not necessarily the same as baud rate. Nor does it represent the number of computer characters sent per second, since each character is composed of more than one bit.

Bulletin Board System (BBS) A personal computer-based telecommunications system that takes calls from other computers and provides public and private messaging services, file transfers, etc.

Broadcast Sequentially sending FAX documents to more than one FAX machine.

Byte A group of bits handled by a computer as a discreet unit; a computer data character. A byte representing a data character is normally composed of either seven or eight bits.

Carrier A tone transmitted over telephone lines that can be modulated to carry data. A carrier tone is an analog signal.

Character A letter, number, space, punctuation mark, symbol, or control character. A representation of the same encoded in groups of binary digits.

Command An instruction or set of instructions that tells a program or electronic device to perform a specified function or operation.

Communications Link The telephone lines and associated systems that link two systems in data communications.

Communications Parameters A group of changeable settings available in a computer communications program. These settings determine how your computer will communicate with another and include baud/bps rate, parity, duplex, character length/data bits, and number of stop bits.

Communications Software Dedicated computer software that enables and facilitates data communications. Sometimes called terminal software.

Connect The point at which two modems are first connected and mutually acknowledge the same.

Connect Charges The cost of time spent on a commercial online service, usually calculated on a per-minute basis.

Contrast The relative sensitivity of a scanner to shades of gray. As an adjustment, contrast makes a scanner more or less sensitive to gray (the greater the sensitivity, the more shades of gray are perceived as black).

Cover Sheet An option page added to the beginning of a FAXed document that may contain information such as the name of the intended recipient of the document, the sender, or other data.

Data Information of any type. Addresses are data; so are names or groups of numbers.

Database An organized collection of related information stored on a computer, usually searchable by keywords and/or other criteria. The information may be stored as a group of related files or in one file.

Data Bits The number of all bits sent for a single character that represents the character itself, not counting parity or stop bits; it is normally seven or eight bits. Also a communications setting.

Dedicated FAX Machine Also called a standalone FAX machine, it is the standard configuration for a FAX machine. A dedicated FAX machine is a specialized device that includes a scanner, a printer, a modem, and associated electronic circuitry to transmit and receive/print *facsimiles* of documents via data communications, using special communications protocols designed for facsimile transmission.

Delayed Transmission A FAX feature that allows a document to be transmitted unattended at a prescheduled time. This feature requires document storage in memory and/or a document feeder. Also called scheduled transmission.

Demodulate To recover data from a carrier wave; it is the opposite of modulate.

Dial Up The process of calling one computer with another via telephone.

Dial-Up Modem In general, a modem designed to operate within a bps range (0 to 9600) that is effective in transmitting data via voice-grade telephone lines.

Digital Refers to the binary system or its use.

Digital Signal A discontinuous signal, identified by specific levels or values, typically on/off or low/high. An electrical signal in which information is coded as a series of pulses or transitions.

Digitizing The process of scanning a picture and encoding it as binary data.

Direct Connect Modem A modem that connects directly to a telephone line via a modular jack.

Directory A summary list of available messages in an E-mail area. `DIRECTORY` is frequently a command used to display such a summary list.

Display To "print" to the computer screen. Also, the computer's screen or monitor.

Dithering Another name for a halftone or gray-scale scanning process that produces varying shades of gray.

Document One or more pages transmitted via FAX during a single transmission. A document can also be described as the sum total of information transmitted during a single FAX transmission. The information transmitted can consist of text and/or graphics.

Document Feeder A mechanism that feeds document pages to a dedicated FAX machine's scanner.

Document Storage A dedicated FAX machine feature that stores incoming or scanned documents in memory until they can be printed or transmitted.

Dot-Matrix Printer A printer that produces characters and lines by placing patterns of dots on paper.

Download To receive data from another computer. On some systems, `DOWNLOAD` may be a command that initiates a file transfer via ASCII or binary file-transfer protocol.

ECM Acronym for Error Correction Method. ECM is a method of transmission that automatically corrects errors during transmission. ECM is built into many newer Group 3 FAX modems.

Electronic Mail A computer-based messaging system used to deliver messages from one online service user to another. E-mail files are usually private (i.e., accessible by the sender and recipient only), and often the user must go to a special online area to read E-mail. Most E-mail systems handle ASCII text files only, but some will transfer binary files. Usually referred to as E-mail.

Electronic Mailbox The private storage area or portion of a database on a BBS or online service where E-mail messages are stored.

Electrostatic Printing A printing process that attracts particles of ink or toner fluid to specific locations on a sheet of paper, then fuses the particles to the paper. The combined dots produced by this process create characters, lines, and other elements of an image.

External Modem A self-contained desktop modem connected to a computer via a serial interface cable plugged into the computer's serial or RS-232 port. An external modem can generally be used with any computer, provided the proper cable is used, and may be acoustic or direct-connect.

Facsimile A duplicate, or copy, of something. In data communication terms, facsimile refers to a document transmitted electronically.

Fallback The ability of a FAX modem to adjust its transmission speed downward to compensate for poor telephone-line quality and thus ensure an error-free transmission.

FAX Short for facsimile transmission, which is the process of electronically transmitting a duplicate of a document from one location to another, using special scanning and data-transmission equipment. FAX is used to refer to transmitted documents, the equipment used to transmit them, and the act of transmitting facsimiles.

File Related data (program or information of any type) stored in binary format on a defined area of a computer disk and accessible by a computer program or computer operating system.

Flatbed Scanner A scanner whose configuration is similar to that of a photocopier.

Folder In E-mail systems, a group of related messages, stored and accessible separately from other messages. E-mail systems automatically store new, unread messages in a separate group and move them to the main group once they've been read. On most systems, you can create your own folders and move messages into them based on arbitrary criteria.

Graphics The elements of an image on a sheet of paper or a computer screen. Graphics may include characters, lines, dots, curves, angles, and cursive writing.

Gray Scale See *Halftone*.

Group A designation, followed by 1, 2, 3, or 4, that alludes to the FAX standard and transmission techniques in use by the FAX machine to which it is applied. The current generation of FAX machines are designated Group 3, and are characterized by digital data scanning and transmission techniques, as well as a 9600-bps maximum transmission speed. Group 4 FAX machines are specialized devices, requiring sophisticated digital data transmission lines to use.

Halftone A method of scanning and printing that distinguishes between 8 and 64 shades of gray, rather than the straight black-and-white scanning and printing techniques used by most FAX machines. It is used by some advanced Group 3 FAX machines. Halftone can be used to transmit photos—color or black-and-white—with nearly full contrast.

Handheld Scanner A type of scanner used with computers. Literally, a handheld device that is capable of scanning a standard page in 4-inch increments as it is passed over the page.

Hardcopy A printed document of any kind, but the term usually refers to FAXed or E-mailed documents that have been printed. Also printout.

Host System The computer system receiving a call from another system. Host system is also a computer system on which an online service is based.

ID A name or number by which online service users are identified. Various information is tied to an online ID on a host system, including the user's password, E-mail address, screen display parameters, and billing information. A user ID may be a number, a name, or a series of letters and numbers.

Image The contents of a page of data transmitted via FAX. Specifically, the electronic form of a scanned page (i.e., the binary or analog data in which a page is stored and transmitted).

Internal Modem A modem installed inside a computer, usually in the form of a printed circuit board or card.

Keyword A word used to index files in databases and other information retrieval areas on online services.

Kilobyte A unit of computer memory, normally referring to the number of bytes in RAM or the size of a file, equal to 1024 bytes.

Laser Printing A printing process whereby charged particles of ink or toner fluid are fused to a sheet of paper by a laser beam at specific locations to create an image.

Lines Per Inch A measure of the resolution of a FAX image (literally in dots per inch). The more dots that a scanner can scan or a printer can print in a horizontal line or the more lines (or dots) in a vertical inch, the finer the resolution. Also called pels, picture elements.

Main Menu The highest level of an online system. A main menu lists as selections the major categories of services or areas provided by an online service. Each main menu selection leads to further menus, called sub-menus. Also called the top menu.

Memory Dialing A feature on many dedicated FAX machines that allows you to dial a preset phone number by pressing one or two single buttons.

Menu A listing of commands and/or options available in a particular area on an online service.

Message Any communication from one computer user to one or more others via the facilities of an online service. Messages can be electronic mail messages. Message also refers to short documents sent via FAX. Message does not necessarily refer to a text-only message where FAX is concerned.

Modem A device used to translate binary signals from a computer or FAX machine into analog signals for transmission via telephone line, and vice versa. FAX machines and computers use entirely different kinds of modems.

Modem/FAX Service A computer-based service that serves as a go-between for FAX document transmission between modem-equipped computers and dedicated FAX machines. Most (not all) modem/FAX services are one-way–computer to FAX only.

Modulate To alter some characteristic of a carrier wave or tone according to an established protocol, in order to transfer information via the carrier.

Offline A state in which a FAX machine or computer's modem is not connected with another modem.

Online A state in which a FAX machine or computer's modem is connected with a modem; the opposite of offline.

Online Service A commercial service that provides any or all of the following services for a fee: communication, database, and information storage and retrieval. Online services are usually multiuser. Examples of online services include CompuServe, DELPHI, GEnie, and MCI Mail. Sometimes referred to as networks.

Optical Character Recognition (OCR) Software Special computer software that converts the characters in scanned images or incoming FAX data into their ASCII character counterparts for storage in a computer. OCR software is the key to converting FAX data format, which is entirely graphic in nature, into computer-readable data.

Optical Scanner Another name for a scanner used with a computer.

Packet-Switching Network A data communications service that transmits data from one computer system to another in the form of packets, or coded groups of data. Most packet-switching networks provide a nationwide system of local telephone numbers (called nodes) to enable users to access online services without incurring long-distance charges. DataPac, Telenet, and Tymnet are packet-switching networks.

Page A sheet of physical paper scanned or printed by a FAX machine. A page is also a unit of information transmitted via FAX (i.e., the information content of a sheet of paper, which can be text, graphics, or both).

Password A string of letters and/or numbers used to verify the identity or authorization of a user calling an online service or BBS. Use of a password prevents unauthorized use of an online ID or unauthorized use of a system. Ideally, passwords are known only to those who own the ID or account with which they are associated.

PC FAX Board A device that, with the help of specialized support software, translates computer data into FAX format, and vice versa. PC FAX boards are equipped with special FAX modems so that they can send and receive FAX data, as well.

Pels See *Lines Per Inch*.

Peripheral An ancillary or auxiliary device attached to a computer for the purpose of performing specialized tasks under the control of the computer and its software. Printers are computer peripherals, as are modems and PC FAX boards.

Personal Computer A microprocessor-based computer characterized by its relatively small size (desktop-size or smaller), keyboard input, and monitor output. Also called a microcomputer.

Pixel Short for picture element, the smallest element of a picture.

Polling The capability of a dedicated FAX machine to call another FAX machine and request that a document be transmitted to it (to the calling FAX).

Printer A computer peripheral designed to print computer data (text and/or graphics) on paper.

Printout See *Hardcopy*.

Protocol A mutually agreed-upon set of data-transmission conditions (transmission speed, format of data, etc.) under which two computer or FAX modems exchange data.

Repeat Dialing A feature on dedicated FAX machines that redials a busy number until a connection is made.

Resolution The relative fineness of detail captured by a FAX scanner or reproduced by a FAX printer. Usually measured in lines per inch or dots per square inch.

Serial Port A device that provides a physical data connection between a computer and another device (usually a modem) and that handles various data translation and exchange tasks. Also known as an RS-232 port.

Scanner A device that converts the image on a piece of paper into representational binary data by assigning a specific value of lightness, darkness, or grayness to each dot or pixel (a tiny area or location on the paper). Dedicated FAX machines have built-in scanners; scanners may be added to personal computers. Scanners come in several configurations, including flatbed, sheet, and, handheld.

Scanning The process of converting an image (text and/or graphics) on paper into a binary data representation of the image. Also called digitizing.

Scheduled Transmission See *Delayed Transmission*.

Script File See *Auto-Logon File*.

Selection An item on a menu. Selection is also an item chosen from a menu.

Sheet Feeder A mechanism that feeds single sheets of blank paper into a FAX or computer's printer.

Sheet Scanner In dedicated FAX machines, a scanner whose configuration is such that sheets of blank paper must be fed into it. The paper is pulled through the inside of the FAX machine and past the scanner by rollers (platens). A document feeder is often used with a sheet scanner to automate completely the process of supplying document pages to a scanner.

Sign On The process or event of connecting with and identifying your computer to another computer system. Signing on typically involves sending a user ID and password to the answering system when it prompts for them.

Store-and-Forward A FAX transmission procedure in which a document is transmitted from one FAX machine to another (or to a computer), held for a specified period of time, then retransmitted to one or more other FAX machines.

Support Software Personal computer software used to perform tasks (e.g., data translation or conversion), that enable other software or hardware to use certain data or that make using other software or hardware easier.

System Any computer (and its peripherals)–particularly a computer that is connected with another computer, whether as a host or as an originating system.

Telecommunications Data communication over telephone lines via computer or FAX modem.

Telex A specialized international telecommunications system that carries messages to and from nearly two million Telex and computer terminals worldwide.

Text Data composed exclusively of letters, numbers, punctuation, and spaces.

Text File A file in ASCII format, as opposed to binary format.

Thermal Printing A printing process whereby heated wires darken dots (pixels) on heat-sensitive paper to produce an image.

Time-Sharing System An antiquated term used to describe computer systems that are accessed by more than one user at a time.

Transaction Report A report printed by a dedicated FAX machine listing incoming and outgoing calls and their duration, as well as the numbers dialed for outgoing calls, and other information, as an aid to tracking FAX usage.

Turnaround Polling The ability of a FAX machine to reverse the direction of information flow during a transmission. That is, the ability of a FAX machine that is sending a document to request the FAX machine to which it is sending data to transmit a document.

Upload To send data to another computer. On some systems, a command that initiates a file transfer from your computer to a host system.

Voice/Data Switching The ability of some FAX machines to switch between FAX transmission and voice-telephone communication during the same call.

User Someone who dials up, or uses, an online service.

Xmodem A special error-checking file-transfer protocol that transfers files in blocks, or packets, of 128 bytes. Xmodem transfers are virtually error-free. It requires Xmodem capability on the part of your terminal software and the remote system.

Answers to Quizzes

1 | 1-c, 2-b, 3-c, 4-b, 5-c, 6-a, 7-a, 8-a, 9-b, 10-a, 11-a, 12-d

2 | 1-c, 2-d, 3-a, 4-b, 5-c, 6-c, 7-a, 8-a, 9-b, 10-a, 11-a, 12-d

3 | 1-a, 2-d, 3-a, 4-b, 5-a, 6-b, 7-d, 8-c, 9-d, 10-b, 11-d, 12-c, 13-(a, c, and d), 14-c, 15-b

4 | 1-b, 2-c, 3-c, 4-d, 5-d, 6-a, 7-a, 8-a, 9-c, 10-d

5 | 1-c, 2-c, 3-c, 4-c, 5-b, 6-d, 7-c, 8-c, 9-d, 10-b

6 | 1-b, 2-c, 3-c, 4-b, 5-c, 6-a, 7-a, 8-b, 9-a, 10-c

7 | 1-b, 2-d, 3-c, 4-b, 5-d, 6-d, 7-d, 8-a

8 | 1-b, 2-c, 3-c, 4-a, 5-d, 6-a, 7-b, 8-c, 9-b, 10-c

11 | 1-a, 2-b, 3-d, 4-b, 5-c, 6-c, 7-c, 8-b, 9-d, 10-d

Index

B

Background operation, 69–70

Backup number dialing, 43

Binary
    data, 36
        in computers, 120–124
    file transfer, 140
        user-to-user, 203
    numbers, 123–124
    signals, 37

BIX, telephone numbers, 243

Board(s)
    dedicated PC FAX, 90–93
    FAX, PC, 3, 18–20, 59–71, 87–96
        installation, 88–90

Broadcast FAX, 55–56, 66

Bulletin board(s)
    computer, 4, 104
    MCI mail, 199

Business applications, 15–16

C

Callback, automatic, 42

Care and maintenance, fax machine, 83

Channels, E-mail, 110–114, 132

Characters
    control, 61
    graphics, 61

Choosing service, 229–238

Command summary
    CompuServe, 215–216
    DELPHI, 219–220
    GEnie, 224

Commands, E-mail, 135–137

Commercial electronic messaging,
    105–106

Communications
    computer, how it works, 119–125
    equipment, data, 125
    hardware, computer, 125–131
    links, 124
    software, computer, 131–132

Compatability, Group 1 and Group 2
    modems, 48–49

CompuServe, 212–216, 215–216
    access, 216
    command summary, 215–216
    connect charges, 226
    EasyPlex E-Mail, 213–214
    E-mail enhancements, 214
    help, 216
    message surcharges, 226–227
    service overview and features, 212–214
    telephone numbers, 243

Computer(s), 125
    bulletin boards, 104
    communications
        how it works, 119–125
        software, 131–132
    communications hardware, 125–131
    connections, E-mail, 129–130
    data format, 61
    FAX, via online services, 20–22
    messaging, 103–104
    -to-computer messaging, 104–105

Connect charges
    CompuServe, 226
    DELPHI, 226
    online services, 226

Connections
    FAX machine, 3
    modem/FAX, 152–153
    physical, 39–40
    telephone-line, 128

Contrast control, scanners, 45–46

Control characters, 61

Conversion, data, with modem, 37–38

Copier function, 54

Correction mode, error, 40–41

Cost(s)
    E-mail, 114, 207–210, 232–233
    online services, 225–228, 232–233

Courier services, 108

Cover sheets, automatic, 58, 68

Creating messages, E-mail, 170–171

Cutter, paper, 53